Passion and Pride

The Official Biography of Davy Fitzgerald

with

Jackie Cahill

BLACKWATER PRESS

Editor
Adam Brophy

Design & Layout
Paula Byrne

Cover Design
Karen Hoey

ISBN
1-84131-647-4

© 2005 Jackie Cahill

Produced in Ireland by
Blackwater Press
c/o Folens Publishers
Hibernian Industrial Estate
Tallaght
Dublin 24

DAVY'S
ACKNOWLEDGEMENTS

I simply have to start with my family. My father Pat, mother Nuala and my sister Helen – I thank you from the bottom of my heart for all your love and support down through the years. My son Colm is the main man in my life. Colm, I am proud of you and I hope that when you grow up, all your dreams come true. I love you son.

Olivia, you have been a massive support to me in everything that I do. You mean so much to me. My uncle John is another huge part of my life. John, I took great inspiration from you as a young child, watching your passion and pride for this great game.

Fr Harry Bohan, I want to thank you for your assistance with this book. You helped me through the good and bad times. Journalist, Vincent Hogan has been a real friend to me. Vincent, thanks for your assistance, you are a great guy. I would also like to thank Peter Shanaher for all the help he has given me.

Martin Donnelly, the main sponsor of this book and a true GAA supporter, deserves a special word of appreciation. And I would also like to give special thanks to Alan O'Donoghue of Umbro.

In my business dealings, Michael O'Keane from Bank of Scotland has always been a tremendous help.

To my co-author Jackie Cahill – you put up with my stubbornness but never complained. Thank you for your patience. I could not be happier than to have a person of your qualities writing this book for me. Please God, we will remain friends for life.

For all the other fantastic people that I have come across through the years, many of you are mentioned inside. Thank you all for what you brought to my life.

To Kevin 'Trixie' Twomey and Sheila Considine, two fantastic people who I miss more each day, I continue to be inspired by the way you both cherished your lives.

Jackie's Acknowledgements

My close pal in journalism, Damian Lawlor, summed it up just a few short weeks ago. He said to me, 'Jackie, you have written the story of a hurling legend.'

I have always admired Davy Fitzgerald and in recent years, I have enjoyed chatting to him on a regular basis as we cemented our friendship. Naturally, assisting him in the writing of his life story was a real honour. Davy, I hope that I have done you justice. To Davy's parents, Pat and Nuala, his sister Helen and young Colm, a sincere thanks for your warmth and hospitality. You are friends for life.

A special thanks to my girlfriend, Chris. You have always encouraged and supported me and I love having you in my life. Tina and Liam, Chris' parents, have always made me feel welcome in their home. You are two fantastic people. To Damian Lawlor and Vincent Hogan, two proud Tipperary men, I will never forget your assistance during the writing of this book. You were there when I needed a hand. I can't forget my good friend in Dublin, Brian Carroll, for his early assistance, and my editor, Adam Brophy, who was a tremendous help towards the end, and John O'Connor, Margaret Burns and Paula Byrne from Blackwater Press. In Clare, Seamus Hayes, Des Crowe and Fr Harry Bohan were always available to give advice. Close to home, I have some good people around me. Iver, my best buddy from childhood, constantly encouraged me. Liverpool FC is our common denominator! The two Jimmys know who they are, the big man, Colm Keys, is a great man to talk to about all things journalism and, down in Cork, they don't come much better than the great Colin Corkery.

Thanks to John Kelly and Sportsfile for permission to reproduce photographs. Cover photographs were supplied by Sportsfile and M Donnelly.

It all started for me in Rathclogheen, Golden. My father, John, and mother, Angela, have put up with a lot from me down through the years! Thanks for your support. I am extremely proud of my sister, Rose, and my two brothers, Brian and Andrew. I hope life is good to you all.

Finally, I would like to dedicate my work to my great friend, Derek Egan, who passed away in 2002. Derek, you will always live on in my heart.

ABOUT THE AUTHOR

Jackie Cahill comes from Golden in county Tipperary and is the Gaelic Games Correspondent with the *Irish Daily Mirror*. He graduated from Dublin City University in 1999 with a BA in Journalism. He is a current Vodafone Allstar hurling selector and has displayed a deep interest in sport from a very young age. This is his first book.

DEDICATION

C, O, S, T, S, Ⓕ

CONTENTS

PROLOGUE

We have nothing to fear but fear itself.

Franklin D Roosevelt

It's dark in here, difficult to breathe. In my right hand lies a buzzer and I feel like pressing it. Minutes seem like hours, I am gripped by fear and paranoia and I itch to call out for help.

It is St Patrick's Day 2004 and I am on my back in an MRI chamber at Limerick's Regional Hospital. I close my eyes and think of the good things in life. My son Colm, hurling, friends; my mind is racing. Two days ago, I took a bad turn after Clare's national hurling league match against Galway in Salthill. At a post-match dinner, I felt dizzy at the table. I told our manager Anthony Daly to call the doctor, I thought I was a goner. Gulping the cool evening air outside, I felt that something horrible was in my head.

I had a brain scan taken at the Regional Hospital the next day which revealed a three-centimetre cyst on the wall of my brain. An MRI scan would tell me more. So here I am. 25 minutes of sheer hell and the waiting game begins. It will be three and a half months before I get the all-clear at Dublin's Blackrock Clinic. In the meantime, I can only hope. This could be the toughest match of my life, and there's no way of predicting the result.

***

Tuesday, June 29 2004. Point Theatre, Dublin. *The Corrs* are on stage and Andrea looks beautiful. I think that everything's going to be ok. Next morning, a taxi arrives at the Burlington Hotel to take me back to the Blackrock Clinic. An unusual sense of calm descends on me, the concert was good, I am feeling positive. The doctor gives me the good news. 'The cyst won't do any harm, don't worry,' he tells me. I have just won the All-Ireland.

***

I now realise how precious life is. When I am out there hurling, everything is good. But there are things in life that I have to re-evaluate. I have been pushing myself for years as a sportsman. Playing with hurling teams, training others, finding new rungs on the property ladder. It has been a rollercoaster ride through marriage and break-up, sickening abuse from opposition supporters on the terraces, Munster finals, All-Ireland finals, Allstars, prizes won and prizes lost.

There is more to life than hurling, but it has taken me a while to realise that. Burning the candle at both ends in search of the next glory took its toll and almost rendered me helpless. Health scares opened my eyes. But in the weeks leading up to big championship matches with Clare, nothing else matters.

I am David Fitzgerald, originally from 3 Thomond Terrace, Sixmilebridge, now living on the Castlecrine Road just outside the village. Possessed on the pitch, nice guy off it. Hated by some, loved by others, there is no in-between. I have been playing inter-county hurling for Clare since 1990 and, even though I am 34 years of age now, I have no intention of giving up this great game. It has been good to me: two All-Ireland medals, three Munster titles, Allstars and a place on Clare's Team of the Millennium. In there ahead of Seamus Durack, Mick Hayes, Pascal O'Brien and Dr Tommy Daly. Great men, great honour.

Those men blazed a trail, I merely followed in their footsteps. But the imprints I have left behind are visible for generations to come. My uncle John, Kevin 'Trixie' Twomey, my family, and John Lynch in the local Mill, were all influences on my career. Trixie was special and his death in July 2004 rocked me to the core. He was my mentor, friend and golfing buddy. He drilled me before championship matches, he brought Liam Fennelly down from Kilkenny for specialist work before the 1995 All-Ireland final, he always had a trick up his sleeve. I like to think I have too.

My playing career will come to an end soon enough but I have already cut my teeth as a coach. I am player-manager with my beloved club, Sixmilebridge, and Trixie told me that if I could deliver a junior county title to Ennistymon hurling club, I could do anything. He wasn't there to see it, but he would have been proud. He should have been with me too when Limerick Institute of Technology won the Fitzgibbon Cup in 2005. But he helped to plot that great success, and he knew that we would get there.

Trixie handed me a Clare jersey for the first time when I was just a teenager and from there, my career blossomed. The Clare hurlers blew off the shackles and won the All-Ireland title in 1995, I was between the sticks and saw it all. Two years later we did it again, but then it turned sour for a while. Who dares to speak of 1998? In many ways, it was our greatest year.

Passion and pride – watchwords in the Clare dressing room. Watchwords in my life. Victories, defeats, suspensions, controversy, drama. Join me for a look inside.

1 THE BANNER ROARS AGAIN

Biography is the only true history.

Thomas Carlyle

Welcome to my world, it is just about to cave in. The time is fast approaching 5 p.m. on Sunday, August 14 2005, and referee Dickie Murphy has blown his whistle to signal the end of the Guinness All-Ireland hurling semi-final. I am David Fitzgerald, Clare's senior hurling team goalkeeper and I am in shock. Reigning All-Ireland champions Cork have beaten us by a single point (0-16 to 0-15), but we are the architects of our own downfall after letting a six-point lead slip away in the second half.

With only 23 minutes of normal time left to play, Tony Carmody's point had put us 0-13 to 0-7 ahead. We were surging towards another All-Ireland final and it seemed that nothing could stop us. Then, Cork manager John Allen took off two Allstars, Ronan Curran and Brian Corcoran, and reshuffled his team. John Gardiner moved into centre back and suddenly, every puckout that I launched into the Cork half of the field was coming back at me just as fast. The tide was turning.

We were starting to lose it and I couldn't get instructions up the pitch to our half-forwards to just pull on the ball in the air and drive it through. Stop trying to out-catch the Cork half-backs because it just wasn't working. Two, two, two, I was dividing my puckouts evenly across the Clare half-forward line but Seán Óg Ó hAilpín was catching ball, John Gardiner inside him was plucking them out of the skies and Tom Kenny was back from midfield mopping up. Our manager Anthony Daly sent word up the sideline to me to keep the ball away from Kenny but no matter what I tried, it kept coming back. Cork were murdering us. I was going down Seán Óg's wing and down the centre but Cork by then had a serious momentum from their half-back line and we could not smash our way past them.

Andrew Quinn and Tony Carmody pinched a couple of scores for us but they only served to delay the inevitable and Cork drew level in the final minute of normal time. Then Jerry O'Connor cut through from midfield and put them ahead. There was still time for Colin Lynch at the other end but he shot wide. The ball was switched to the other end of the field and I dove at the feet of Cork substitute Neil Ronan to prevent a goal. It was my second good save of the day but it meant fuck all to me.

Then, it was over. Murphy blew the final whistle and I was absolutely distraught. I have seen the TV pictures where the cameras are on me, capturing the look of shock and sheer desolation in my eyes. I thumped the ground with my hurl and took off running, towards Murphy. My head was spinning. We had been less than two minutes away from a place in the All-Ireland final, so close I had its smell in my nostrils. The massive occasion, 80,000 spectators, the people of Clare roaring us on to glory as Brian Lohan, Colin Lynch and Seánie McMahon rolled back the years. But that's all gone now and my thoughts have changed. Am I finished? Will I ever get back here again? Will I ever play in another All-Ireland final? Is this it?

It is hard to describe the exact feeling but I will do my best. I had built myself up to incredible mental and physical levels and I was convinced that we were going to beat Cork. When we didn't, I imploded. I work all my life to play for Clare, I devote everything to this game, my dream is so close that I can almost touch it but then, in an instant, it has vanished. I can't believe it and I feel so empty inside.

I was very pissed off with Dickie Murphy at the final whistle and the TV cameras disappeared somewhere else as I made my way towards the Wexford referee. In Clare later, a lot of people heard that the reason that I was so angry was because Colin Lynch had hit some wides during the game. There was talk that I had gone after Colin after the game, but that is simply not true. Colin Lynch and I are like brothers and I never saw him playing as well as he did at midfield against Cork. His work-rate was incredible and, with any luck, a few of those wides would have gone over the bar. If he had scored two of those, he would have been man of the match. That's how fine the line is. That's hurling.

***

I am beside Murphy now, roaring at him. 'For fuck's sake! You screwed us in 2001 [against Tipperary in the Munster championship] and you're after doing us again today.' I meant every word of it. In the closing stages against Cork, I took a quick puckout to Lynch but Murphy blew me back and ordered a re-take. Yet he had let Cork goalkeeper Donal Óg Cusack away with a succession of quick puckouts, despite telling our captain, Seánie McMahon, before the game that he would be keeping an eye on Donal Óg. With Donal Óg getting away with it, I curved a ball and stuck it in Lynch's hand at midfield with the game on a knife-edge. But what does Dickie do? He blows me back.

The game was getting away from us but we kept trying to burst through. Niall Gilligan and Diarmuid McMahon were pulled back at different stages towards the end of the game but no free was given. In a final attack, Lynch hand-passed to Tony Griffin, Griff turned and his jersey was given a quick tug. Here's Dickie's chance to give Clare the free and secure another few bob for the GAA. More importantly, give us the replay we richly deserve. But the whistle remains silent, until that final shrill blast.

Looking back, we were a bit naïve. Not breaking ball through up front and doing a few little things wrong. When I slumped to the Croke Park sod, a Cork supporter approached and placed two consoling arms around me. He was talking but I was hearing nothing.

'No problem, fair play to ye, well done,' I mumbled. He wouldn't go away and I lost patience. 'Will you go away will you?' He meant well but I was there with one of the lowest feelings of my entire life and this fella hanging off my neck. I needed to be alone with my thoughts. Donal Óg came down and said that Cork shouldn't have won the game. He was right, but I had to admire Cork. They never gave up; they worked hard and they stuck to their gameplan. They are good champions and a professional outfit – I respect that, I really do.

My hurley survived the walk back to the dressing room. God only knows how because I hammered it off the tunnel walls four or five times. I hit the dressing room table a lash, fired my jersey up in the air and fucked my father out of it when he told me to calm down. How unfair can this game be?

The dressing room was deathly silent. There wasn't a word spoken and I was looking at fellas with tears streaming down their cheeks. There wasn't a dry eye in that dressing room but in a funny kind of way, I'm happy inside. 'Every one of these lads cares so much,' I thought to myself. Dalo got up and said a few words telling us how proud he was, and Seánie McMahon spoke too. I couldn't let the opportunity pass. 'I'm proud to be from Clare today,' I said. 'I've always said to ye about fighting the fight. We fought the fight today, we didn't come out on the right side but we'll go on from this. We're not gone in Clare, we'll never be gone. And for the fellas that are thinking of hanging up the boots, I'm proud to have played alongside ye.' With that, I went to the warm-up area and cried buckets.

***

We stayed at the Burlington Hotel that night and I just could not get my head around the defeat. I was in the lobby area around 12.30 a.m., sitting on a couch by myself. My son Colm came over, lay down beside me and put his head on my lap. 'We lost today but this is more important,' I thought. I was going to stay up a bit longer but Colm had other ideas, 'Dad, I want to go to bed.'

'Colm, I don't know if I want to go,' I replied, feeling a bit sorry for myself. 'That's ok Dad, I'll stay up with you if you like.' Then it clicked with me. 'Come on, let's go to bed.' We went to our room and Colm moved towards the television. 'What channel do you want on, Dad?' he asked. 'Are you hungry Dad? I'll order room service for you.' My heart was full of love. I knew that I would be gutted for a few days after losing to Cork, but having Colm there with me was helping to soothe the pain. His support was incredible and that special little man helped me more than he will ever know that night. 'Go on there and get yourself to sleep Colm,' I said. He came over and gave me a hug goodnight. I ordered a chicken sandwich at 3 a.m. Then I tried to get some sleep.

I woke around 8.30 in the morning and the full pain of championship defeat hit me straight between the eyes. The body might be sore and bruised but the mental anguish is much worse. Then there's that gut-wrenching feeling in the pit of the stomach. There was no chance of getting back to sleep and I wasn't hungry either. I was just numb. I showered, shaved and stared vacantly at my reflection in the mirror. Then I remembered I had committed to training kids in Fingallians that morning for a good friend of mine, an ex-Sixmilebridge man, Derry Murphy. Derry collected me at 10 a.m. and I left Colm at the hotel with his grandfather Colm and Mike Collins, or 'Gazzy' as he's better known, a vital member of our backroom team.

Coaching kids in Swords was the last thing that I wanted to do that morning but I had made a commitment and there was no going back. 'I don't feel like doing this Derry,' I said, 'but I'll do it.' I spoke to the 70 kids that were present for ten minutes and divided them up into different groups for some coaching. I started with them at 11 a.m. and left just before two o'clock in the afternoon. And in hindsight, those few hours got me level again. I had to come around quickly because I was due back to training with my club, Sixmilebridge, on the Tuesday night. And as the team's manager, I had an even greater responsibility. Getting back to the club helps the wounds of a championship defeat with Clare to heal quicker but club-mates sometimes don't understand just how high we get for inter-county hurling. They can't relate to that mental state, how psyched up we are before a match against Tipperary, Cork, Kilkenny or Waterford.

We are expected to be in perfect shape when we return to our clubs but it never works out like that. The freefall from the heat of inter-county battle to the first round of the local club championship is some shock to the system. You'll hear the usual buffoons with their tuppence worth on Sunday's defeat too, of course. One particular clown in Ennis couldn't resist but I met fire with fire. 'Do you know who John Gardiner is?' he asked. 'What were you hitting the ball down on top of him for?' I explained calmly, and without losing the head, that John Gardiner hadn't done a thing on Alan Markham but when he went in centre back, he caught a few balls and cleared them up the field. Seán Óg caught a few, Tom Kenny went back from midfield and caught them. Fuck it ... I've gone through all this before and I'm not wasting my time with this ape.

Those final minutes are still killing me now as I write these words, and the pettiness of the GAA's rule-makers is gnawing away at me inside. Let me explain. For the past few years, different lads have been with me behind the goals at league and championship matches to help me with my hurleys. As a goalkeeper, I have different sticks for shot-stopping and general play and I like the transition to be as smooth as possible after pucking the ball out. I want to keep focused on the game at all times, I don't want to take my eye off the field for one second and that's why I have a personal helper behind the goal handing me the correct hurley for the next passage of play. A goalkeeper can get distracted rummaging in the corner of the net for a hurl so this is a practice that I introduced over the past few seasons. However, the GAA took issue this year. My good friend at Limerick Institute of Technology, Jimmy Browne, looks after my hurleys during championship matches. And for this year's league campaign, I was helped by a young lad from Killaloe, Dwayne Sheedy. Dwayne lost his younger brother Noel at an early age from meningitis so when Syl Adley told me that Dwayne wanted to help me out on match days, I was more than happy to oblige. Dwayne's a lovely chap but during the league matches, he got hassle from umpires and various officials who insisted that he shouldn't be behind the goals. I was getting my usual fair share of stick from opposition supporters on the terraces and Dwayne didn't like that either, so for the championship Jimmy Browne was back in my corner.

A real problem surfaced before the All-Ireland quarter-final against Wexford. The Clare county board was warned that a fine was in the offing if I persisted with using helpers. We went ahead anyway and Clare was fined €2,500 for a breach of match regulations. So, for the Cork game I was by myself again and as our half-forward line struggled to make any headway towards the end, I had nobody to send instructions up the field, which Jimmy would normally do.

I have a fair idea which county was behind the move to deny me an assistant for the All-Ireland semi-final. If the GAA is going to get that professional about the game, then it should start paying the players. I look around Croke Park and it seems that everybody bar the players is being paid. There are people working in the shops, officials on the field and lads on the stiles, and they're all getting a few bob. Why don't the powers-that-be take a look at lowering ticket prices and getting people back into the GAA? We're going down the same road as rugby and soccer and I would rather not see that happening.

We have a unique, passionate sport and if a manager is training a team all year, he should be allowed onto the pitch to tell his players what he wants them to do. I have nothing against soccer and rugby but we do not have to take after them. We are so caught up in technical stuff with all these committees. There's a need for some of them but they could be a lot more effective with their time. Referees do have a tough job but they have to be more accountable for their actions. They should sit down with the two managers involved the day after a match and discuss problematic incidents. I do not think referees should be put on the spot with the media straight after a game but instead, the manager who has trained his team for a year should be in a position to ask whatever questions he deems appropriate when the dust has settled. Referees have to make decisions on the spur of the moment but they get so many wrong, and some of them get personal. In my opinion Aodán MacSuibhne is the top referee in the country at the moment, an honourable man and match official.

I like honourable people in the GAA but our former All-Ireland winning manager Ger Loughnane has lost a lot of respect in Clare over the past few years for comments that he made about the county team in his newspaper column and on TV. There will only ever be one Ger Loughnane, he brought us two All-Ireland titles in 1995 and 1997 and I had incredible respect for the man. I might not always have agreed with his methods but he delivered results. However, in recent years, he has turned against us and I just wish that he wouldn't go in so hard. His criticism has not inspired us, in fact it's done the complete opposite – it has hurt us. Loughnane openly criticises the county board and the make-up of Anthony Daly's backroom team, but Ger is speaking from a pedestal that he has built for himself.

If Ger has so much to say, why isn't he in the thick of it with us, helping us out? This is a shame because I think he still has plenty to offer to Clare hurling. And it is a pity that he has made enemies because as a trainer and a manager, I will always have respect for him. Before my story was published, some people advised me that I might be better off not mentioning Loughnane at all, but I am fiercely loyal to my team-mates. I've seen how they train and the sacrifices that they make so I hate to see them cut down. I am not going to overly criticise Ger Loughnane, he will always do what he wants anyway, but hopefully in time he will realise that, as a Clare man, he should back the team to the hilt. And if he believes there is something so badly wrong, why doesn't he try to put it right? Hopefully the lads that he has hurt will forget about it and move on, but I can tell you that a few of them are unwilling to forgive and forget.

I admit that it is Ger's prerogative and he is entitled to say what he wants about us. I am a straight talker myself in many ways, and Ger makes a few bob for trotting out his opinions. But he seems to have a very short memory. As a panel of players, we were always very loyal to Loughnane and never let him down. He was a superb manager for Clare and certainly a big part in our All-Ireland wins but he didn't win them by himself. Loughnane had a great TEAM with him, people who wanted success for Clare every bit as much as he did. I will always respect Ger but I think he was wrong to cut down our players on TV and in print. We knew that he had completely written off some of our players after the Waterford game in 2004, but I would like to think that we proved him wrong later that year. He stuck the knife in after the Tipperary defeat in the 2005 Munster championship but he seemed to be singing from a different hymn sheet after the Cork defeat.

The last thing I want to do is get embroiled in a war of words with Ger Loughnane but he should not, under any circumstances, criticise Clare hurlers who give their all, just to entertain the rest of the country and to make a few quid for himself. When Ger was with us, I knew what he thought of the other teams we faced in championship hurling: very, very little. His philosophy was simple, Clare were number one and the rest were nobodies. So now, when he sticks the boot in, it smacks of hypocrisy.

***

Anthony Daly is our manager now and he is a man I have great time for, even though relations between the pair of us were somewhat frosty when he took the job after Clare were knocked out of the 2003 championship by Galway. Dalo held his counsel when Loughnane was criticising him in 2004 and the season ended on a respectable note as we exited the championship after a quarter-final replay against Kilkenny.

Just a few short months later, Dalo rang me to go back training in November ahead of a new season. He reassured me that he didn't want to push me; he just wanted me back doing a small bit, some power weights in St Flannan's. I was not asked to do much running or a pre-Christmas fitness test, which was good. There was no point anyway because I wouldn't be at the same level as some of the other lads. We had the Christmas break and Dalo told us to be ready for action on New Year's Day at 8.30 a.m. on Spanish Point beach. On New Year's Eve, all I could think about was the beach the next morning. And those thoughts were killing me. I would train all day hurling-wise, working on my drills, but these long runs do not make much sense to me because they are of no benefit to my game. I went to bed at 7 p.m. that night but couldn't sleep. I was in my apartment in Lahinch and the next morning wind, rain and hailstones were beating off the window. 'Oh Jesus, what am I doing?' I thought to myself. I sat on the corner of my bed for a few minutes and asked myself 'Will I go, or won't I?' Eventually, I decided to throw on my wet gear and driving in the car, I asked myself again: 'What am I doing? New Years Day and here I am, driving to run on Spanish Point beach.' It was madness really and I didn't even switch on the car radio, I just listened to the wind and rain pelting the car. There was a full turnout that morning and our trainer Johnny Glynn had everything marked out. We ran the length of the beach, with the wind at our backs and then back into it. We were bombarded with a welt of hailstones on our very first run and it was rough going. But it was character-forming stuff …

It was down to serious business after that, gym work at St Flannan's and running on the Fair Green in Ennis. Johnny gave me a different running programme to the one the other lads were following. It was made up of short, fast sprints, which made sense to keep me quick on my feet. I was doing a bit in the handball alley by myself too, in Sixmilebridge or St Flannan's, and working with my own personal trainer, Darren Ward, at the Shannon Shamrock Hotel in Bunratty. Jamesie O'Connor and Ollie Baker had announced their retirements from inter-county hurling before the new season and it felt different without them. Brian Lohan, Seánie McMahon and Colin Lynch were still there but the older crew were getting scarcer. I was sad to see Ollie and Jamesie go but they were gone and that was it. We just had to get on with it.

Our first match of the year was a challenge against Limerick in Meelick. I played out of my skin, the best I had played in a long time. That same weekend, as coach of Limerick Institute of Technology, I was supervising a training camp for the LIT players. It was a hectic schedule, late with LIT on the Friday night, up at six on the Saturday morning, and same again on the Sunday. I was wrecked and, before we played the match against Limerick on the Sunday, I had already covered five miles in Cratloe Woods with the LIT lads. I dashed back to the jacuzzi in the Shannon Shamrock to get some bit supple for the Limerick game and it worked. I played well and I made a few good saves. We drew the game and it was a useful workout.

Our National Hurling League campaign began on February 19 against Laois. Philip Brennan played in goal because LIT were involved in Fitzgibbon Cup action against Cork Institute of Technology on the same day and I asked to start on the sideline for Clare. We played badly that day, Dalo was not a happy camper at half-time but we scraped through 1-16 to 2-11. Laois played good stuff, their manager Paudie Butler had them well prepared but we were poor. My first outing was against Dublin at Parnell Park a week later and we won that game convincingly, 2-19 to 0-14. We had two wins under our belts but Galway brought us right back down to earth with a bang at Cusack Park on March 13. After a couple of relatively straightforward matches, we were caught by the pace of Galway who had played a tough match against Kilkenny the week before. We wanted to do well but it didn't happen for us. We lost 3-11 to 1-13 and we took a fair bit of stick locally after the game. In the dressing room, Dalo got stuck in. He told us that neither our performance nor our attitude was good enough, that we would have to up the tempo. I felt very down after the Galway game because Dalo was right, it was a terrible performance. After matches like that you always wonder what the future holds.

The perfect fillip arrived a week later against Kilkenny at Nowlan Park. It was the first competitive meeting between the two teams since the 2004 All-Ireland quarter-final replay and we were expecting a ferocious battle. I could feel a tension on our team bus and we wanted to go there and tear into them. The attitude was good and in the Hotel Kilkenny before the game, lads were really up for it. You don't see that too often for a league game. I felt wired-up myself and Dalo told us to go out there and give it a right lash. We beat them 2-13 to 1-8 and it could have been more. They got a goal at the end that I am positive was a square ball, but I was busy enough throughout and

I made a few saves. It was a good day to be a Clare man in Kilkenny. It was the first time we had beaten them for a while and, although I had expected a rough atmosphere, it wasn't too bad. The Kilkenny supporters were shocked to see their team losing like that and it lifted us and lifted our year. Six days later, we beat Waterford in Dungarvan and the atmosphere that day was one of the most hostile that I have experienced for a long time. The abuse was flying from the terraces in my direction and it was the first time I got that kind of personal stick in a league match. But I take no notice of it at this stage and thankfully, Colm wasn't there to hear it. It was intimidating and on the sideline, Dalo and Waterford manager Justin McCarthy had a go at each other. It was brilliant to come out of there with a 3-14 to 2-10 victory and it consigned Waterford to the relegation section in the league. The pace of the game was close to championship, with good tackling, blocking and both sets of players going at it hammer and tongs. The standard of hurling was poor at times but we wanted to stand up to the Waterford lads and show them what we were made of. The championship defeat against them in May 2004 had been humiliating and it was nice to make some amends. Those league matches against Kilkenny and Waterford really stand out, finally I felt that things were coming together and my puckouts were right on the money.

That night we flew to La Manga in southern Spain for a week-long training camp. Each morning, we were up by 6.30 to eat breakfast and gone by 7.30. We were told that the run down to the training facility was roughly a mile, but we soon found out that it was a three mile stint. The first morning, we set off as a group and the pace was unreal. Dr Padraig Quinn and Dalo decided to come with us but just a few hundred yards down the road, the Doc ran out of steam. I passed him out and he was down. 'What's wrong Doc?' I asked, laughing. 'Hamstring, gone,' he wheezed! He was under a bit of pressure but the hamstring was a good excuse and that was the end of the Doc's run. The pace of the run was unrelenting and I thought 'whoa, Davy'. I slowed down to my own pace and I let the lads off. The only thing that mattered to me was finishing the run ahead of

Dalo! He had set off way behind us and I was tipping along at the back of the field. I could see Dalo coming in the distance and he was making up ground on me, rapid! I put on a bit of a spurt and Dalo told me later that he thought he was going to pass me until I shook myself up a small bit.

That was one hell of a depressing run, every morning at 7.30. The training centre was something else though: indoor and outdoor running tracks, superb gym and training fields. We trained well, it was sharp and fast and our first morning was all touch work. We rested, then had a team meeting before going back for some gym work and more running. Each evening we hit the beach for running, jogging and stretching. The routine was good and varied. We didn't neglect our hurling and we ran a league with four different teams involved. East Clare was one team, Sixmilebridge and Tulla were put together, as were the Eire Óg and Clarecastle lads, while Kilmaley and St Joseph's Doora-Barefield had their own team. They even got their own kits made! The Shannon lads had a team of their own and they roped in Crusheen's Gerry O'Grady. It was seven-a-side hurling and nobody was holding back. The four managers were Dalo, selectors Fr Harry Bohan and Alan Cunningham, and county board treasurer PJ Kelly. The hurling was highly competitive and the ground was perfect, hard and with the grass cut to the bone. We bonded as a panel of players with team meetings where we aired our views, asked questions and talked.

It was a well-organised trip and our backroom men played their part. The heart and soul of the week was Mike Collins, who takes care of everything from keeping the gear clean to collecting sliotars and looking after the water supplies. 'Gazzy' is a great lad to have around the team and my son Colm adores him. But for me, the real unsung driving force behind the Clare team is our long-serving physiotherapist Colm Flynn. What Colm has done for players down through the years is unbelievable. A lad might be struggling for form and Colm will have a word in his ear to help him along. And if there's trouble in the camp, Colm will try to patch things up. Aidan Looney and Dan McNamara give the players rubs at training and on match-days, with Colm and Ger Hartmann looking after the physio. But Colm is much more than a physio, he is the link that holds everything together and, most important of all, he is a friend. Naturally, I have that special bond with Colm because I married his daughter Ciara and my son Colm is named after his grandfather.

There was time for relaxation during our week away, but just for one night. We took a bus to a pub that I part own in Praia da Rocha. We ate at the nearby 'Dockside' restaurant and when we got to the pub, music was in full swing. The lads sat back and enjoyed themselves but didn't overdo it by any means. We had planned to leave at 12.30 a.m. but when the craic got going some of the lads found it hard to leave! Nobody wanted to go home but everybody was on the bus by 1.30 a.m. We had a sing-song on the bus back but the routine never changed, the next morning we were up and ready for that horrible three-mile run down to the training camp.

We were tired when we arrived back in Ireland and our first league game in the second phase of the competition was just over a week later against Tipperary at Semple Stadium on April 10. We could have won by a lot more than we did (1-16 to 0-15) but they were just back from a training camp themselves. All-Ireland champions Cork were our visitors to Cusack Park a week later and, for the first twenty minutes, we couldn't handle their running game. They were killing us, but we changed tactics and went man for man. Cork got back to within three points of us towards the end when I was faced with the type of ball that a goalkeeper dreads: a high, dropping ball lobbed in between Brian Corcoran and Brian Lohan. They were pulling but the ball was coming under their heads and I knew it was coming in on top of me. It's the last thing you want in a game but I caught it, ducked out and cleared the ball. We held on for a 2-15 to 3-9 victory and that virtually sealed our place in the league final. We pulverised Wexford in our final group game, winning by 13 points, and we were set up for a league final showdown with Kilkenny on Bank Holiday Monday, May 2.

The last time we met Kilkenny in a league final was back in 1995. After losing, Ger Loughnane boldly proclaimed that we would win the Munster title that summer. We all thought he was off his rocker but of course, Loughnane was proved right. Those old memories surfaced in the build-up to this year's final and it was a game we were itching to win. We had given them a fair trimming up in Nowlan Park in March and it had transformed our season. But Kilkenny were a changed team after that game and they had embarked on a ruthless winning streak since. Now, we were due to meet again and I badly wanted to win a National League medal, the one major accolade missing from my collection. We trained hard and did a nice bit of work in the days leading up to the game itself. On the way to Thurles, we stopped at Inch House in The Ragg and I could feel that the lads were tense. We were ready for it and I was awfully wired-up myself. This year, I got into the habit of listening to music on a personal CD player on journeys to away matches, I have to thank a very special person who picked the right music, you know who you are. I sat on the front seat of the bus on my own every time because I am a bad traveller. I listened to my music and concentrated on my own mental state. When I do that, I can work things over in my head on the way to the game. I like my own space and time and don't want to talk to too many people while preparing mentally for a big game. This year in particular, I worked much harder on staying focused.

I wanted this league medal and I wanted to stand up to this Kilkenny crowd again. I expected that they would have a right go at us but I felt that our mood was right. In the first half, we played well. I know I made a couple of good saves from Henry Shefflin and Eoin Larkin but we played out of our skins. We should have gone in at half-time well ahead but instead, we were level. And a different Clare team came back out for the second half. People say that Kilkenny were awesome but ultimately, the sheer class of DJ Carey changed the game. He made Kilkenny's second and third goals but never got the credit that he should have. People want to see DJ racking up big scores but those days are gone. He does a different job for Kilkenny now and some of the stuff that he did on league final day was superb. He set up Larkin's goal with a hand-pass and he cut a ball into Henry Shefflin's hand that set up another one. Henry got a lot of credit for Kilkenny's victory but DJ was the real inspiration. Kilkenny went to town on us, but they were able to because we sat back. I can't put my finger on what happened but it was a loss that pushed us to ask serious questions of ourselves afterwards. 'The most important thing is what's coming up,' Dalo said to us later. 'Championship is everything.'

We went back to the drawing board after the Kilkenny knock. After a disappointing end to a good league run we had a month to get ourselves back together in preparation for our championship opener against Tipperary on June 5. We took the opportunity to get away for a training weekend in Waterford but before that, I made a guest appearance on RTÉ's *The Den* along with Dustin and Soky! I told nobody about this but some of the boys had seen me on the television so when I arrived down to the team hotel, I went straight to my bedroom. The lads were eating at the time but there was no way I was going into the dining room! Colin Lynch (who had accompanied me to Dublin) said to me, 'They're all looking for you, Dustin!' I faced down the boys eventually but they had a field day.

We trained in Waterford on the Saturday and Sunday before we convened for a team meeting. Dalo had his tactics ready, written out on sheets of paper on the clipboard. But Gerry Quinn was up to his usual devilment. When we discuss team affairs at brainstorming sessions, each member of the panel is portrayed as an egg. A basket is drawn on a sheet of paper and all of the eggs should be in the basket as a symbol of team unity. The eggs were in the basket on the clipboard all right, but outside the basket was the comment: 'Gerry Quinn for captain.' There were other comments of course (some of them unfit for public consumption) and written beside my egg was 'Dustin'. Dalo came in, pulled up the sheet and was greeted by Gerry Quinn's handiwork! Gerry's the real joker in our pack but he has had his troubles down through the years. He was dropped off the panel for a spell in 2004 but in fairness, his attitude was spot on in 2005.

June 5 finally arrived and the championship was upon us. On the morning of the Tipperary game, I felt good. There was a bit of tension in the camp but the only downer was that it was pissing rain. Some people seem to think that wet conditions suit us but we prefer dry days because we are well able to hurl. Tipperary adapted better at the

Gaelic Grounds and they took their two goal chances early on. Michael Webster was causing us all sorts of problems at full-forward for Tipp in the first half. We missed four clear-cut goal chances and we shot some dreadful wides. Even in the second half, when it looked like our goose was cooked, we kept on going. Nothing was falling for us but we kept plugging away, and that was encouraging. I was up for the game big-time from the very start and in the pre-match parade, I told each and every one of the Tipperary players what I thought of them. 'Let's have a fucking go at these boys,' I roared. People look at me on television and from the stands and terraces and think I must be some kind of nutcase. But there is always method behind my madness on the field of play. Everything is designed to try to give Clare an edge. I was booked by referee Pat O'Connor in the second half for nothing. It was an absolute disgrace. Webster never stopped mouthing at Brian Lohan all day long and, very early in the game, he came in and stood around my goalmouth, trying to intimidate me. I was only laughing at him because I was expecting something like this. He was having the odd kick at me and walking in front of me. It only drove me on even more. Anybody that knows me knows that the last thing a player should do is try to mix it with me because I get so fired up I will let nothing past me. I love that stuff. That was Webster's mickey mouse way of trying to upset me, but what really pissed me off was his constant chat to Lohan. As I was walking past Webster I left the end of my hurley out and he walked against it. I did not jab him with the hurley, he didn't feel a thing, and yet I got booked. The umpire called Pat O'Connor over, the same umpire that gave Seánie McGrath two points when we played Cork in 1997, two points that were as wide as could be. I'm not talking inches here, these were real wides. I bet Seánie still remembers those 'scores' to this day because he must have had some laugh to himself. We could not believe it.

Webster had a good game against us though, I must give him credit for that. He showed a lot of fire but I didn't agree with his antics and I would love to come across him again. The man wanted to know about it against Clare but a fiery Brian Lohan against Michael Webster would have been a different story. If Brian had played against

Tipperary in the same way that he played in his last three championship matches, Webster would have been anonymous. When Brian is performing the way I know that he can, there is no full forward that can touch him. Webster caught two or three balls and waved the ball in his face on one occasion and Brian had a swipe. I don't know how rattled he was but it pissed me off seeing that. Webster had a good Munster final against Cork and he had a good first half against Galway in the All-Ireland quarter-final. His heart and soul is in it, he gives everything for Tipperary but I am looking forward to meeting him again. We had a good battle, we shook hands afterwards and we moved on. He patted me on the head during the game too but that didn't bother me in the slightest, he can do whatever he wants. But God help him if I had stopped a shot because I would have laid into him. I am well able to handle lads like that. When I started on Webster, I wanted to draw his attention away from Brian because I wanted to take him myself. I could do nothing about the two early goals and I didn't get a shot to save for the rest of the game but I was dying for action. I knew this year that I had enjoyed a good league campaign and I was itching for the championship. But there is nothing worse than shooting yourself in the foot and we only had ourselves to blame. I was disgusted after a 2-14 to 0-14 defeat but we had to pick ourselves up quickly. Before the game, I had been speaking to Eoin Kelly and I told him that I felt Tipp were there or thereabouts. They have the hurlers but they will only be successful if they apply themselves properly. At half-time against Cork in the Munster final, they were heading for a pasting. But in the second half, they tore into it. I don't buy into the theory that Cork took their foot off the gas – Tipp upped their game. They never threw in the towel and I respect them for that.

Incidentally, my father and I happened to find ourselves seated beside Waterford hurling manager Justin McCarthy at the Munster final. As we made our way to our seats in the Covered Stand at Páirc Uí Chaoimh, Justin basically ignored my father. 'How's it going Justin?' I asked. Surely a salute wasn't too much to ask, but not one word was spoken between us for an hour and twenty minutes. I know that my father was very pissed off with Justin because he had had a go at our manager Cyril Lyons during the 2002 All-Ireland semi-final. My father hit back at Justin the following year when we met in the league and the whole thing has festered ever since. But I was annoyed with McCarthy because he never even acknowledged our presence at the Munster final. That is sad, he is no better than we are and knows no more about hurling than we do, even though he might like to think he does.

***

It was difficult to focus in on a new championship but we could go one of two roads, let all our training go out the door or knuckle down hard and try again. We were wary of a trip to Dublin on June 18, they had a new manager (Tommy Naughton) but we did what we had to do at Parnell Park. A 1-23 to 0-9 victory was a nice tonic but the big tests in our qualifier group were yet to come, Offaly and Waterford. Kilkenny roasted Offaly in the Leinster championship and gave them an absolute pasting. I didn't read too much into that result, Kilkenny got on a roll and hit the net a few times. When Kilkenny do that, it's almost impossible to hit back. They could have beaten us by 20 points in the league final and we would not have deserved that. Kilkenny demolished Offaly by 31 points but the scoreline was harsh on them. Then, Offaly had only six days to recover before they played Waterford and finished up losing by eleven points. We now had a situation where Offaly had been well humiliated and were being told that they were gone and that they were absolutely useless. How would their players react? I knew they would fight on their hands and knees against us. I know their manager John McIntyre and the man has fierce pride in what he does. He is a good manager and I knew he would have the team ready. In Portlaoise on July 2, we beat them by a single point, 1-12 to 1-11. 'Ye were poxed lucky.' 'Jaysus, if ye couldn't beat Offaly well ye might as well forget it.' Those were the comments in Clare after the game. Weather-wise, it was a brutal night and when we arrived in Portlaoise, I felt that one or two of our guys were not tuned in. 'Greasy ball here kid, you're not handling anything,' I remember saying to myself. 'Anything that comes your way, just deal with it safely.' This was a big championship game for Clare and I avoid catching anything I am unsure of on a slippery night. Do the simple things right and, on a night like that, take no chances.

I have never come across a team as wired as Offaly were. They were up for it against us in 1998 but this was something else. They were roaring and shouting at each other and McIntyre had them hopping out of their skins. They were fighting for their respect and the Offaly guys are proud hurlers. They're not bad players either when they decide to let it go, and sometimes people forget that. It was a rough game but after finding ourselves six points down, we fought our way back to pip them. We won a battle and deep down, we were thrilled. It's very hard to play a team on a wet night on a tight pitch. They blocked, tackled and harried us and they played eight defenders in the second half. We had hammered Offaly at the Gaelic Grounds in the qualifiers a year before but their attitude then was nothing compared to what it was now. They got their respect back but, even though we were in trouble, I never felt that we were going to lose. Very few teams would have come out of Portlaoise that night with a victory, Cork and Kilkenny maybe, but nobody else. That Offaly team was so fired-up that it took me back to when we played Waterford in the Munster championship in 2004. I knew coming away from Portlaoise that we were going places. People said that I was crazy.

The Offaly win secured our place in the All-Ireland quarter-finals but our remaining qualifier was a serious game because the winners avoided Cork and Kilkenny in the last eight. As far as we were concerned, we still owed Waterford some serious payback for the humiliation they had inflicted on us in May 2004. We were in our own back yard but we knew that Waterford would travel in their droves. It was probably the first time that Clare fans were ever outnumbered at Cusack Park but the atmosphere was absolutely electric. And we started to hurl. We attacked the ball, sent good deliveries to our inside men and we went for goals. We scored four of them and came through comfortably, 4-14 to 0-21. I was psyched that day, I made a good early save and I felt really good. Waterford had Eoin McGrath sent off but I think that it made them play even better if anything. The Waterford lads were annoyed about that decision but McGrath tumbled to the ground and when he did, he flicked back with his hurl and connected with Gerry O'Grady's helmet. 'Ref, for fuck's sake,' I roared. I was straight to the umpire and I asked him to take notice. The Waterford players were pissed off because we were complaining but what was I supposed to do? On *The Sunday Game* later that night, it was proven that McGrath struck Gerry O'Grady across the head. I didn't think that McGrath would be sent off but when you're on the pitch, you will take whatever advantage you can get. Besides, if I had done something wrong, the Waterford boys certainly would not have let me away with it. When McGrath walked, Waterford rallied and worked a bit harder. Having the extra man made little difference to us, but we were delighted with the result.

The quarter-final draw pitted us with Wexford on July 24. A week before, we travelled to Dublin for a training session at Croke Park and got there for the second half of the Dublin v Laois Leinster football final. The atmosphere was fantastic. I love Croke Park and only Kilkenny had beaten us there in the previous decade, before Cork this year. We got a good feel of the place afterwards and we felt that we had to up our work-rate considerably to compete with Wexford. We were confident of beating them but they had played well in the Leinster final against Kilkenny and we knew we would need to maintain our intensity for the full game to get that victory. I suggested to Dalo that it would be a good idea to go to Croke Park the day before to watch the Armagh v Tyrone Ulster football final. That was a savage encounter, full of focused, controlled aggression. It got us right mentally for the Wexford game and we headed for our base at the Portmarnock hotel, where Armagh had stayed on the Friday night. The night before games I prefer not to mingle with the other lads so I had a steak in my bedroom. I went for a puck-around with a few of the boys later and, at a team meeting, Dalo told us that he wanted us to be more intense and to work harder on the basics: tackling, blocking and hooking. At 11 p.m. I changed into my wet gear and made my way to Portmarnock beach. I had been running on the beach in Lahinch before Munster championship matches and I decided not to change from my settled routine. I spent 45 minutes on Portmarnock beach and it did my head the world of good.

On the team bus to the game the next day, the mood felt right and it reflected in our performance. The result was never in doubt from early on and we won in style, 1-20 to 0-12. The pundits said that Wexford were poor but we felt we deserved more credit. The chasing, the blocking, tackling and the amount of work we did off the ball was unreal. 'We're coming right,' I said to myself. Wexford never got the chance to execute their gameplan, their small forwards couldn't get loose to get their shots away.

Cork pulled away late on against Waterford in the day's second quarter-final and I was happy with that. We were itching to have a go at Cork, but even people close to me said we hadn't a snowball's chance in hell. We had three weeks to prepare and I upped the ante. I was training twice or three times daily, stretching, alley work and sessions with Darren Ward in the Shannon Shamrock. After a game, I tend to chill out for a few days, then increase the intensity in training again. I wind down and relax for a week before the next match. In the final few days leading up to games, I work on my head.

In training, we were gearing up for what lay ahead of us. We have a fantastic panel and the fringe players really came to the fore. The second team played the Cork running and hand-passing game and we had to counteract that. We were back to the old days with 6.30 a.m. starts at Cusack Park – every Friday, Saturday and Sunday morning for a couple of weeks before the game. My view of Cork is that they are not the most outstanding team I have ever seen but tactically, they are very good. They are organised and they work hard, and that counts for a lot. That's why they have contested three All-Ireland finals in a row.

We knew that Cork were good but I was still very confident. I honestly could not see us being beaten because our preparation was spot on. We were so right and I fully believed that this was our year to win the All-Ireland title. I wasn't the only Fitzgerald psyched up for the challenge that lay ahead. I had my gear packed, ready to go and my father produced a smaller Clare gear-bag for Colm. My son packed his bag, picked up his two hurleys and now, he was ready too. When we have a championship game in Dublin on the Sunday, our bus driver Donie makes the trip to the capital early on the Saturday morning. But the team bus is always fully loaded up with the team's gear on the Friday night.

Colm said to my father, 'Pat, I gotta drop my gear up to the bus.' My mother smiled and said, 'Colm, where are you going with your gear and those two hurleys?' He replied, 'Nuala, I'm part of this team. I've been with them all year, there's a match on Sunday and I'm ready.'

The next morning we ate breakfast at the Great Southern Hotel. At Shannon airport we chilled out in the VIP lounge before boarding the plane for Dublin. When we touched down, Donie took us straight to Croke Park for the Dublin v Tyrone football championship match and once again, there was a superb atmosphere.

After the game, we encountered two unhelpful Gardaí as we tried to make our way out of Croke Park. 'Where do ye think ye are going? Who do ye think ye are?' was the line of questioning as Donie tried to manoeuvre the team bus out of the stadium. Luckily, the Dublin team bus emerged with a Garda escort and motorcycles. We linked on to the back of that cavalcade and made three miles before the cops realised what we were doing!

Our base on the Saturday night was the luxurious Castleknock Hotel in Dublin but, just like the Wexford game, I preferred not to eat dinner with the rest of the lads. Instead, I went up to my room and ordered steak and chips with a glass of Coke. We went through a few tactics at a team meeting later but the real work was already done, we had Cork's running game well sussed.

I was itching for another run on Portmarnock beach so Jimmy Browne drove me forty minutes across the city. I took in the sea air as I powered up and down the beach but my absence had created a certain amount of panic back in Castleknock. We got there just before midnight to find Colm had told one or two of the lads that I wasn't feeling great. It is amazing how much Colm will pick up when I am restless before a game and even Dr Padraig Quinn was ready to examine me, which of course was not necessary.

Normally, I find it easy to sleep the night before a match but that night was different. I was restless because I could not stop thinking about what lay ahead. I ignored breakfast the next morning, instead grabbed an apple and went for a walk on a deserted golf course.

We had plenty of time to kill before we left for Croke Park so I went back up to my bedroom and watched a film on TV, *Seabiscuit*, the story of the long-shot horse that captured America's heart during the depression. The movie struck a chord with me because in the public's eyes, Clare were the long shots.

I was completely focused and listened to music on my headphones all the way to Croke Park. I saw nobody on my way in and found myself walking aimlessly around the place because I was unable to sit down. I laid out my gear on the dressing room table, grabbed my sub-goalkeeper Philip Brennan and headed to the warm-up area to get going. I took a cold shower after that, threw the gear on and I was buzzing. I ran out through the tunnel and into the light, hit the crossbar a rap and I knew I was feeling good. The world was still just fine then.

2 NEAREST AND DEAREST

If you don't know [your family's] history, then you don't know anything.
You are a leaf that doesn't know it is part of a tree.

Michael Crichton

Hurling is a massive part of my life but without my family, I am nothing. I would now like to introduce you to the Fitzgerald clan, the special people who helped to shape and mould me into the person I am today.

My parents, Pat and Nuala, were married in 1970 and after a few months living in Limerick City, they settled at number 3, Thomond Terrace in the village of Sixmilebridge. I was born in Limerick's Maternity Hospital on August 2, 1971, tipping the scales at 5lbs 15oz, and my childhood days at Thomond Terrace were happy ones. I was first introduced to a hurley at four years of age by my uncle, John Fitzgerald, and my next-door neighbour, Jack Lynch, made my early hurls. These days, well-known hurley-maker John Torpey looks after the job. John is one of my closest friends.

My sister Helen arrived in 1973 and the Fitzgeralds spent 16 happy years in Thomond Terrace before moving to Mount Ivors on the Castlecrine Road on October 11, 1987. Our present base is just outside the village, literally a 30-second drive.

My father Pat, who hails from Truagh in Sixmilebridge, played a bit for Clonlara but made his name in GAA circles as an administrator. His brother John, a massive influence on my career, enjoyed a long and distinguished career with O'Callaghan's Mills. John hurled for 34 years.

Pat's administrative career in the GAA began back in 1983 with the Bórd na nÓg. He was the last Clare hurling board secretary before the hurling and football boards amalgamated in 1990 and he has served as county board secretary ever since. It is a demanding role for my father and he seems to be on the go non-stop. He has somehow managed to combine that role with his work in Aer Rianta in Shannon. He has worked there since the 1970s.

Pat's interest in the GAA deepened as I became more and more involved in hurling. After every match, since I was U-10, I have always asked Dad for his honest assessment of my performance during the game. I knew myself if I had made a mistake but Dad always remained positive and told me that I had done well. Young kids need that type of encouragement because if they are harassed or abused, they will quickly turn their backs on the game. I have watched parents on sidelines and some of them are too intense. They push their kids to the limit and then they wonder why the kids give up the game.

During my formative years, Dad was never afraid to give me a necessary kick in the arse when it was needed. I had a healthy fear of my father and a keen respect for his authority. He never allowed me outside the door until I was well into my teens and I was one of the later starters on the disco scene. When he discovered that I had taken a drink, he let loose with both barrels and I decided not to become a regular drinker. Thankfully, I have never had a problem with the bottle. I can have the occasional one if I want, but drinking is something that has never interested me. I choose not to drink and I enjoy a good quality of life without the liquor.

My father is a man of principles and he likes things done in a straight manner. Those traits have rubbed off on me to a certain extent but I am much more of a risk taker. Business-wise, he always looks out for my best interests but sometimes I think he despairs of my decisions. But he never judges and he has always stood firm behind me.

Pat leads a double life to a certain extent. During the day, he devotes his time to Aer Rianta and at night, Clare GAA takes over. I would like people to know that he never claims a single cent in expenses from the GAA, even though our phone bill is always colossal. My mother always shudders when the most recent statement drops through the letterbox. From six o'clock in the evening, you will always get Pat Fitzgerald on the home number. On the off chance that he is not available, he is either on another call or away on county board business. He has taken a fair bit of stick from certain clubs in the county who believe he's only working for the good of Sixmilebridge, but our club gets the same treatment as any other. My father is the most honest man I know and he does not deserve criticism from other clubs and from people who should know better. Pat loves Clare GAA and will always endeavour to do his best for the county. I think genuine players, supporters and officials know that. The people who know him best certainly appreciate his efforts. Ger Loughnane asked my father to launch his autobiography in November 2001. That's some indication of the respect Loughnane has for Pat Fitzgerald.

I do regret that my father and I are both so busy. I take my fair share of holidays throughout the year but my parents have never been abroad together. I remember a time when my father worked himself so hard that he spent almost a month in Dublin's St. James' Hospital. It was scary to see him in that condition but typically, he bounced back. Clare hurling is now his main passion in life and one of the best days of his life was July 9, 1995, the day we won the Munster hurling title for the first time since 1932. He ran onto the pitch, lifted me up in his arms and I could see tears in his eyes. That was the first time I had seen a display of emotion like that from my father and it meant the world to me. It showed how much he cared for Clare and how much he cared that I was part of this great day.

He has always fought my corner and when I was looking to nail down a permanent place on the Clare hurling team, he always kept me straight and told me what people were really thinking. 'You're under pressure,' he would say. That was a valuable tip-off and a serious piece of motivation rolled into one. But Dad had faith in me and he knew I could handle whatever was thrown in my direction.

A lot of the Clare players do not realise that my father would do absolutely anything they ask. He has the best wishes of the players at heart and if they look for anything, he will take care of it. The Clare county board are lucky to have him because we hear more and more horror stories from other counties where players are treated like dirt. Clare is different and the players respond brilliantly because they are treated in a proper manner. Gear, gym membership, transport and meals after training are the basic issues and the players cannot quibble. That is the way it should be and my involvement with Clare is good for my father because he can see things from a player's perspective.

My mother Nuala has stood loyal beside Pat through the years. When I was a kid, I remember my mother out in the back garden, hurling with me. She enjoys the game but my sister Helen tells me that when the pressure comes on during a big match, my mother hates it. She will bury her head between her knees and switch off from the action for a few seconds. My mother has a softer nature than Dad but you would be wise not to underestimate the tough streak in her. She has had to be strong because there has been a lot of tragedy in her life.

Nuala Mulvihill, a native of Shannagolden in West Limerick, enjoyed a lively upbringing in a large family. She was one of five girls and they had seven brothers for company. Along the way, Mam lost three brothers long before their time. Pat died aged 29 from a heart attack, John suffered a similar fate at 42 and Denis, better known as 'Fonnie', was just 43 when he died of cancer. Another brother, Conor, underwent heart bypass surgery at 38, so there is a clear history of heart problems in the family. I went for an angiogram in Galway's Bon Secours hospital in 2000, just to be on the safe side, and I needed another one in 2003 at Limerick's Regional Hospital when I thought I was in serious trouble.

The Mulvhills were a talented lot and Nuala's father, John, played football for Limerick. Her brothers Donal and Fonnie were both good enough for trials with English soccer club, Queens Park Rangers, but she swears that Conor was the best footballer of the lot.

My mother is a very supportive woman and has also immersed herself in the GAA. She works in my pub, the Bellsfort Inn, and in the days leading up to Clare matches, she enjoys filling out the official team lists that must be submitted with the players' names written down in Irish and English. Translation is no problem to her and she has a trusty Irish-English dictionary for the job!

My sister Helen is a tough nut who took a few belts during her camogie playing days. She is very loyal to me but unfortunately, she has heard an awful lot of the abuse that the lager louts fire my way on nights out. It upsets her but she will stick up for me no matter what, even if the odd row develops. I am very close to Helen, who is two years younger than me. She is much more relaxed than me but if she has something on her mind, she speaks out. We sometimes fight like cats and dogs and we might not speak to each other for days, but eventually we get over it. I like her stubborn streak and she has a savage temper that can sometimes bubble to the surface. When we were kids, she once threw a concrete block through the window at me, missing her target by inches!

My parents and my sister Helen have formed a special bond with my son Colm who is now part of the furniture in Sixmilebridge. Colm was born on March 11, 1997 and he is the best thing that ever happened to me. I am separated from Colm's mother Ciara but she is very flexible about access to him and I can see him pretty much whenever I want. I pick him up at any time to bring him to see a match or off for a drive. I found the first few years after Colm was born quite difficult, but in recent times the two of us have really bonded.

Colm is the most important thing in my life but I am the first to admit that I don't spend enough time with him. He knows that I love him and he comes to all of my matches and training sessions. It is great to see him involved in the Clare set-up, I keep a close eye on him and his hurling is constantly improving.

Colm loves to help out and when training comes to an end, he helps Mike Collins to collect the sliotars dotted around the pitch. He is a sociable kid and has made friends with Colin Lynch's son and Alan Cunningham's young fella. It would be great if some day the three of them could stand side by side, wearing the saffron and blue. Colm loves being part of the Clare scene and after training, he dines with the rest of the players and staff. The lads treat him well and that means a lot to me. They have almost adopted him as their own by now.

On the surface, Colm is a happy child and I just hope that beneath the surface, he is truly content. I am quickly realising that I need to become more involved in what he is interested in. He loves all sports and Ciara handles him superbly, giving him the leeway that he needs. I will never push Colm and tell him what to do because he has to discover life for himself. I do realise that he will come under a certain amount of pressure just because he is my son. It is not a situation I want to see develop but unfortunately it is out of my control.

He will never be a goalkeeper if I get my way because people would forever be comparing him to me. I want him to be his own man and to enjoy his hurling if he wants to pursue a career in the game. It doesn't matter to me what sport he plays, whether it's hurling, football, soccer or rugby, I will be fully supportive of his choices and he will not be pushed into anything. I was wary of bringing Colm to Clare matches until the last couple of years because I thought it would be unfair on him to hear the abuse I get. I have to put up with it but there is no need for Colm to be listening to these apes booing me. I doubt he has fully grasped the situation yet and down around the dugout, he might not hear the worst of it.

It seems that Colm is a hurling fanatic now, like his father. I tested him one day and the response gladdened my heart. 'I'm thinking of not playing next year,' I said to him. 'Dad, you play next year,' he quickly replied. I do worry about Colm because I was picked on in St Flannan's. I don't want Colm to be picked on and I never want him to pick on another child. I have watched his development closely and he is a friendly child who has a lot of time for other young kids. I have never had much time for smart young fellas, the lads that think they know it all. I prefer the unassuming types with a genuine love for life and the game of hurling. I look into their eyes when I arrive to take a coaching session and I realise just how fortunate I am to be able to give a bit back. I think about how lucky I am to live a full and active life. A very special lady made me realise just how huge a gift life is.

Watching her battle against all odds inspired me to keep on going through the hard times.

****

I first met Sheila Considine at a training session before the 1995 All-Ireland final. Our preparations were in full swing and as I trained, I glanced towards the tunnel area at Cusack Park and spotted a girl in a wheelchair, protected from the evening chill by a shawl. She was taking everything in and her thirst for hurling seemed as great as the hurlers out on the pitch going through their paces. As I was coming off the field, my father beckoned me over. 'This young girl wants to talk to you, David,' he said. Sheila was dressed in her Clare jersey and immediately, a special bond was formed.

Sheila suffered from spina bifoda and unfortunately, she could not travel to any Clare matches, not even the 1995 final. Instead, she sat glued to the television as we beat Offaly and later that night, she hit the record button on the VCR as my father and I were interviewed on TV at the post-match function. Sometimes, when I called to visit Sheila at home in Dangan, she played that same video. It was humbling being in her company. The family home was a shrine to me and the amount of Clare hurling memorabilia she collected had to be seen to be believed. Sheila also took a great deal of pride in putting together scrapbooks of my career as Clare's goalkeeper. To this day, I still enjoy leafing through those pages. Old memories flicker into life once more and it is all thanks to Sheila.

Before every big championship game, I always visited Sheila for a good luck kiss and a chat with her parents, Biddy and Pete. In 1997, I was dropped for a league match against Galway and I was feeling down. Hearing Sheila was in hospital put things in perspective. Biddy asked me to visit Sheila because at the time, she was very ill. 'What should we do with her?' Biddy asked me, despair in her eyes. 'They're saying she has no time left. Should we bring her home?'

I couldn't believe that Biddy was asking me for advice and that she valued my opinion so much. I felt a real love for Biddy just then, but I also felt a deep sorrow because I was helpless in that situation.

'Maybe she would be happy at home,' I whispered. The three of us travelled back to Dangan by ambulance. Sheila was finding it very difficult to breathe and the doctor did not hold out too much hope. We played Galway that same day and I told Clare FM's Matthew McMahon to mention that I was asking for her. Sheila was given just days to live, but she was an incredible fighter and she rallied.

I had always told Sheila that she would be present at my wedding. Biddy never believed it could happen, but on July 11 1997, Sheila was beside myself and Ciara at the altar as our special guest. The woman that had been written off so many times continued to defy the odds until November 1998, when she was called from this world.

As her health deteriorated rapidly, I spent many an evening at her house. Around that time, I had booked a holiday to Spain but I was reluctant to go because I feared the worst. Biddy persuaded me to fly out on a Friday night, the night Sheila passed away. I touched down in Malaga airport and contacted home for the latest. Distraught at her passing, I stayed up all night and boarded a plane straight back to Dublin. I arrived back in Dublin at six o'clock in the evening and, even though the funeral was due to leave Tulla at seven, Biddy waited until I arrived. I made it from Dublin to Tulla in two hours and I immediately noticed the massive crowd outside, waiting for me. I had never entered a mortuary in my life because I am uncomfortable in those situations but Sheila's uncle Pat whispered quietly, 'Davy, you have to go in.' I faced my fear and the sweat rolling down my cheeks was soon replaced by tears. I entered the mortuary and walked over to Biddy and Pete, embracing them in a warm hug. Then I went to Sheila and kissed her gently on the forehead. Before the funeral departed for the church, the family played a tape of GAA radio commentator Mícheál O'Muircheartaigh. He was describing moments in big matches like only he can, moments in which I was involved. The last words in the mortuary were about me. That was some compliment and I was just grateful that I had made Sheila's final years a little bit happier. At the funeral mass, the family invited me to sit with them in the front pew and I was deeply honoured. I helped to shoulder her coffin to her resting place and wished her a fond farewell. I may have had an effect on Sheila Considine's life but it was a two-way street. She had a massive impact on my life and made me realise just how valuable life and family are.

Before big championship matches, I still visit Sheila in the graveyard in Tulla, just to chat for fifteen minutes or so. Sheila was always there for me when she was alive and I know that she is still there for me now. She is one of the first people I turn to for help before a big match. She never lets me down.

I am glad that I shared so much of my life with Sheila and there is a special place in my heart for people less fortunate than myself. I have taken part in charity work in the past and it gives me a great sense of fulfilment. Frank Keogh, a Sixmilebridge man, developed a serious illness at 43 years of age and I decided to embark on a 100-mile cycle to raise some money to help fund his treatment. A few of my Clare team-mates mucked in too, Anthony Daly and Brian Lohan, and we came up with £23,000. We have raised in the region of €50,000 over the years but we are not looking for any kudos. It is important to remember those less fortunate, and if my profile enables me to raise awareness and badly-needed funds, I will gladly use it. I like to give of my time generously and I have visited many sick people in hospitals. If I can make them feel happy, even for a few minutes, it has been a worthwhile visit. Some people are very unselfish with their time and shine like beacons when it comes to charity work, but there are others who could do a lot more instead of frittering away their spare hours.

For the People in Need Telethon in 2000, a helicopter ferried me from Bundoran in Donegal to Tory Island for a fundraising challenge. I had expected a car to meet me on the island but tractor was the preferred mode of transport and I was unceremoniously bundled into the back box! In the middle of a field, I was stuck between two sticks and the idea was simple. Every goal that was scored past me meant a few quid for People in Need. We continued along the west coast of Ireland, stopping at various islands to raise more money, and it was a fantastic day. The highlight for me was the helicopter ride over the Cliffs of Moher and back into Lahinch.

I will continue to do my bit for charity and I admire people like JP McManus who can set aside money for a good cause. I am in awe of JP because, even though he is one of Ireland's wealthiest men, he remembers his roots. I had a chance to say hello to him in Thurles before the 2003 Limerick v Waterford Munster championship match but I bottled it! I was itching to approach him because he seemed very down to earth and levelheaded. He came from a gambling background and I can relate to JP because he has taken more than a few risks. I read that he spends most of his time in Switzerland now but he regularly travels back to Ireland to organise golf tournaments and other fundraising events for local charities.

****

Kevin 'Trixie' Twomey was without question the biggest influence on my hurling career. He was my best friend, my biggest critic and my trusted mentor all rolled into one. When I was just fifteen years old, Trixie handed me my big break with the Clare minors and that cemented a lifelong friendship that lasted until he passed away in July 2004. Trixie was a member of the great Newmarket team of the 1960s and won a number of county titles in goals. When he came to live in Sixmilebridge, he took me under his wing straight away and taught me everything he had learned.

But I was hooked on this great game long before I met Trixie for the first time. My uncle John Fitzgerald was also a massive influence during my formative years, and every Friday night he would call to see me in Thomond Terrace. I looked forward to John's arrival all day long and when he got there, I was always togged out in my gear, ready for a game of 'end to end' in the hall. John was barely in the door when he was nabbed and he would often spend two hours at a time playing with me. Later, the pair of us went to his house in Truagh, stopping to pick up a bag of chips along the way. As we were driving, I knew when to drop the hints. 'I could eat a horse,' was a particular favourite of mine. The word 'chips' was never actually spoken but John knew that the belly was rumbling!

It was the little things about John that made me love him - when I was a little bit older, I found out that he had given me a calf for my first birthday. Presents never mattered to me because it was his company that I wanted most of all. I slept in the same bed as John on those Friday nights, grabbing a couple of hours sleep ahead of the early morning milk run. We got up at 6 a.m. and I loved the entire milking process. My favourite part was bottling the milk and, after spraying the bottles with water, they were trailer-bound for Limerick City. We would arrive into Limerick at half past eight in the morning, 25 or 30 crates on the trailer. Our very first stop was across from Thomond Park, Munster's famous rugby ground, and at the end of the run, John would give me money to buy sweets for the journey home. When we got back, he made the breakfast, scrambled egg and toast – a traditional dish that I love to this day.

Our work wasn't finished yet and after the breakfast, it was time to clean the cowsheds. It was a messy job but I loved it. As the hours passed, I started to really come alive. It was soon time to change into my football boots, togs, socks and jersey. There was a field, just down from the house, and I always ran down to it through two gates, my very own tunnel. I had sticks as goalposts and lost count of the amount of matches I played on that field, alone with my thoughts and a hurley and sliotar. I always managed to coax John down for a few pucks and from day one, I was the goalkeeper. When John wasn't around, I was every player under the sun: Clare great Seán Stack, my idol Gerry McInerney, Cork's Jimmy Barry-Murphy. I could stay out there for up to two hours by myself, hurling the ball up and down the field. But when John came down, I was always the goalkeeper, Clare's Seamus Durack or Kilkenny's Noel Skehan.

I knew from my very first day in Sixmilebridge National School in 1976 that it was not for me. I hated the place and never concentrated that much because all I wanted to do was hurl. I remember that our old Volkswagen had no exhaust and I was mortified going to school because of the noise! I always pleaded with my mother to let me off twenty yards from the school. I would walk the rest of the way.

Mr Shannon, originally from Corofin, was a great man for hurling in Sixmilebridge but he was also the man the sixth class pupils dreaded. He liked to give lads the odd poke of a biro into the ribs but we didn't mind. It was just his way. Mr Shannon drove hurling in the school along with Mr Bradley, the headmaster. We were lucky to have two men with such a keen interest in the game. I didn't care much about the books in primary school. When I got home in the evening, I dropped the bag and picked up the hurl.

John liked to bring me to a local match after dinner on Saturdays. His club was O'Callaghan's Mills and he introduced me to the game of hurling. I vowed that I would hurl for O'Callaghan's when I grew up and John was my inspiration. He was a versatile hurler, not the most skilful but he was tough and hard. Not the biggest lad in the world, it must run in the family, but what he lacked in size, he made up for with sheer heart. The Mills jersey at the time was a distinctive one, green with a diagonal saffron stripe. They don't wear it any more but I used to love the shirt that John wore for the 1977 Clare county senior hurling final, O'Callaghan's Mills v Sixmilebridge. Ask me now who to support when these two sides meet and you know where my loyalties are but for that match, I was a Mills man. I will never forget that game which the 'Bridge won to land their very first county senior title. John was a substitute for O'Callaghan's Mills and throughout the game he was crouched on the sideline in Tulla, a bag of nerves. I don't recall much of the actual match itself because I was too transfixed by John and his passion for the game. I remember the disappointment etched all over his face in the dressing room after the game. Heads were bowed and through the walls, the players could hear the Sixmilebridge celebrations in full swing. The raucous laughter and shouting must have sounded like jackhammers in their heads. I know that John still regrets not winning a county championship medal.

John took me to see the 1978 Munster hurling final at Semple Stadium in Thurles, a game that attracted an attendance in excess of 54,000. I was on what is now the New Stand side of the field but back then, there was no stand to cover patrons. We were at the mercy of the elements on an open bank. John held me in his arms for the entire game and he nearly lost his cool when I was struck by an apple on the back of the head. But I didn't care what happened to me that day because I was bitten by the bug, captivated by this big game. Watching the match gave me a huge rush and Cork corner back John Horgan, so distinctive with his blond hair, drove the ball an absolute mile with those monstrous frees down the field.

That was one of the first Clare matches I saw live and the league games in Tulla were special with the big crowds that followed the team. The Clare half-back line at the time was made up of Seán Hehir, Ger Loughnane and Seán Stack and it was a superb unit. Clare won two league titles in 1977 and 1978 with Fr Harry Bohan as manager, but they never quite made it in the championship. It is a pity because the talent was there.

When Clare played in Tulla, I stood behind Seamus Durack's goals. I idolised the man and when I got home, I went straight to the Old Mill in Sixmilebridge, not far from our home in Thomond Terrace. I honed my early skills in the Mill and there, I was Durack. The gates of the big factory wall were my goals and with cardboard boxes scattered on the ground, I could dive without fear of injury. A special guy, John Lynch, lived beside me. His father Jack was my hurley-maker in my early playing days. John was Clare's minor captain in 1981, right corner forward when they won the Munster championship and he was another early influence on my career. John showed no mercy as he peppered me with shots from 15 and 20 yards, but he toughened me up. If I got a slap of the ball on the head, there was no room for sympathy. 'Get up, GETTT UP!' John roared. He would never let me stay down. 'Come on Davy, you're much harder than that.' I had bags of respect for John because he was an excellent player and well known locally. I loved watching him perform for Clare and I felt privileged that he would spend time with me in the factory.

I was eight years of age when I played my first match for Sixmilebridge, introduced at wing-forward for the last ten minutes of a challenge game against Cloghaun in Limerick. I was different from the other kids because I was desperate to be a goalkeeper. My wish was soon granted and I played my first full match for Sixmilebridge, an U-12 game against Feakle in Tulla. We won by a cricket score, 13-2 to 0-0 and we beat Éire Óg in our next outing, 15-2 to 0-0. I have no problem remembering those scorelines, obscure as they may be. The reason is simple – I could never forget them.

I hurled away with the club during my primary school days and I had my first real taste of the harsh side of the game against Newmarket in an U-12 county semi-final. I was replaced at half-time after letting in two goals. That hurt but it made me work even harder and two years later, we had our revenge against Newmarket in the county decider. I went on to captain the Sixmilebridge U-13 side that won an All-Ireland Community Games title, beating Piltown from Kilkenny in 1983.

When I was in fifth and sixth class, we were often given half-days to watch the secondary school team from St Flannan's in action. I knew that I would be going to the famous Ennis hurling academy after primary school and Harty Cup hurling was my new Holy Grail. I went with my father Pat and Dr Padraig Quinn to the Harty matches. I was well prepared when I entered St Flannan's in September 1984 but it would turn out to be an often gruesome five years. Other pupils distanced themselves from me, I could not relate to them and I never mixed. It was difficult because secondary school is a daunting place for a young boy. Every morning the bus pulled up outside my house and it was 40 minutes of hell from Thomond Terrace to Ennis. I never sat beside any of my tormentors because I did not feel wanted. Instead, I made sure I sat up the front in the first or second row. Some lads used to smoke on the bus and I often wondered what it was like. I often wondered about asking them for a pull of a fag but I wasn't going to do that just to gain acceptance. I faced up to the fact that other local lads did not want anything to do with me and the first two years in St Flannan's were tough. I hated the journey home on the bus every evening from school. The bullies sat down the back, targeting lads weaker than themselves. They had different ways of terrorising their victims, painting them with markers or taking off their shoes before throwing them the length of the bus. I dreaded this treatment and I was caught a few times. On one occasion the bus pulled up outside my house and my shoes, shirt and jumper were thrown through an open window. I picked up my stuff with tears streaming down my face. Sometimes there was hope, like the time when they invited me for a game of indoor soccer. But the only reason they did was to give me a good kicking. Seven or eight of them brought me into a room with the sole intention of kicking the shit out of me. I felt terribly alone. Thank God for the hurling because it was the only thing that kept me in St Flannan's.

I bottled up in school, but the experience hardened me and hurling was a release. I can still see the faces of my tormentors clearly and, even now, if I see a child being picked on, it brings it all back. If I become aware of bullying when I am coaching young players, I try to nip it in the bud immediately. In St Flannan's, hurling helped me to forget and on that level I worked very hard. I forced my way onto the school's hurling teams through sheer perseverance and that made me feel good because none of the 'hard men' made it. I felt like I had finally got one over on them. When I got home in the evenings, I headed straight for the Mill and the books always played second fiddle. Homework meant copying from somebody else the next morning at quarter to nine. I had little or no interest in studying and I failed the vast majority of my exams. Hurling was the number one priority and it kept me that one step ahead of the bullies. I was determined not to let them break my spirit. I spent five years at St Flannan's and finished with a decent medal haul. I won an All-Ireland Colleges title in 1987 after we hammered St Kieran's of Kilkenny, two Dr. Harty Cups in 1987 and 1988 and a Dean Ryan (Munster) cup in 1988.

During my time at St Flannan's, my inter-county career also took off. I pulled on a Clare shirt for the very first time in 1985 and it is still difficult to fathom that I am the only player, still hurling for Clare, who played on the county's very first U-14 hurling team. My first game was against Waterford in the annual Tony Forrestal tournament for U-14 county teams and, although the competition ended in disappointment for Clare, I still felt a massive sense of achievement having made it at 13 years of age. In 1986, I was thrilled to be selected on the East Clare U-16 team that captured the Munster title and our 1-12 to 0-5 victory over mid-Tipperary in the final was my first real taste of the big time. On the bus to Killarney, on Munster senior hurling final day, my stomach was churning but the moment I hit the field, I loved it. Fitzgerald Stadium was my first taste of a provincial venue and I embraced it. That game was a curtain raiser to the main event, the Munster final between Clare and Cork which Cork won by three points. The next time Clare were involved in a Munster senior hurling final, I would have a much bigger role to play.

My hurling career went into complete overdrive in 1987. St Flannan's pulled off a Harty Cup and All-Ireland Colleges double and I was just 15 years old when I made my county minor debut against Cork in Kilmallock on May 19. I was called in by Éire Óg clubman, Paddy Duggan, on Trixie's recommendation. Trixie was a member of Paddy's backroom team and after he gave me my break in the early days, I always hated letting him down at any point in my career. I felt that I played pretty well in Kilmallock that evening, even though we lost the game by five points. I was still eligible to play for the East Clare U-16 team and it was perhaps inevitable that we would meet our great rivals from mid-Clare in the Munster final less than two months after making my minor debut. Mid-Clare had been crowned Munster U-16 champions in 1985 and it meant a huge amount to our players to succeed them a year later. This 1987 meeting was now a battle for local bragging rights and, with Paddy Duggan in charge of mid-Clare and Trixie involved in our backroom set-up along with John Nihill, Danno Doyle and John Wall, there was plenty of pre-match banter. The venue could not have been much bigger, Semple Stadium in Thurles before the drawn Munster senior hurling final between Cork and Tipperary. Even though I was captain, I had no speech prepared and it was left to John A Sexton, an Irish-speaking officer with the team, to hand me two pages of hand-written 'Gaeilge' after we had beaten mid-Clare. The problem was I couldn't read what John had written down so I had to go up, accept the cup and rattle away the 'cupla focail' I had myself. I had no idea what I was saying, the words were flowing but I was elsewhere, floating away on a natural high.

Paddy and Trixie were over the minor team again in 1988 but I feared that my championship was over before it had even begun, after breaking my hand training with the club. Less than two weeks before we were due to play Tipperary, the cast came off and on the same Friday evening, I played a minor league semi-final for Sixmilebridge against Éire Óg. The cast came off at 4 p.m. and I played two hours later. Paddy was on club duty looking after Éire Óg and he hit the roof when he saw me lining out. I badly wanted to play to prove myself ahead of the Tipp game. I had no feeling in my left hand and our full-back Alan Murphy, my best mate, was taking the puckouts. But I wasn't happy with Alan's deliveries and I took over, a move that almost cost me my place on the Clare minor panel. Sod's law ensured that against Tipperary in Bruff, I took a belt on the hand very early in the game. I thought it was broken again but I strapped it up and came through the game, which we lost by seven points.

In 1989, we would be crowned Munster minor champions and it was about time too. The signs were there that we were an emerging force after our successes at U-16 level. The successful St Flannan's teams were also backboned by Clare players so we knew that it had to come good soon. Mike McNamara took over the minor team in 1989 and we never did as much running in our entire lives. Mac brought a whole new approach, each player was treated equally but there was only one way to do things – Mike's way. If Mike Mac told you to run 20 laps, you ran 20 laps, so physically we were in terrific shape. Two years after losing to Cork in the Munster final, we annihilated them 7-8 to 0-7 in a Kilmallock semi-final.

Our Munster final showdown against Limerick on July 7 was the curtain-raiser to the senior decider between Tipperary and Waterford at Páirc Uí Chaoimh. We were well in control of the game but Limerick kept plugging away and we were left hanging on for a one-point victory, 2-13 to 2-12. I kept out a 21-yard free right at the death and when the final whistle blew we went mad. Winning a Munster minor championship was one hell of a feeling. Not many from that team went on to win All-Ireland senior medals, Jamesie O'Connor played at centre-forward in that minor final, Conor Clancy was in full-forward and my club-mate Christy 'Rusty' Chaplin covered the ground at midfield.

We had little time to reflect on our achievement as on our first night back at training, Mike Mac put us through an hour and a half of physical work. I struggle with the physical stuff at the best of times but this was something wicked, and some of the lads ended up vomiting. We played Galway in the All-Ireland semi-final on August 6 and that was my first experience of Croke Park. On the very same day, Antrim shocked Offaly in the senior match. I was blown away by Croke Park and as I looked around, I struggled to take it all in. With just minutes remaining in our game, I came off my line 15 yards to contest a 50/50 ball. I got there first but I came off second best in the collision and I ended up down on my knees, struggling to get to my feet. Stephen Marsh, who drove the team bus, was behind the goals and he ran out, picked me up and put me back in. We won the game by two points and slowly it began to sink in that we were through to an All-Ireland final.

September 1 approached and the hype around the county of Clare was huge. Big crowds flocked to our training sessions. We were mini-celebrities. We received sponsored gearbags and tracksuits, the best of everything, and we were also fitted for suits. We left for Dublin on Saturday, picked up in Sixmilebridge, down to Cratloe station and on from there to catch the train from Ennis to Dublin. No ordinary train mind you, this thing was a luxury machine with couches! My father decided to drive up instead, he is fussy like that. He never travels by train or plane and feels that everything is more in control when he's driving. We were ferried by bus from Heuston Station to the plush surroundings of Dublin's Montrose Hotel. Sleep was hard to come by that night for all of us, just hours before the biggest game of our young lives. We had a team meeting the next morning where Mike Mac drilled home some final instructions and then we were back on the team bus for the ride of a lifetime. We pulled away an hour and a half before throw-in and two Gardaí on motorbikes must have told the bus driver to drive as fast as he possibly could. The Garda escort was a great buzz and, as we whizzed through the streets of Dublin, I was in heaven. The sirens blared and we almost fell out of our seats as the bus roared on at breakneck speed. Some players tend to let this side of a big day distract them but I love those moments. I love the rush. Getting off the bus and walking proudly into Croke Park in our new suits was something I had always dreamed about and finally, I was here. I had a quick look through the tunnel to convince myself that it was for real. We came out from the far corner of the old Hogan Stand, at the Canal End side of the field; and I took everything in. The camera in my brain clicked away as it recorded as many images as possible. The match itself was one we would rather forget as Offaly beat us by 2-16 to 2-12. We missed plenty of chances and Brian Whelahan was inspired for Offaly. We would meet a number of their players on the playing fields of Ireland again in the following years. Johnny Dooley also performed well and John Troy was in their goal.

The next day, we were taken to Kilmainham for the traditional Monday reception, a practice that has been dispensed with in recent years. A free bar was available and the lads could not believe that they could drink as much as they wanted. The Tipp seniors were there, parading the Liam McCarthy cup. Their beaten opponents Antrim were at another table and we were also joined by the victorious Offaly minor team. I didn't think this type of get-together was necessarily a bad idea but, with everybody sticking to their own groups, I felt uncomfortable. I was envious of Tipperary and I wished that the Clare seniors were here. Looking at the Liam McCarthy cup perched on the Tipp table was something to drive me on. We stayed in the Montrose Hotel again that night before taking the train back to Ennis the next day. It was the first time I had ever paraded through the town and I was so sorry that we hadn't come back with the cup. Around 3,000 people had gathered in the square and it was a nice pick-me-up. It lifted the spirits again.

I was back hurling with the club soon after and a good spell of form brought me to the attention of the Clare senior management team. Five men were in charge at the time: Tony Kelly, Jim Cullinane, Donal O'Grady, Eamonn Long and Michael Kelly. Jim, who hurled for Clare in the 1960s, relayed the good news to my father that I had been drafted in as sub-goalie for the league game against Carlow at Cusack Park in October 1989. I had to wait until February 1990 for my first appearance in the team, against Down in Ballygalget, and Lady Luck played a big part as I grabbed hold of the jersey. Leo Doyle, a brother of Liam from Bodyke, was Clare's regular goalkeeper at the time but the week before the Down game, Leo's appendix burst. I was flabbergasted when I got the call because I had only kept goal for Sixmilebridge a matter of months. I was only 18 and this rapid rise to the top was an awful lot to cope with in such a short space of time.

I avoided socialising for ten weeks before my first senior championship game for Clare against Limerick on May 13, 1990. Villagers would often see me on the streets of Sixmilebridge, knocking around with friends or heading into Gleeson's pub for a game of pool. I was not to be seen from March onwards as I built myself up, crucifying myself every night with sit-ups and push-ups. I had remembered Terence Kenny hurling for Limerick club champions Ballybrown against Sixmilebridge in the 1989 Munster club final and I thought this guy was an absolute giant. Kenny was a mainstay of the Limerick senior team and I pictured him every night as I drifted off to sleep.

Eventually the big day arrived – my first senior championship match for Clare. I had butterflies in the stomach but this was a dream come true for me, representing my county at Cusack Park in Ennis. I will never forget the moment I hit the field and heard the Clare fans roar, it was the ideal place to make my debut.

I can clearly remember my first taste of championship action, grabbing the first ball that dropped near my goal before driving out through a group of players. Limerick's Leo O'Connor decided to put manners on this fresh-faced upstart and arrived to hit me a shot. Although he didn't hit me very hard, I went down like a sack of potatoes and Leo was booked.

We were hammered that afternoon, 2-16 to 1-5. I was happy that I had performed well but it was a terrible result for Clare hurling and a radical overhaul was needed. The county board decided to look outside and appointed a Tipperary man as team manager, Len Gaynor. I had heard of Len but I was surprised that the county board had plumped for an outsider. When Len took over, Clare hurling was at rock bottom. He had a massive challenge on his hands but he showed a real enthusiasm for the job and his attitude impressed me. Len's daughters would often accompany him to training sessions, Eimear, Sinead ('Pooch') and Ciara.

Len called us together as a panel of players for the very first time in the Newmarket-on-Fergus clubhouse and I could tell that he was passionate and determined to see Clare succeed. He was not afraid to introduce new players, he gave everybody a chance and I don't think people fully appreciate the work he did for Clare hurling. I was sickened when Len was subjected to horrific abuse from a section of the Clare support at Cusack Park when he returned to Ennis as manager of Tipperary in 1997. Genuine Clare followers would never condone that type of behaviour because they realise what Len gave to Clare and I know that Len himself was upset because he could not understand why these morons had turned on him. What these idiots failed to remember was that Len Gaynor laid the foundations for our 1995 All-Ireland success.

Len is a very honest person and did what he thought was best for Clare. Before every game, he used to visit the players at their houses. He was checking to see how we were on the eve of a big match and that was a nice touch. His heart and soul were in the job and he brought us together as a unit. The Clare hurlers with All-Ireland medals owe so much to Len Gaynor. I hope Len, and the girls, remember the good times they had in Clare. They were part of us for four years and I cherish the memories. I love a man who wears his heart on his sleeve and is passionate about his work. Len was like that with Clare and he was the same with Tipperary. He burst a gut for Tipp and I thought he was badly treated there. After all, he was only a puck of a ball away from winning an All-Ireland title in 1997.

During Len's time with Clare, Anthony Daly began to emerge as a real leader and the likes of Fergie Tuohy, PJ O'Connell, Jamesie O'Connor and Brian Lohan burst onto the inter-county scene. I had a couple of early run-ins with Len because I felt that he could be easily swayed by certain players. We were losing matches and because we were conceding goals, I was the prime target for criticism from both inside and outside the camp. My club-mate John O'Connell approached Len and told him that it was about time people stopped picking on me. 'The backs and forwards need to be looked at,' said John. 'There are problems all over the field.' Len was not happy to see John taking my side like that.

I knew that my understudy Eoin McMahon was pushing hard for an extended run in the team and, ahead of the 1991 Munster championship, the competition between the pair of us was fierce. 'You can't afford to make a mistake, David,' my father warned, and he was right. Bishop Willie Walsh, a selector with Len, was leaning towards Eoin and wanted him in the team; that was the feedback I was getting. I was aggressive in training and pushed Eoin to the limit. I wanted him to know that I was prepared to do anything to hold onto my starting position. I knew that in every game I played, I was under pressure to perform with Eoin breathing down my neck. One mistake and I was history.

We met Limerick in the first round of the Munster championship at the Gaelic Grounds and after a mighty battle, we lost out by a goal, 1-15 to 0-15. But this was progress. In 1990, Limerick had beaten us by 14 points but 12 months later, we stood up like men. Technically, it was not a great game but at least we were in with a shout, we were competing. Clare hurling seemed to be on an upward curve and I was raring to go when winter training came around.

My club-mate, the great Gerry McInerney, was coming towards the end of his career and he wasn't quite so enthusiastic. I always travelled to training with Gerry and one night, as we pulled up in Crusheen at five to seven, I was ready to go. 'Are we not going in Gerry?' I asked. 'It's too early,' he replied, five minutes before the start of the session. Gerry was looking deep inside himself, wondering if he wanted all this again. We drove for a bit, parked up and chatted for a few minutes. I eventually persuaded Gerry to turn the car around and drive back to Crusheen. The nights in the rain and hail were indeed wicked, but we were making progress. And with men like Gerry McInerney in my corner, I always felt safe.

The 1992 goalkeeping battle was between myself and Leo Doyle, the man whose misfortune handed me my big break in 1990. I was dropped for a league match against Waterford in the spring and my world crumbled. Len phoned to tell me and I was shocked. I felt that management had been biding their time, waiting to shove Leo in and to push me out. I was now a man possessed, working harder than ever to get my place back. When Leo was preparing for work in the morning, I was training. And Leo knew it, because he saw me. Nothing else mattered.

Leo made a couple of mistakes during the league and I was back in pole position. My first game back in the side was a huge one – Waterford in the first round of the Munster championship. A Thurles replay was required to separate the two teams but we lost by two points, 0-16 to 0-14, following a high-scoring draw first time around. Less than 10,000 people turned up for the replay, a tiny crowd for a Munster championship tie, and the atmosphere was somewhat surreal. I could even hear Clare FM's Matthew McMahon in the commentary box.

In 1993 we tried again and our first championship game was another showdown against Limerick in Ennis. They were reigning league champions and, if you believed the hype, were now set to reap the rewards from their great U-21 teams of 1986 and 1987, with the top players from those teams now reaching their peak. Their former All-Ireland winner Phil Bennis was manager of a perceived team of superstars to our no-hopers; but they were in for one hell of a shock. Ger 'Sparrow' O'Loughlin got his chance from the bench and he played an absolute blinder. We won a fantastic match by four points, 3-16 to 3-12, and Cusack Park erupted. Nobody in the county had expected this, except the players themselves.

We needed to get straight back down to earth because Cork were waiting for us in the Munster semi-final at the Gaelic Grounds. For that game, I had a new full-back in front of me, Anthony Daly. Kevin Hennessy was Cork's star turn at full forward but Dalo was ready for him on a wet day that made underfoot conditions extremely difficult. Nobody gave us a hope of beating Cork but we took the game to them. Our battling qualities, our tackling and our blocking were superb. Dalo was outstanding on the edge of the square in one of the best games I ever saw him play. He was in Hennessey's ear for the entire 70 minutes. Dalo could hurl but he was well able to yap too and he didn't give Hennessy a moment of peace.

Observers were now beginning to take notice of this Clare team but the 1993 Munster final was a game I would never forget, the hype was unbelievable. I trained like a dog but Tipperary hammered us by 3-27 to 2-12 on July 4. Eighteen bloody points. I didn't have a prayer with any of the goals, buried past me from close range, and Tipp were popping points over from every angle. They were passing the ball over their own heads, sticking it over our heads and really rubbing it in. But looking back, it was a major turning point for us. Our supporters were leaving early and the Tipp lads were having a joke among themselves out on the field. That made us feel twice as bad and the sight of a grinning Nicky English is an image that never left our minds. Nicky has since denied that mocking our efforts was his intention, but on the pitch it felt like he was laughing at us. I just wanted to get out of the Gaelic Grounds as quickly as possible and Nicky has to accept that later, we used his smile to our advantage.

The atmosphere in the dressing room after the game was terrible. We sat stunned for a quarter of an hour, not sure what to do, afraid to even step outside the door. As a goalkeeper, there was nothing I could have done to change the result but we rise and fall as a team and collectively, we were destroyed. Tipperary were on fire that day, their touch was good and their shooting exceptional, but beforehand I had felt convinced that we were going to win. After all, we had beaten Limerick and Cork.

We had a full eleven months to reflect on that demoralising defeat. We worked much harder and Ger Loughnane had come on board as a selector with Len. Loughnane was now building himself up for a crack at the top job. I didn't realise it at the time but Loughnane was biding his time in typically shrewd fashion. There was only one thing on his mind, he wanted to manage the Clare senior hurling team.

Many hurling followers refer to Nicky's smile as our main motivation as we looked to erase the memories of the 1993 Munster final, but John Moroney's tragic death in a car crash in 1994 was the real driving force. John, a fantastic hurler, played at corner back in the 1993 final. He was a lovely lad, a solid fella and before we met Tipperary again in the championship on May 29, Dalo expressed his deep feeling of loss in the dressing room. 'We have to do it for John,' Dalo urged. We huddled together in the shower area before the game, locked in a circle. It was a tight, confined space but perfect for Dalo's message. He reminded us of John and the day of the funeral and he told us that we were going to honour John's memory in the best possible fashion. We beat Tipp by 2-11 to 0-13, one of our greatest ever victories. Walloped by the same opposition the year before, four point winners now – hurling is some leveller. I swapped jerseys with Ken Hogan after the game, he was Tipperary's sub-goalie and he wanted my shirt. That was an honour for me too. I always admired Ken as a player and I feel that he was hard done by when he took charge of the county. In 1993 the then manager, Michael 'Babs' Keating, had come into our dressing room to commiserate with us, but there was no sign of him now. I was disappointed he didn't come down because we were looking forward to seeing him. Managers are great to enter dressing rooms as winners but they should be gracious enough to enter as losers too. That defeat for Tipperary spelled the end of Keating's reign, so perhaps he didn't feel much like talking. I have good time for Babs, one of the GAA's real characters. It is good to see him back in charge of Tipp and there are interesting times ahead. But back then, he wasn't a happy camper.

With Tipperary out of the equation, we were in confident mood once again ahead of the Munster final against Limerick, who we had beaten in 1993. Expectation levels were at an all-time high in Clare but at Semple Stadium, Limerick blew us off the park. They ran out 0-25 to 2-10 winners and there was nothing we could do to stop them. They were on fire from the first whistle and, for some reason, we were off the pace. Preparations had gone according to plan, I felt the work was done, but obviously we hadn't done enough. Len was gutted, for us more than anything. He wanted us to win every match when he was in charge of Clare, even when we played Tipperary. I felt desperately sorry for him because he had guided us to two successive Munster finals but lost both.

Once again, it was time for change and one man was waiting in the wings, ready to pounce. This man knew that something special was happening in Clare. He knew the stuff was in us and he felt he was the man who could bring it out and make it happen. That man was Ger Loughnane.

3 BYE BYE BIDDY

Every great achievement is the victory of a flaming heart.

Ralph Waldo Emerson

September 1994 – enter Ger Loughnane to change the course of hurling history. Twelve months later, we were sitting pretty at the top of hurling's summit with Munster and All-Ireland medals in our back pockets. How did it happen? Sheer bloodymindedness, power hurling and a burning desire to win fuelled by Loughnane. Len Gaynor had laid the foundations, but now Loughnane and his team of contractors were in to complete the job. We had lost two successive Munster finals, heavily, prior to Loughnane's appointment and I was beginning to despair of ever winning one. I suppose what we were really lacking was a deep-rooted self-belief. And by God, did Loughnane instil that in us. He was a new voice, a tyrant in many ways, with fresh ideas and a fresh approach. Hurling, hurling, hurling was the key to success and Loughnane could touch our inner souls in a way that only the Clare men that played for him could fully explain.

Loughnane's appointment was relayed to the players via the county board and we were informed that he was bringing in Mike McNamara and Tony Considine as selectors. He was a highly respected figure in Clare hurling circles, having played in the National League winning teams of 1977 and 1978. He won an Allstar award in 1974 and he repeated the feat in 1977, honoured on both occasions at right halfback.

Loughnane was sacked as U-21 manager in 1992, which was harsh in my opinion. We had been making good progress under Loughnane and for the 1991 U-21 championship, he appointed me as team captain. We were due to play Limerick, who had beaten us a year before, but it was a game I should not have played in because I had only just recovered from a bout of pneumonia that kept me in bed for six weeks. But as captain, I was desperate to play and when Limerick beat us again, I was devastated. In 1992, we got revenge on Limerick and that set us up for a crack at Waterford in the Munster final. That was a classic game and our team was firmly based on the great minor string from 1989. The final in Thurles produced a game of hurling that Waterford people still talk about to this day, arguably the greatest game of hurling played in 1992, in any grade. That was scant consolation for us as Waterford came in from the cold to win a provincial title. Waterford went on to win the All-Ireland U-21 title that year. Loughnane's reward was dismissal. At the time, he had also been working as a senior selector with Len Gaynor and the players enjoyed Loughnane's coaching. We had no quibbles with him whatsoever. Loughnane returned to the senior backroom team after the 1993 Munster final when he was invited back in by Len. It was now clear to the players that Loughnane was angling for the top job, and one of the conditions for his return as a selector was that he got the manager's job after Len. There weren't too many other people around willing to take the job after Len and Loughnane was a good coach, so why not? There are better coaches than Loughnane out there but to me, the most important thing that a coach should have is a real presence. When he talks, he will have the full attention of his players. Loughnane had that. A lot of coaches out there think they are good and know their drills, but what is important is how you hold a training session, and what you do with it. If things are going badly, how do you turn it around? I often have a plan for a training session and change it halfway through as the session develops. That was one of Loughnane's good qualities – he could adapt. I was never afraid of Loughnane but there were players who had a genuine fear of him. He commanded respect but sometimes, he went over the top. I did not like the way he treated Ollie Baker, as he outlined in graphic detail in his book.

Mike McNamara was no stranger to me either, he was the man who guided us to the 1989 All-Ireland minor final. I knew he would train us hard and felt we needed his drive, enthusiasm and powers of motivation. I wasn't personally familiar with Tony Considine, but he was a well-known figure on the local club scene. Tony was always on the lookout for a possible edge for Clare. At training sessions, Tony studied everything and expressed his views to Ger and Mike afterwards. The three worked so well together and Tony was a vital cog in the wheel.

Ger Loughnane's first competitive game in charge of the Clare senior hurling team was a league match against Kilkenny in Sixmilebridge on October 8, 1994. Normally we played our matches at Cusack Park in Ennis but the ground was unavailable due to redevelopment work and the game was switched to the 'Bridge. It was a very cold day but a few thousand hardy souls braved the elements. Naturally enough the atmosphere was muted after losing two successive Munster finals, but playing for Clare on my home pitch in the National League meant a lot to me. We beat Kilkenny, 0-14 to 0-9, a fantastic result. They were All-Ireland champions in 1992 and 1993 and still regarded as a top-quality side so it was an ideal start for Loughnane. We beat Galway, Antrim and Limerick before the winter break to record maximum points from our opening four matches before getting down to some serious stamina training.

Training in Crusheen was tougher than anything we had previously experienced. Mike Mac introduced a killer 30-minute run in 'figure eights' around the pitch and I absolutely hated it. Some of the lads dodged half of the runs, shattered from the exertions. After the half-hour run we moved on to sprints, 100m, 300m, 400m, McNamara crucified us. He put us through hell and if he saw the Clare footballers training, we had to remain until they were finished. We started before the footballers and finished after them, simple as that. Mike was never happy and sometimes I felt that he wanted to kill us. An average training session could range from an hour and forty minutes to two hours and twenty minutes. Press-ups, sit-ups and every sort of run imaginable. Our warm-up consisted of twenty laps of the pitch and we used to dread it. I did not enjoy the hardship, I hated some of it, but pulling on the Clare jersey made it all worthwhile.

Loughnane and McNamara soon came up with the idea of the Hill in Shannon. I will never forget the first night of this new form of torture. A full-pelt run from bottom to top took roughly 30 seconds to complete and after seven, I was absolutely shattered. Mike Mac ambled over and informed us in his monotone voice, 'Well girls, 28 more to go.' I was convinced that he was winding us up but no, this was for real. It was agony and each lung-bursting run to the top of the Hill made me hate the place even more. The last 30 yards was the real killer because it's very steep and every time we reached the top, Mike Mac bellowed, 'Girls, back down the Hill, back down to the start!' Loughnane always stood at the bottom to start us off, Considine roared us on at the halfway point and Mike Mac waited at the top. There was no hiding place and we were under intense scrutiny all the way up. I remember one night being in a group with Jamesie O'Connor, PJ O'Connell and Conor Clancy, all quick lads. On our last run Loughnane roared at me, 'Fitzy, you might as well be at home the way you're running. It's terrible!' I told myself that I was going to win the last run, just to show him. I was flat out when I got to the top of the Hill but I won the race. Of course Loughnane knew what he was doing; the mind games had worked to perfection. I dry-retched for 15 minutes with Loughnane at the bottom of the Hill, laughing at me. He knew he would get the best out of me by winding me up, taunting me into a reaction. After that gut-wrenching run, I couldn't drive my car and John Chaplin had to take me back to the changing rooms. I will never forget the pain I felt, doubled over on my knees, but Loughnane never caught me like that again.

'Sparrow' hated training more than I did and when we ran the Hill, he was completely cheesed off. He used to walk down the path and into nearby bushes, waiting for 10 or 15 minutes before rejoining a run. He would stay for another few circuits before escaping into nearby bushes again. He wasn't the only man to go missing in those bushes; such was the intensity of the long-distance training.

The vast majority of the players were afraid of Loughnane. Sparrow and myself were the only two that ever gave him backchat, but if I was late for training, I was better off turning the car and heading for home rather than going in. If you were late, Loughnane made your life hell. He could be really insulting when he wanted to be but it was all designed to get the best out of players. One night, Eamonn Taaffe drilled a ball past me from six yards, an unstoppable shot into the top corner. Loughnane roared his displeasure at our defence. I shouted back, 'For fuck's sake Ger, how do you expect me to save that?' The next voice I heard was Brian Lohan's. 'Relax Davy, he was having a go at me, not you!' Training sessions were dog eat dog affairs. I took a belt one night and blood began to seep from the wound. 'How many stitches do you think he'll need?' Loughnane asked our physio Colm Flynn. 'I would say six or seven, Ger,' Colm replied. 'Fuck it, he'll be fine.' Loughnane expected me to play on despite the fact that blood was pouring down my face. He was ruthless.

Endless hours of being flogged by Loughnane and Mike Mac hardened our resolve. There was the torture of the Hill, the long sessions in Crusheen on that quagmire of a pitch and 7 a.m. starts became the norm. Some lads had never seen that early in the morning, never mind training, but this was all part of the new approach, designed to sort the wheat from the chaff. The bar was raised ten-fold but even though the players were treated like dogs, they responded like men. The new regime was absolutely savage, fellas puking their guts up, then forced to forsake dinner later in the night as the body slowly returned to normal having been put through the mill.

We beat Laois in our first league game back after the winter break in February 1995, followed by victory over Tipperary and a defeat against Cork at Páirc Uí Rinn, our first defeat in the competition. We had done enough to qualify for a semi-final meeting with Waterford in Thurles. At half-time, an official came into our dressing room to tell us that we had to get back out on the pitch in good time for the second half. That poor man never ventured inside a Clare dressing room again because Loughnane told him he would break his neck if he didn't leave immediately. Paddy Casey was the next in line for a Loughnane tongue-lashing, castigated for letting the official inside the door in the first place! Paddy, who passed away in 2003, was always with the Clare team and if anybody needed a lift to training, he was the man. Paddy was recognisable by his bald head and glasses and he was a great friend of the family who rarely, if ever, missed a Clare match. He was always there for us and gave us many nights of great entertainment in his Sixmilebridge hostelry. He will never be forgotten. Paddy could not do enough for Clare but that didn't matter to Loughnane on that occasion as he sent him packing along with the chastened Semple Stadium official!

We were on fire that day against Waterford and we knew we could upset their star forward Paul Flynn by needling him. Flynn was driven mad and he didn't puck a ball. We beat Waterford comfortably, 2-14 to 0-8, and Clare had qualified for a first National Hurling League final in seven years.

The final against Kilkenny on May 7 was our third big match in as many seasons, after losing Munster finals in 1993 and 1994. Kilkenny, who we had beaten in Loughnane's first game in charge, were a different team on this occasion and, after rocking us with two early goals, they ran out 2-12 to 0-9 winners. We may have lost the game by nine points but the more I thought about it, the more I realised that we had not given up and that was a really positive sign. In the dressing room after the game, Ger Loughnane changed the face of Clare hurling forever. He stood on top of a table and ordered us to our feet, asking us to face him. With media representatives also present, Loughnane told us that we would win the Munster hurling championship later in the summer. 'We will win the Munster championship,' he said. 'We are going to do it.' He was certain, I could see it in his eyes and his demeanour suggested that he had nothing else in his mind. It was tunnel vision on a grand scale and his fiery declaration naturally made headline news in the papers the following day. Leaving Semple Stadium with my sister Helen, I turned to her and said, 'Do you know what that nutcase Loughnane said in that dressing room? He told us that we would win the Munster final.' Jesus, we hadn't won Munster since 1932! Helen could not believe that Loughnane had come out with that, especially in front of the media, but his belief in us affected me deeply. In training we knuckled down and worked that bit harder, training like dogs for Cork in the first round of the Munster championship on June 4.

I have looked back on the video of that Cork match, just one tape in a vast collection under the television in Sixmilebridge, and even though they were better hurlers than us on the day, we beat them with sheer commitment. Our blocking, tackling and passion were unbelievable. The game itself was nip and tuck all the way through, real tit for tat stuff. In the closing stages we were rocked by a Kevin Murray goal and they thought they had us. Seánie McMahon's collarbone was broken and how he stayed on the field, I will never know. He moved from centre-back to corner-forward, now merely a passenger, and I remember Eamonn Cregan on the video. He was in a state of disbelief, asking, 'What are they doing leaving Seánie McMahon on the field? He'll only get hurt, get him out of there.' But Seánie showed unbelievable guts, forcing Timmy Kelleher to concede a line ball. Fergie Tuohy cut in a super delivery and Ollie Baker got the crucial touch, deflecting the ball into the back of the net. Cork hit back immediately and it was only a combination of an upright and Frank Lohan that saved us. We held out, winners by a single point, 2-13 to 3-9. We were through to another Munster final thanks to a man with a broken collarbone, and a midfielder popping up with the match-winning goal. We had done to Cork what they had been doing to us for years and I was ecstatic. We stole the game from them and it was one hell of a sweet feeling.

Limerick edged out Tipperary by a point in the other semi-final to set up a repeat of the 1994 provincial decider. Loughnane got inside our heads before the game and the intensity went up a notch. Training games were savage affairs, kill or be killed as players battled for positions on the match-day panel. In training games, some lads were split open but Loughnane would not allow them to come off. We had

36 players on the extended panel and, as only 30 could compete in full training matches, six lads were on the sideline, itching for the chance to impress. We could only bring 24 players to Thurles on the day; competition was fierce.

We drove to Thurles for a training session two weeks before the final and Loughnane used a unique form of transport. He contacted Mr Pickwicks, a restaurant in Shannon, and managed to get the use of a van for the trip to Tipperary. Loughnane packed bins full of soft drinks, water and sandwiches. As we trained, Loughnane asked us what the difference was between Semple Stadium and Cusack Park in Ennis. 'Same size field, two sets of goalposts, there's nothing to do only go out there and play hurling,' he told us. The training session at Semple Stadium was a good one and it relaxed us. Training in general was incredibly fast, we were hitting more balls than ever before and physically, we had never been in better shape. Tony Considine liked to speak with every player but we knew that whatever Tony said to us, he had heard from Loughnane. In the Loughnane/McNamara/Considine hierarchy, Tony was at the bottom but he was brilliant at lifting the spirits in the camp with a few words of encouragement or by cracking a joke.

Sunday, July 9, and Munster final day had finally arrived. I had worked myself into a frenzied state. I could think of nothing else for ten days before the game and on the Friday night, I could hardly talk because of the nerves in my stomach. My family tried to interact with me but I was like a zombie, in a world of my own and tuned into what lay ahead. I surprised myself by sleeping for nine hours the night before the match because I had expended so much nervous energy. Some of the other players used sleeping tablets but I never did that. My mother called me early in the morning and I was ready, mad for road. We had the warm-up in Leahy Park in Cashel and in the bus on the way to Thurles; I turned to Sparrow and said to him, 'It's today or never, if it doesn't happen today, we've had it.' We drove up beside the stadium and the Limerick supporters, who outnumbered our own, were beating their fists off the bus. Anthony Daly stood up and roared, 'Today's the day to stand up and be counted! Let's drive those fuckers back! Like they did to us last year.' The mood was right and everything was positive in the dressing room. Loughnane produced the Clare jersey, waved it in the air and told us what it meant to each and every one of us. We needed no further motivation and tore onto the pitch.

Before the game I had made up my mind that if Damien Quigley got the ball and ran straight at goal, I would confront him immediately. Quigley was a real threat for Limerick and when he gathered possession for the second time, he decided on the direct approach. I was out like a flash but myself, Quigley and our corner back, Michael O'Halloran, all collided. I burst a blood vessel above my right thigh and I could immediately see there was a problem, blood was visible through the skin. I had never experienced such pain in my life and, although I managed to make a few saves, I was hobbling around the pitch. Not long after getting injured, I was summoned towards the other end of the field to take a penalty ten minutes before half-time. I had never hit one before in a competitive game, Seánie McMahon was our regular penalty-taker, but before the final Loughnane had asked me to hit a few in training. I never once thought that I would have to take one for real, and in a Munster hurling final. I was in agony as I ran the length of the field for my moment of truth, but I was focused. Tony Considine later told me that he came out on the field to offer words of encouragement but I didn't hear a word. I looked at the goal before I lifted the sliotar and picked my spot over Joe Quaid's right shoulder. I stepped back and put everything I had in my body into that one strike. Bang! I never felt such a rush as when the ball hit the back of the net. The pain above my thigh subsided immediately as adrenaline coursed through my body. I raced back to my goal, embracing the effects of a complete and natural high. You have to take into account that I had never before scored a goal in a competitive match and yet here I was in a Munster final with Clare two points behind before I nailed that penalty. Talk about pressure. But it didn't bother me, I had a job to do and after that goal went in, the boys started to believe.

The penalty was the undoubted turning point in the 1995 Munster senior hurling final but I did not realise at the time just how much it actually meant. If I had missed, I shudder to think of the consequences. After I scored, I felt no pain in my leg for almost five minutes. Quaid took a short puckout and Ollie Baker nailed Gary Kirby, allowing me the opportunity to get back between the sticks before the play switched to our end of the field. I never realised that adrenaline could remove so much pain but when my initial elation began to wear off, the pain returned and it was unbearable. At half-time the feeling in the dressing room was positive. Loughnane roared, 'They're for the taking, they're gone, we have them!' Our physiotherapist Colm Flynn confirmed that I had indeed burst a blood vessel. 'I don't give a shit, he's not coming off,' Loughnane snapped. Colm iced the affected area and he hit me with a painkilling injection. Back out we went and early in the second half, Damien Quigley had a great chance but fired wide. Loughnane was right, Limerick were gone. PJ O'Connell blitzed Ciaran Carey, Jamesie O'Connor was popping up everywhere, Fergal Hegarty was scoring freely ... we were on fire.

I asked the umpire how much time remained and he told me four minutes. Four minutes! And we were leading by ten points. The one thing I had always wanted since I was a youngster was just four minutes away and here was this umpire telling me how close it was. With two minutes left I made one of the best saves of my life but it was lost amid the growing euphoria of the Clare supporters. Pat Heffernan gathered possession 14 yards out, turned and fired it towards the top right hand corner. I dived full-length to make the save, but half of the spectators in Thurles missed it because they were simply preoccupied by thoughts of Clare's first Munster title for 63 years. When the final whistle eventually sounded I stood on the pitch shellshocked, blown away by the sheer scale of our achievement. I will never forget the sight of my father racing onto the pitch and the feeling as he lifted me up and hugged me. He's not an emotional man by any means but I could see tears in his eyes and that moment will live with me forever. Clodagh Lennon, a Clare camogie player, was my girlfriend at the time and hours of training with her had paid off. I was lifted from the goalmouth by Clare supporters and carried shoulder-high to the podium. My feet didn't touch the ground once. It was an amazing sight as we gazed upon the sea of saffron and blue from the New Stand in Thurles. Grown men were crying and I could not take everything in. I had seen what success meant to the people of Clare when the footballers won the Munster title in 1992, but we had not won a provincial hurling title since 1932. Looking down on former players from the 1970s and 1980s, huge smiles lighting up their faces, was a special feeling and when Dalo finally lifted the cup, I was in heaven.

We returned to the dressing room as Munster hurling champions and on the bus back to Clare, we had an amazing singsong. I can't sing for nuts but, carried away on a tide of emotion, I rattled out a few bars that must have made for painful listening for the rest of the lads! The first spot we hit on the way home was the Two-Mile-Inn, on into Setrights to greet the people of Meelick but the first real taste of it was in Newmarket where we were mobbed. We got back to the West County Hotel in Ennis at two o'clock in the morning and the place was still swarming with people. We had been on a high since that afternoon and it remained constant.

The county partied all night long and the celebrations continued on the Monday when we visited Crusheen, Tulla and my native Sixmilebridge. We arrived into the 'Bridge from the Kilkishen side and it was a hugely emotional moment for me. I spotted Jack and Mary Lynch in the crowd; Jack made my hurleys when I was a youngster. I remember my club-mate and Clare panellist Christy Chaplin saying to me that one man should have been up on that trailer with us as we paraded the Munster trophy, John O'Connell. John had just finished hurling and I rated him as highly as any hurler that ever played with Clare and one of the finest the 'Bridge ever produced.

We were soon whisked into Ennis for a reception on an open-top bus through O'Connell Street. Dalo told us to live the moment, to take it all in and to remember it. When I am feeling down, when supporters have a go and when people pry into my private life, I think back to those good times and it keeps me going. That night in Ennis will live with me forever, Micháel O Muircheartaigh doing his thing on the trailer as he introduced the players individually. Len Gaynor wasn't forgotten either, carried shoulder-high through the streets. We covered the rest of the county over the next few days, Lisdoonvarna, Inagh, Ogonnelloe, Killaloe, and Scarriff before finally getting back to training on the Wednesday night. The last time we had seen Clarecastle, we were being carried over the bridge in the middle of the night but now we were back for a physical session with Mike Mac. It was some comedown, rough stuff and I was very glad I missed it due to my thigh problem. The first training session after a big win is always ugly viewing with lads trying to get three or four days liquor out of the system. But we were soon tuned in again, preparing for an All-Ireland semi-final against Galway on August 13. The hype around the county was incredible and the colour was breathtaking wherever we travelled. Loughnane now wanted even more out of us, and the thought of playing at Croke Park naturally excited us.

We flew to Dublin on the morning of the Galway game and ate breakfast at the Forte Crest Hotel, where the Republic of Ireland soccer team used to stay before home internationals. We did some light training at the Aer Lingus grounds before boarding a coach bound for Croke Park. Another Garda escort, six years after my first one before the 1989 minor final, and the buzz was exactly the same. I was extremely nervous, but in hindsight, it was a match we were never going to lose, and Loughnane had no doubts about us. I savoured the roar from the Clare crowd when we hit the pitch and Croke Park erupted. It was a tense, close match but we hurled well, Sparrow scoring an excellent goal following a neat series of passes. That was typical Sparrow, always good for goals at the right time. Fergie Tuohy, Seánie McMahon and the Lohans were flying and we won 3-12 to 1-13.

The county of Clare went mad before the All-Ireland final and Loughnane reminded us that what was at stake was the chance to end an 81-year wait for the Liam McCarthy Cup, the chance to shatter the curse of Biddy Earley. The story goes that Biddy cursed the 1914 All-Ireland winning team and said that Clare would not win another championship until all the players were bachelors. The first team to consist entirely of unmarried men happened to be ours in 1995. We were ready to consign that particular piece of folklore to the scrapheap.

We enjoyed ourselves after the semi-final victory over Galway but it was soon down to business again, preparing for Offaly, the reigning All-Ireland champions. The hype around the county was massive and impossible to put a lid on. Sometimes three thousand people would show up for training sessions at Cusack park and it could take up to three hours to get out of the place after training as we mixed with supporters and signed autographs.

Every night at training in Cusack Park was like a press night. There were TV cameras everywhere and it was difficult to concentrate with so many people in attendance. Sometimes it was difficult to get into my own house as my father tried valiantly to cope with an incredible demand for match tickets. Queues of people turned up outside the house, begging and pleading for the precious passes and unfortunately, not everybody left with smiles on their faces. The doorbell could ring as late as one o'clock in the morning, supporters expecting tickets. My father tried to keep everybody happy but it was impossible. We received enough playing gear from the county board to last us for an entire decade but it was all greatly appreciated as All-Ireland final fever took a firm grip.

Trixie brought former Kilkenny forward Liam Fennelly down to Clare for a training session before the final. Liam certainly put me through my paces, peppering me with shots as Trixie kept a close eye on my movement. I was in good nick, perhaps even over-confident.

On final day, September 3 1995, we followed our semi-final routine and flew up in the morning. With time to kill, I shared a room in the Forte Crest with our corner back Frank Lohan. I beat a sliotar incessantly against the wall and focused on what lay ahead. The Clare hurlers were the centre of attention on All-Ireland final day at Croke Park and it was something quite alien to the county, and indeed the country. In the dressing room Loughnane produced the jersey in time-honoured tradition and told us what it meant. He was confident that we were going to win and, in a famous TV interview at half-time, he actually told the watching millions that we would. It felt to me like Clare owned Croke Park when we emerged from the tunnel, the supporters had a massive impact on us. I felt great but looking back, it was the hardest day of my life between the sticks.

I caught the first two balls and cleared them but just before half-time, Michael Duignan hit a shot from 20 yards out, at a decent height to my right hand side. I reckon Duignan was trying for a point but mis-hit his shot and it dropped short. The sliotar came to me and I felt so good, I decided to kill it dead on the bas of my hurl. To my horror, the ball spun off my stick and dropped a yard over the line. It was the worst feeling of my entire life. We had been motoring so well but my mistake brought Offaly right back into the game. I could see it on the big screen above Hill 16, I must have looked at it three times. Fortunately after I conceded the goal, we replied quickly with good scores, Sparrow popping over a beauty just before half-time to leave us trailing by two points, 1-6 to 0-7. I made a beeline for the toilets in the dressing room. I was distraught and slapped myself around the face a bit, vowing not to let the lads down again in the second half. Anthony Daly placed a protective arm around me and assured me that he had no doubt that I could stand up to the challenge in the second half. When we got back out there, I dealt perfectly with two of the most difficult balls a goalkeeper can ever deal with. One right under the crossbar, a real tester, followed by one that bounced three yards in front of me. I regained my composure and felt back on top of my game but I had put myself under so much unnecessary pressure. I knew that one more mistake from me and Clare were out of contention for an All-Ireland title. Talk about doing things the hard way!

Thirteen minutes into the second half we were level at 0-10 to 1-7 but soon after, Johnny Pilkington was on hand for another Offaly goal. We hung in there and the crucial score arrived with less than five minutes remaining, supersub Eamonn Taaffe poking home the decisive goal. When Anthony Daly stood over that late 65, there was no doubt in my mind. He was going to nail it. Cool and cocky, that was Daly. As the final whistle went, the relief was incalculable. I asked a steward to look after a special hurley as supporters quickly engulfed me. He promised me that he would but I was the fool to believe him. He was a Clare man and that hurley represented one hell of a prized memento. It was the stick I had scored the penalty against Limerick with, I had used it throughout the entire championship campaign but it disappeared with that steward and I never saw it again.

The Clare supporters were going absolutely berserk on the Croke Park pitch as we climbed the steps of the Hogan Stand. Daly's speech was emotional, he summed up the feeling of the entire panel of players and I was moved to tears. It was as good a speech as I have ever heard and Dalo was beginning to make a habit of them. 'In Clare we love our traditional music,' Dalo boomed. 'But we also love our hurling.' It just shows the calibre of the man to come out with a speech like that on All-Ireland final day, straight off the top of his head. Tony Considine sang *My Lovely Rose of Clare* from the podium and the thousands of supporters clad in saffron and blue swayed and sang along.

At Dublin's Berkeley Court Hotel later that night, we tucked into our victory meal beneath the glare of the RTÉ cameras. *The Sunday Game* had arrived at the Clare hotel for the very first time on All-Ireland final day and it felt good. Every Clare person present was on a high and the chat flowed freely. Seánie McMahon was honoured with the man of the match award and that capped a super day. I was busy taking everything in, minute by minute as best I could. I must have spoken to every single person in the hotel, pulled and dragged from pillar to post, but it was enjoyable. As a group of players, we stopped short of mentioning the future, preferring to concentrate on the present, having just atoned for the past. I got maybe an hour's sleep at most before the celebrations continued early the next morning, many people not having slept at all. We flew home that evening and the atmosphere at Shannon Airport was electric. Thousands of Clare people had gathered to greet us as we disembarked from the plane and we were applauded all the way through arrivals and onto the team bus.

The celebrations in the county were out of this world and we gave generously of our time, not wishing to forget the magnificent Clare supporters who had cheered us to victory. We visited every single school in Clare with Liam McCarthy in tow, a process that seemed to take an eternity but I would gladly do it all over again just to get my hands on that trophy. I attended at least one function per week but the hectic schedule did not bother me in the slightest. Seeing the joy on the faces of the people of Clare made it all worthwhile.

With the Clare party still in full swing, we were brought right back down to earth by Kerry in the opening round of the National Hurling League, just weeks after winning the All-Ireland. We hired a bus for the journey from Ennis to Tralee and on the way down, we had to leave the doors open because of the fumes. Loughnane nearly lost his life. Normally preparations for any match were perfect but everything that could go wrong that day, did go wrong. It was some kick in the backside after our Croke Park heroics, our lads thought they were real heroes but Kerry were up for it and turned us over. Still, the limbs were weary and the last thing we needed at that time of the year was hurling. We were in the mood for a holiday and it arrived in the form of a trip to Boston and New York in early December. Tom McGann (RIP), a Clare-born businessman, who had made his mark in America where he had acquired a number of pubs, invited us over. We brought our resident singer Kieran McDermott with us, armed with his trusty guitar and he sang his heart out. Kieran, who has penned a number of songs inspired by Clare hurling teams, had nothing more to give by the time we arrived back to Ireland after a fantastic holiday.

Our trip to Thailand was another one of the perks associated with winning an All-Ireland title. During the course of that break, we spent three nights in Bangkok in a first class hotel. The open sewers in the city were an eye-opener but they didn't spoil my fun. The locals would do anything for five 'baht', the local currency, which is a pittance in real terms. Jamesie O'Connor and myself took on PJ O'Connell in a race, dodging through cars on the tuc-tucs driven by the local lads eternally grateful for a few quid. A tuc-tuc is a local form of transport, a type of motorbike with a cab attached to the back, and we enjoyed the ride! PJ had long hair at the time but he decided to visit a local barber's shop for a number one blade all over. In a typical show of solidarity, the rest of the team quickly followed suit. Clare without the hair if you will …

Another highlight of the two-week trip was a soccer challenge against a local team that gave Ger Loughnane a clear indication that, although we were All-Ireland hurling champions, we had lost none of our competitive edge. Loughnane patrolled a dusty touchline, I was in goal and Frank Lohan was the only decent soccer player we had! Still, we beat the locals 3-1, kicking them all over the place and forcing two of their players to retire injured!

When we arrived home, refreshed and raring to go, we did so as All-Ireland champions. It was a completely new feeling and we were cocky. As kings of Ireland, we felt truly invincible.

4 TRIALS AND
TRIBULATIONS

We can decide to let our trials crush us, or we can convert them to new forces of good.

Helen Adams Keller

The history books have recorded that we lost our Munster and All-Ireland crowns against Limerick in June 1996 as Ciaran Carey popped up with a wonder score to win the provincial semi-final. We went from being All-Ireland champions to nobodies and it was difficult to accept because we had been in great shape. Confidence was high but looking back, perhaps it was too high. We were cocky but that was only natural because we were All-Ireland champions and we felt unbeatable.

That Limerick game was another massive one because, after we had beaten them in the 1995 Munster final, they were out to nail us. With time up, I pucked out the ball but after Carey grabbed it, there was no stopping him. He soloed up the field and I was helpless as he put the ball over the bar. That game will always be remembered for Carey's point but it shouldn't be forgotten that Gary Kirby dragged Limerick back into contention with a vital goal at a time when we were cruising.

Few people in Limerick begrudged us our All-Ireland success in 1995 but it must have been hard for them to take. They knew they were close to making the breakthrough and, after losing the 1994 final, those few years were do or die for Limerick as they searched in vain for Liam McCarthy. Carey's point catapulted them to a second All-Ireland final in three years but once again, they couldn't complete the job. The Limerick fans I saw leaving Croke Park had haunted expressions on their faces. Their team struggled badly to reach the heady heights of the Munster championship, but what made it worse for those gaunt supporters was the fact that Wexford played most of the final with 14 men. There is no way Clare would have let Wexford off the hook like that.

I was happy when Wolfe Tones beat us in the 1996 Clare county championship because I did not want to see a hurley for six months. I had been on the go constantly from September 1994 until August 1996 without a breather. Still, I envied the Wexford players as they ended a 28-year wait for All-Ireland glory. It was boom time for hurling with the less-fancied teams basking in the sunshine. Offaly in 1994, Clare in 1995, Wexford in 1996, it was a nice change from the traditional Cork/Kilkenny domination. Clare 1997 was soon added to the list of All-Ireland champions. We were steeled up for a fresh assault on the game's top honours but it was a tough time as my wife Ciara was expecting a baby that March.

I was training on the dreaded Hill in Shannon the night Colm was due, March 10. I was wrecked after a savage session and had only been in bed for two hours when Ciara woke me to say that our son was on the way. Having a baby in the middle of training for a new championship season pushed me to the limit, and the last thing I needed was Loughnane on my back. But he had a problem with me at the time, dropping me for league matches for no apparent reason. We were carrying three goalkeepers on the Clare panel and one night at training, I was the odd man out, positioned at wing forward for a practice match. I had started off in goals but after missing my target with a puckout, Loughnane started to roar abuse at me. I pucked the ball out again, missed my target by inches and Loughnane declared he had seen enough. He roared at me to get out of goals and I was incensed.

I approached Loughnane and asked him what the problem was because I felt that I had done nothing wrong. He reassured me that I was his number one but I found that hard to believe because he had made my life hell for a month. I was going through a rough time at home and I could have done without him on my back. Not many people would chat back to Loughnane if he was in full flow but I wasn't afraid of him. He is on record as saying that he always knew what I was saying about him because his son Conor used to stand behind the goals at training sessions. I knew Conor was there and I used to hope he would go back and tell Loughnane. Being played at wing forward in that training session was demoralising particularly with Loughnane roaring in my ear, because I am my own worst critic anyway. I have no idea what his motives were but I will never forget it.

In training, Loughnane could really get under my skin and he used to love having the rest of the players lined up to bombard me with shots from the 14-yard line or the 21. Sliotars whizzed at me from all angles; I often took a few belts and Loughnane loved it. The madder I got, the more Loughnane liked it. Those sessions were brilliant for my reflexes and some nights, I felt unbeatable from close range.

I got back in for a league game against Tipperary in Ennis, the same day our former manager Len Gaynor took some terrible and unwarranted abuse from some small-minded Clare supporters. I was on the receiving end of stick myself after handing Tipperary two crucial scores. In the first half I hit a short puckout to Anthony Daly but John Leahy intercepted and stuck it over the bar. In the second half a long ball dropped in from midfield but, as I went to collect it, it dribbled past me and into the net. Cusack Park was full, we lost by a point and I was directly responsible for 1-1. Three lads behind the goal were roaring at me, telling me how bad I was. The same trio came up to me after the 1997 All Ireland final, clapped me on the back and told me I was the best thing since sliced pan.

It is amazing how the wheel can turn full circle; take myself and Leahy for example. I gifted him a point in that league game but, with time running out in the All-Ireland final, I saved his goal-bound shot. After the league game, I rang Loughnane to apologise for my display.

'You're the best in the country, Davy,' he said. He had no worries about me.

Loughnane kept training going at a fanatical pace and, as Anthony Daly once said, he had us driven demented. The thought he put into every last detail was second to none. I had great respect for the way he handled us. Maybe I didn't always agree with everything he did but he was light years ahead of other managers and raised the bar to a new level. He might not have been the most approachable of men but he knew how to get the best out of us.

Cork in the Munster semi-final was a massive match for us. Loughnane summed it up perfectly afterwards when he said that our whole hurling lives had been at stake. We needed to answer a lot of questions after losing our titles in 1996 but I think we answered those questions in emphatic fashion. It was also nice to silence the doubters at the Gaelic Grounds, the same venue where Ciaran Carey had buried us 12 months before. We now had the Indian sign on Cork having beaten them three times in five championship seasons, and now this special group of Clare players had the chance to beat Tipperary in a Munster final for the first time.

There was a savage atmosphere for the final against Tipperary on July 6 at Páirc Uí Chaoimh and in the first half, we pulverised them. We were hurling with fire and fury and some of the stuff was as good as we have ever produced. We let them back into it in the second half and, although only a goal separated the sides at the end (1-18 to 0-18), we were by far the better team. It was a special day, especially for older supporters in the county who would never have seen a Clare team beat Tipperary in a Munster final. We needed to beat them to earn respect but, as 1997 was the first year of the back door system, Tipp were still in the championship and remained dangerous opponents. I got married to Ciara five days after the Munster final but we were finding the going tough. We had moved in together, we had a new baby and with hurling on top of that, I was feeling the pinch.

Kilkenny also availed of the back door to qualify for an All-Ireland semi-final against us after beating Galway in the quarter-final. DJ Carey was on fire, scoring 2-8 against Galway, and we knew he was the man we had to watch. The score stood at 1-8 to 0-6 at half time and three early points in the second half sealed the issue. We led by 1-14 to 0-7 heading into the final quarter before DJ rattled in 1-1. Our foot was slipping off the pedal but we still managed to win by four points, 1-17 to 1-13. Jamesie O'Connor was at his brilliant best, creating havoc in the Kilkenny defence with his energy while also contributing 0-9, 0-5 from play.

Loughnane reckons that the penalty save I made from DJ Carey in that game is the best that he has ever seen. As DJ told me after the game, he hit the ball as well as he could but I just knew that I was going to stop it before it even left his hurley. Loughnane was behind the goals roaring but I heard nothing. I was buzzing.

That save may have been the best, but I will probably never make a more important save than the one that denied John Leahy late in the 1997 All-Ireland final. Leahy connected perfectly with that ball and, to those who believe he fluffed his shot, I say watch the tape again and note how far the sliotar travels off my hurley after I make the save. Loughnane said it on countless occasions; the save in the 1997 All-Ireland final was everything. People think it was a Leahy mis-hit but the ball hopped 15 yards off my stick, such was the power in his shot. He did everything right, hopping the ball in front of me, across my body to my right hand side. He was thinking the way he should have been, and went for glory. Leahy is like that, he is a winner and he thinks big. If the ball hit the back of the net, Tipperary were All-Ireland champions. I have looked back on that save thousands of times and I know it was a good one. I took a step to my right just as he was striking the ball and got down behind it. If it had been an easy shot, it would never have hopped yards off the bas of my hurl. I was speaking with Jamesie later in the year and I joked to him, 'My save got you the hurler of the year award!' And I didn't even get a bloody Allstar …

After winning the All-Ireland, we only returned to county training in the first week of February 1998, but Loughnane worked us to the limit again. Our training was a month behind schedule but we still had a decent league run, qualifying for a semi-final against Cork at Semple Stadium in early May. We trained hard the week before the game and I could see no reason why. On the day of the match, we travelled by car and headed to Templemore, something we had never done before a game in Thurles. The warm-up lasted longer than usual, tough going in fact, but there was method behind Loughnane's madness. We were promptly spanked by Cork (2-15 to 0-10) and that gave Loughnane something to hold over us. He flogged us and the routine was five nights of successive training, two off and then five in a row again. He reminded us that we had been useless against Cork, who he built up as supermen ahead of our rematch against them in the Munster championship, when it really mattered.

On Sunday June 21, we blitzed Cork with one of our greatest ever displays. We hit them with fast, hard hurling and even though they led by a point at half-time and trailed by just two with nine minutes remaining, we ran out 0-21 to 0-13 winners. Subconsciously, we felt we would beat Waterford in the Munster final on July 12 but we saw a different side to them. Waterford tried to 'out-Clare' Clare, and instead of Clare showing all the boldness and arrogance, it was Waterford. They shoved us around the pitch, their mentors on the sideline were full of guff and their players out on the pitch were all chat. They were in our faces from the word go and never let the intimidation up. They were everywhere and Jamesie was even struck before the throw-in.

Waterford were up for it and Anthony Kirwan gave Brian Lohan a torrid time, scoring 2-1. Paul Flynn blasted a 21-yard free to the net two minutes from the end to level the match and could have scored a winner in the final minute, just missing the target with a free from over 100 yards. Waterford were in our faces all through the game but the match was not dirty by any stretch of the imagination. PJ O'Connell was sent off for a high tackle on Tony Browne at the death and it was a shame that 'Fingers' missed the replay because it was a game he would have revelled in.

We realised that we hadn't been fully tuned in for the drawn match and when we returned to training on the following Tuesday night, hardly a word was spoken. Even Loughnane was quiet and I found that peculiar. It was the same again on Thursday and now we were really wondering what the hell was going on. Loughnane hadn't gone mental after our performance on the previous Sunday? Something fishy was in the air.

The day before the replay, Loughnane called each member of the panel into Cusack Park. He ordered us to stand in a circle on the 21-yard line before he proceeded to verbally abuse us, individually. He called us a bunch of cowards and not one player was exempt from his wrath. I was shocked by this approach but I could see that Loughnane was seriously motivated and it fired us up too. Niall Gilligan, Christy Chaplin and John Reddan were late for training at six, caught in traffic on their way from Sixmilebridge. When they arrived and spotted the circle of shame out on the pitch, Gilly was first to size up the situation. He let 'Rusty' and Reddan out first to take the brunt of it before making his way out from beneath the tunnel. I had never experienced such venom in Loughnane, such bitterness. We were a bunch of little girls for not standing up for ourselves and for our county, and we had let our families down. Waterford had treated us like dirt, Loughnane informed us. Not one of the players said a word but his tongue lashing had the desired effect.

On the way to Cashel the following morning, the bus was silent. We ate breakfast in the Cashel Palace Hotel and retired to the bedrooms we had hired for a couple of hours. That is always the worst time for me before a game, trying to relax but needing to use the toilet constantly due to nerves. We went to the local pitch, Leahy Park, for a warm-up and I could sense that there was power in us. It was a short session, fifteen minutes at most, short and snappy. There was a fierce tension in the camp and looking in the lads' eyes, I knew they were up for it.

In the Semple Stadium dressing room you could cut the tension with a knife. Loughnane had a few choice words but apart from that, we were quiet. I looked around the field before the throw-in and opposition players were stuck in each other. Brian Greene broke a hurley off Jamesie but Jamesie stayed on him, he was giving it back. I felt that it was harmless enough stuff and certain things were being sorted out during those opening minutes. Referee Willie Barrett felt that he had to do something to keep control of the game and so he sent off Brian Lohan and Waterford's Michael White following an altercation. Brian was a huge loss to us but perversely, it served to lift us again. In fairness to Willie, I thought he handled those frenetic opening moments well. He delayed the throw-in a small bit which caused a bit of friction but with so much pent-up anger in Clare, something was bound to happen anyway.

In the Cusack Park circle, Loughnane had put it up to Colin Lynch. 'Are you a coward?' Loughnane asked, face to face with Colin who was ready with an answer at the throw-in. Colin was wired, he pulled wild but he did not strike anybody and the three-month suspension that was imposed on him is the biggest single injustice the GAA has seen over the last decade. Colin was not sent off but the Munster Council wanted to punish him to get at Clare and to put us in our place. A Tipperary GAA official in the stand, Gerry McDonnell, was the man who singled out Colin who had not even hit anybody. What was the problem? No bones were broken nor was anyone seriously injured, but the Munster Council treated us with a disgraceful arrogance. We beat Waterford that day 2-16 to 0-10 with a fantastic performance. We simply blew them away with power hurling. Afterwards, Colin was made a scapegoat and the way the entire affair was handled was a disgrace. He was dragged through the gutter by the media, but how many people saw the entire incident with Tony Browne?

Was the Munster Council out to get us because of what was right for the game or because the top brass couldn't handle the fact that Clare were on top? I can't recall an occasion when a player has been suspended for not hitting anybody because usually, the referee's report is taken as gospel. Instead, the Munster Council took the word of a man in the stand, Gerry McDonnell. Seán Kelly, who was Munster Council chairman at the time, spoke with Colin a few years later. Seán knew that what happened in 1998 was wrong and, in fairness, it appears there was little he could do about the situation.

The night Colin was suspended he missed the Munster Council meeting at the Limerick Inn because his grandmother was very sick.

At that meeting, James Nash from Scarriff, the man nominated by Colin to defend him, was not allowed in. Yet Colin was suspended on video evidence, without any form of representation. The Munster Council would not allow any Clare representatives into meeting, not even my father who knocked at the door. Dad said that he never felt as low as at that moment.

The Munster Council are elected by the GAA people of Munster, they should be working for the good of the entire province but they treated Clare like dirt. I have no time or respect for the Munster Council because of the way they treated a great Clare player, Colin Lynch, and also because of the way they treated my father.

The Munster Council put Colin Lynch and his family through hell. Colin had trouble every time he walked down the street and he was branded a villain. He was in the papers every day but he refused to launch a personal defence and in hindsight, he should have. If I were a Munster Council member at that time, I would be ashamed of myself. They singled out Colin Lynch simply because Clare were winning and they were sick of our attitude and the way we played. When they decided that Colin had a case to answer, it was not because of the referee's report. Why did the Munster Council take Gerry McDonnell's word?

Cork and Tipperary have hammered us down through the years and I want to beat them every time but the only way I should be able to do that is on the field, not in a boardroom. Why then was the boardroom the vehicle the stronger counties were using to wreck our championship season. It was the only way they felt they could beat us. Loughnane addressed the county on Clare FM, told it as it was and yet, for going down that road, he was labelled as arrogant. He told a few home truths which had not been heard before and the whole country turned against us. How would they feel if a player from their county was taken and suspended for three months even though he had not been sent off? Maybe Loughnane should have let Colin defend himself and tell his side of the story, or maybe Ger wanted to avoid Colin being put under that sort of pressure.

Colin remained very much a team player and continued to train with us. He took his medicine but it broke his heart. It was difficult to get the affair out of our heads and certain sections of the media have a lot to answer for. Their coverage of the Colin Lynch case was unbelievably one-sided and bordered on character assassination. My father Pat referred to the Lynch affair in his annual report to the Clare county board later that year. He said that Clare were the victims of a media witch-hunt and that selective video evidence had been used to suspend Colin. He said that it:

> '... was a year in which certain sections of the media cried foul and pursued a hidden agenda. Some bared their teeth, turned viciously on Clare and ended up vilifying the team at every opportunity ... it smacked of a major gripe on their behalf. It was as if they targeted the players in an apparent backlash against Ger Loughnane for feeding them false teams in the run in to important games. The only way they could get at Loughnane was through the players. Consequently they tried but, thankfully, didn't succeed in sullying Clare's success. They demonised but didn't demoralise the players. In a way, they set up a siege mentality, a them against us confrontation.'

The newspapers printed stills of the incident where Colin stood toe to toe with Tony Browne. If that were an offence we could go back over the last twenty years and have half the country suspended. Certain journalists reported in a biased fashion to enhance their own reputations. Did they take a step back and ask themselves why the referee had not reported Colin Lynch? No, it simply made good copy, and journalists could put their own slant on the story. He had to live with what they wrote, keep on training, accept his punishment and take it on the chin.

The man was wronged and the newspapers turned the entire country against Clare. We were nobodies for long enough but why should we have to go crawl back into a hole just because the so-called super counties wanted to get back on top? Was this the only way they could get at us? My father was badly affected by the strain but he was loyal, keeping in touch with Colin and Loughnane throughout the entire saga. My father and Colin felt they had a great chance with the appeal, everything was in their favour but it was like talking to a brick wall. I have difficulty believing an appeal will ever overturn a judgement because Croke Park will not go against the Munster Council. The GAA wanted to put Loughnane in his box after his outburst on Clare FM.

It was now finally settled, Brian Lohan and Colin Lynch would be missing for the All-Ireland semi-final. In protest at Brian's sending-off against Waterford, Loughnane retired the number three jersey for the game against Offaly. Loughnane was also suspended and given a touchline ban following repeated pitch incursions.

The first game, played on August 16, finished level at 1-13 apiece. There must have been more attention on Loughnane than on the actual game itself, as he watched from the bottom tier of the Cusack Stand. We were awarded a penalty during that game and I struck it well, apart from the fact that I hit it at one of the greatest players the game of hurling has ever seen, Brian Whelahan, who saved it. I pulled off a fine save myself during that game, denying Johnny Dooley to my left hand side.

We were on fire in the replay and well in control with just a couple of minutes remaining. We were leading the match by three points when referee Jimmy Cooney blew the final whistle with Barry Murphy in possession in an attacking position. I immediately realised that Cooney had blown up early and the umpire confirmed this. We had been treated badly in the Colin Lynch affair but Jimmy Cooney blowing up early was the biggest injustice of the whole year. We had played a game for 68 minutes, we were three points up with one of our players in possession and suddenly the final whistle blows.

I had watched the Kilkenny v Waterford semi-final and noted that, before blowing for full-time, Pat O'Connor first consulted with his linesmen. Jimmy Cooney didn't do this, he made a mistake and we shouldn't have paid the price for it. It finished his refereeing for all time and, I'll be honest, I felt a real bitterness towards Jimmy for years after that. I didn't meet him again until September 2005 when Galway's 1980 All-Ireland winning team, of which Cooney was a member, were holidaying in Portugal. It was arranged that they would spend a couple of nights socialising in a pub that I part-own in Praia da Rocha and sure enough, I got chatting to Jimmy. Our conversation put a different slant on things for me. I could see how much of an effect the 1998 incident had had on him. Feelings of resentment left me and now I hope that he can just get on with his life because at the end of the day, it was just a hurling match. Ger Loughnane opened up old wounds earlier in the year and I know that Jimmy felt hurt again because he would rather forget about the events of that year. He pointed out to me that he won't be remembered for the All-Ireland medal that he won; he will be remembered for blowing our match up early. That is a shame and it still haunts him to this day. I must say that my heart went out to him and I never thought that I would feel that way before we started talking. I enjoyed the night with the Galway lads and I got to know many of Jimmy's old team-mates. The Connolly brothers, Joe and Michael, are thorough gentlemen. Steve Mahon, Noel Lane, PJ Molloy, Seán Silke, Iggy Clarke and their goalkeeper Mike Conneely were all there. It's funny, because I had a run-in with Mike the week before, he trains Clare club team St Joseph's/Doorabarefield, so there was plenty to talk about! Grabbing the microphone, Joe Connolly issued his famous speech from 1980 all over again and introduced the players one by one. I enjoyed their spirit, their singing and dancing, Joe McDonagh, the former GAA President, got up and sang a few songs. He's well able to sing, a good entertainer. It struck me how close these men have remained since, that bond was the secret of their success.

As I chatted with Jimmy, memories of 1998 came flooding back. I remember the Offaly supporters staging their sit-down protest on the pitch after the game. And I remember being back in the Burlington Hotel later that night in a state of limbo. I was in the lift with Anthony Daly and he said to me, 'Jesus, we're nearly going to have to replay this game.' 'No way Dalo,' I replied. 'We have all the aces here.'

Offaly had beaten Meath and Wexford before Kilkenny walloped them in the Leinster final. Then they got the lucky draw in the quarter-final, pitted with Antrim who they beat comfortably by 10 points. Compare those games with our run: Cork, Waterford (twice) and two more savage battles against Offaly. I felt that if we had to play Offaly again, the odds were stacked heavily in their favour because we were a tired team. We should have taken a step back and analysed the situation in real terms, but Dalo was confident that we would beat Offaly regardless. Loughnane made a big mistake when he met with GAA officials and agreed to another match just a week later. He later intimated that he had received certain assurances from top GAA officials that Clare would benefit from playing again so soon, but he shouldn't have agreed. Would Colin Lynch have been freed for the final if Clare agreed to a quick replay? Maybe, but I remain convinced that if we had been granted a two-week break between the second and third games, we would have beaten Offaly. I had no problem with replaying the game but it should have been on our terms.

At Semple Stadium in Thurles, Stephen Byrne produced a goal-keeping performance that secured an Allstar award and booked Offaly's place in the All-Ireland final. Joe Dooley rolled back the years with a classic performance of forward play and all my worst fears came to pass. We were jaded, we had nothing left in the tank but Loughnane would not listen. I was brutally disappointed because I wanted to succeed for my close buddy Colin Lynch more than anybody else.

I have nothing against Offaly, but we were the better team that year by a long shot. I acknowledge that the 1995 All-Ireland final could have gone either way, we got the breaks and we won it, but we were a far superior team three years later. We received a huge ovation from the Clare fans when we emerged from a desolate dressing room after the lost match. They knew we had gone through one hell of an ordeal that summer. The big counties got their way, we won nothing after 1998 and it was the wrong way to do business. Offaly won the All-Ireland but as far as I am concerned, those players have OUR medals and it was OUR All-Ireland. I was nominated for an Allstar award but Stephen Byrne's great game against us in Thurles swung it for him, and he deserved it.

I have great time for some of the Offaly lads, Brian Whelahan has superb skill and fully deserved his place on the team of the Millennium. His skill, vision and delivery are a joy to watch and he is always a pleasure to play against. Martin Hanamy, a hard as nails corner-back, and Joe Dooley were excellent players. Joe never got as much credit as he deserved.

However, I was very disappointed with two Offaly players at the 1998 Allstar function. They were taking the mick behind my back when I was talking to Joe Dooley. It was an incident I have never forgotten.

5 The Lost Allstars

The greatest losses are unknown and unknowable.

W Edwards Deming

August 31, 1999, a fateful night in Cusack Park and there is poison in the air. I am in charge of the Clare U-21 team for the Munster final against Tipperary at the height of the bitter rivalry between the two counties that surfaced on the back of our great success. We had qualified for the final against Tipperary thanks to a fantastic semi-final victory over Cork, who had won All-Ireland U-21 titles in 1997 and 1998. That was a sweet victory, particularly as I had engaged in pleasantries with the Cork mentors on the sideline throughout the game. On one occasion, I unintentionally stood in front of the Cork dugout and roared at the referee. Frank Murphy, a highly influential GAA official from Cork, shouted at me to sit down and I immediately reacted. 'Frank, I'm not one of your Cork boys. I'll stand where I want.' I would live to regret speaking to Murphy like that but at the time, I didn't care. I wasn't going to let him talk down to me like that just because I was from Clare.

We had only a week to prepare for the Munster final and I was unhappy because Tipperary were fresh following a three-week break. Fortunately, we didn't need much training after the Cork game and it was simply a matter of keeping the lads focused. The atmosphere in Cusack Park on that dark, gloomy night was nasty and a disturbing undercurrent ran through the evening. We were unlucky to lose the game by a goal, Alan Markham was on fire but the Cork match had taken too much out of us. Brian McMahon sustained a serious injury ten minutes in that badly disrupted our gameplan, but the lads fought hard and I was extremely proud of them.

When the game ended, a Tipperary substitute jumped from the dugout. He was waving his arms wildly in the air and roaring obscenities. I heard derogatory comments about Clare and personal abuse concerning my family. It was suggested that I was incapable of taking care of my wife and child, and I flipped. I lashed out and I make no apologies for that because I would do the same thing all over again. The Clare substitutes reacted when they saw me charging at the Tipperary sub and all hell broke loose. I have never intentionally hit a player on the field of play but this was different. The game was over and all bets were off. I take so much abuse about my family and, high on emotion after losing a Munster final, I wasn't prepared to take any more.

After the scuffle, I headed for the dressing rooms and, as I entered the tunnel, I spotted Nicky English who was chatting with a few friends. I flipped when I saw English who, at the time, would not have been the most popular guy in Clare. I remembered his smile from the 1993 Munster final, and seeing him smiling again now flicked a switch in me. High on emotion after what had happened on the touchline, I made a bolt for English and hit him a shoulder. He aimed a few choice words in my direction as I continued on down the corridor and looking back, he was right. I should not have reacted like that; it was the wrong thing to do.

When the dust settled, I decided to get away from it all and went to Galway for a few days. I followed the Cusack Park aftermath in the national press and, true to form, Clare were the bad boys again. *The Star* and *Irish Independent* published photographs of my involvement in the after-match mêlée but they had me pictured boxing on my own. The newspaper pictures caught the glint of rage in my eyes and I looked like a psychopath. I was made a criminal for defending what is precious to me. I paid a huge price for that incident; I was suspended for two months and lost out on the Allstar award that I was entitled to in 1999.

The Munster Council carried out a protracted investigation into the post-match incidents and I was summoned to the Limerick Inn Hotel on Tuesday, October 26 to explain my actions. Frank Murphy approached me and my father before the hearing. 'Davy, we'll forget about what happened in the past between the two of us,' he said. 'You'd never know what will happen in here. You might get away with it.' I knew that Frank Murphy could nail me but I was reassured after that little chat.

During the meeting, I explained my actions to the officials and, as I watched the video of the incident, I outlined the reasons why I had reacted in such a manner. The Waterford and Kerry delegates backed me to the hilt but I was uncomfortable because Limerick's Jimmy Hartigan was nowhere to be seen. I had asked Jimmy for his support and he had promised me that he would be there. Instead Limerick sent Rory Kiely to the meeting and he voted against me. Con Murphy appeared from Cork and where he was sprung from, I will never know. The vote finished all square and, as chairman, Seán Kelly had the casting vote with the power to suspend or free me. Amazingly, Frank Murphy then proposed a vote of no confidence in Seán Kelly and the meeting was adjourned.

As the Munster Council deliberated, I waited in the hotel foyer. I was anxious to learn my fate on the night rather than wait for official notification the next morning. I was disgusted when they decided to suspend me but the so-called 'appeal' in Athlone troubled me even more. I travelled up with my father and Fr Michael McNamara, county board chairman at the time. Our case was firm and we spent an hour and a half presenting it. Joe McDonagh from Galway was GAA President at the time and he was on the appeals committee. I didn't rate him because of his part in the Colin Lynch affair in 1998. During the hearing, mobile phones were ringing, lads were staring out through the windows and it was clear that I had no chance. These officials just did not want to know about an appeal and the most degrading thing was that a decision was made in a few short minutes. Surely they could have given it more thought.

Ger Loughnane was one of the first men to publicly criticise the manner of my suspension. In a newspaper article, he wrote:

> *The timing of his suspension, and the method, is what gets everybody here. There is a sense in Clare, that some officials have it in for them. The fact that they (Munster Council) had their knuckles rapped from Croke Park last year, over their behaviour in the Colin Lynch affair, seems to have angered them all the more, and the perception is that they will now penalise Clare at every available opportunity. I'd say that is the major feeling here.*

Luckily I didn't miss any games of significance during my two-month ban, which began after the county final against St Joseph's, but I was definitely screwed out of an Allstar award. Under the rules governing Allstar selection, there was no ban on players who received suspensions over and above a month. Even though I was under suspension, I was still eligible for an award. I was shocked and disappointed when I was omitted in favour of Cork's goalkeeper, Donal Óg Cusack. I was dumbfounded when I was left out of that Allstar team in 1999 because I had enjoyed a fantastic season.

It was the second time in three years that I felt I had been snubbed by the selectors. 1997 was a good year; I saved a blistering penalty from Kilkenny's DJ Carey in the All-Ireland semi-final and kept out Tipperary's John Leahy at the death in the final. That counted for nothing as Wexford's Damien Fitzhenry got the Allstar. Fitzhenry is a fantastic goalkeeper, one of the best I have ever seen, but 1996 should have been his Allstar year, not 1997. I felt robbed, but the feeling was twice as bad in 1999.

My shot-stopping and ball-handling were of the highest possible standard and the drawn Munster championship match against Tipperary was arguably the finest performance of my career. I stopped Paul Shelley late in the game with one of my best ever saves before scoring the last minute penalty to earn us a replay. I wish the selectors had the guts to really tell me what my position was in relation to the

Allstars. My disciplinary record spoke for itself and at that point, I had only been booked once in my entire career. Why the hell would I end up in a brawl with a Tipperary substitute at the end of an U-21 match unless seriously provoked?

Soon after the Allstar team was announced, Jim O'Sullivan rang me from *The Examiner*. 'Well Davy, you didn't get an Allstar. Have you any comment to make?' he asked. 'Jim, ye are a bunch of cowards,' I replied. Understandably, he was taken aback but perhaps he should have expected my reaction. I was heartened by the support of my team-mates after I missed out. Five of them contacted me and I was grateful for that. With my head swimming, I should have remembered that Colin Lynch had missed out on so much more in 1998. I may not have got an Allstar but at least I had played. Colin was robbed of some of the biggest matches of his career and that is much more difficult to accept.

Remember too that Brian Whelahan was omitted from the Allstars in 1994 and that was one of the craziest decisions in the history of the GAA. To ensure there are no quibbles with the annual selection, the decision-making process should be taken out of journalists' hands. A panel of 20 players that played over the past two generations should come together and analyse games closely. The likes of Declan Ryan, Jimmy Barry-Murphy, Gary Kirby, Ger O'Loughlin should be entrusted with this role because the Allstars are important and must be chosen correctly. Highly-respected players should take over the reins under the chairmanship of a top figure from Croke Park. I was entitled to those Allstar awards in 1997 and 1999, but those misses made 2002 all the sweeter, proving that I could come back seven years after my first award and win another.

Losing out in 1999 was hugely disappointing because I had never trained as hard for any championship campaign. I dedicated myself not only to the Clare cause, but to countless others: the Sixmilebridge club team, the Sixmilebridge camogie team, Liscannor senior footballers and the Clare U-21s. At the time I just could not say no but I was never as fit in my life. I ran the beach in Lahinch, a three-mile stint, five times a week and during the month of March, we trained 24 nights out of the 28 available. The cycle was neverending; bed at night, up for work, going to training, back to bed, getting up again …

Everything was geared towards June 6 and our Munster championship showdown with arch rivals Tipperary. It was Nicky English's first year in charge of the Tipperary team and he had his players psyched for the challenge of Clare. In the days leading up to the game, I knew that I was in super shape and preparation couldn't have been better. Páirc Uí Chaoimh was packed to capacity and I revelled in the occasion. After I caught my first ball, Paul Shelley hit me a belt as I drove out from goal. On the way back in, I hit him back. The Clare crowd roared their approval.

Tipperary were much the better team but I was having one of those days a goalkeeper dreams about. They led by two points with four minutes remaining when Shelley let fly from eight yards, sending the sliotar whizzing towards my bottom left hand corner. I produced a tremendous save but Tipperary converted the resulting 65 and we needed a goal to salvage a draw. Remarkably, Conor Clancy won an injury-time penalty and it was now or never. I was striking into the City End of the ground, where the Clare support was gathered and I was focused. I picked my spot to the left hand side of Brendan Cummins and I knew that if I got the lift right, I would score. When the ball hit the back of the net, it was like the 1995 Munster final all over again, a feeling of sheer elation. I ran back down the field leaping for joy all the way. The final whistle sounded when I got back between the posts and Colin Lynch ran the entire length of the field to embrace me in a bear hug. That was a sign of a great team player.

After my exploits, I was splashed all over the papers the next morning but with the replay looming, I was fully aware that I was up there to be shot at. Hero one week, villain the next? I decided not to read the papers and instead, I held them over until after the replay when I could reflect properly. Before the replay, we held a team meeting and Loughnane told me that I had the most difficult job. He predicted that, because I had performed so well in the drawn match, I would struggle to get up for the replay. But if any Clare players were lacking motivation in the dressing room minutes before the replay, it arrived from an unlikely source. Through the walls Loughnane could hear the pre-match speech Nicky English was issuing to his Tipperary players. 'Ssshh! Listen lads,' Loughnane said to us. We could hear English shouting, 'What do we do with wounded animals? Kill! Kill!' We went berserk. Loughnane never had to finish his own team talk.

From the very first whistle, we were flying. When I collected my first ball and drove out, my nemesis Shelley connected with the pole of his hurley straight across my hand. I am convinced that Shelley was told to take me out of the game early. I thought my hand was broken and when referee Dickie Murphy told me to get up, I turned around and fucked him out of it. I was in huge pain but thankfully, no bones were broken. After the game, I spoke with Shelley for nearly an hour because off the pitch, he is a sound lad. Later that night, a journalist rang me and asked for a comment. The journalist felt that Shelley had hit me with a savage blow but I wasn't going to hang an opponent out to dry. Anyway, Shelley never got near me again during the game because Tipperary were blown out of the water. We were full value for a 1-21 to 1-11 victory; they had missed their chance in the drawn game. Nicky English must have rued not killing off those wounded animals when he had the chance.

Clare had not met Cork in a Munster hurling final since 1986 and we should have realised that the Rebels would have one or two tricks up their sleeves on July 4. As a team, we had developed a habit of coming together in a huddle for the national anthem, but we didn't get that chance on Munster final day. We were lined up in single file behind the band for the parade when to our surprise, the anthem was played. Only high-ranking officials have the power to change pre-match protocol and a cute Cork man had played a trick on us. Even before the throw-in, our routine was disrupted.

Cork went on to take us out cleanly, 1-15 to 0-14. They were more aggressive, very fired-up and we had too much mileage on the clock. We had been Munster champions for the previous two years and this defeat sent us through hurling's 'back door' for the very first time. We didn't mind that one bit, we didn't care once we were still in the championship. We had a second chance and wanted to give it one hell of a lash, but we were tired.

We met Galway in the All-Ireland quarter final on July 25 1999, in a match described by Kilkenny manager Brian Cody as 'a classic'. It looked like our goose was cooked fifteen minutes into the second half as we trailed by nine points but Jamesie's introduction lifted the whole team and Seánie McMahon was imperious from placed balls. A high-scoring 3-15 to 2-18 draw was a fair result and we were confident ahead of the replay, played on a Bank Holiday Monday. Waterford in 1998 and Tipperary in 1999 learned that when Clare are stung and on the rebound, we are capable of wreaking terrible havoc. Back then, if a team missed the boat against us first time around, they were facing a heavy defeat in the replay. Niall Gilligan hit 2-3 as we beat Galway far more convincingly than a 3-18 to 2-14 scoreline suggests. PJ O'Connell scored a crucial goal early in the second half and we never looked back from there. Our 3-18 tally, following on from 3-15 in the drawn game and added to the 1-21 against Tipperary, would suggest that our much-maligned forwards were doing something right. Dalo said it during the year that back then, we always felt that somebody would pop up to get us out of trouble during those years. Champions have that feeling.

We wouldn't have won two All-Ireland titles and three Munsters without good forwards. Nicky English always maintains that we will never score over 0-20 in a championship match, but that total was good enough to win the 1997 All Ireland final and you won't score more than 0-20 in too many championship games. We scored 2-17 against Tipperary in the 2003 Munster championship and I would regard anything over 0-15 as a good score. We may not have the flair forwards that other counties might have, Eoin Kelly in Tipperary, Henry Shefflin in Kilkenny, Joe Deane for Cork, but our lads still get the job done and Niall Gilligan has been a prolific scorer in recent years.

Our victory over Galway set us up for a crack at Kilkenny in the All-Ireland semi-final on August 15. We were confident that we would win the game but we were starting to take matches for granted and we came badly unstuck. Ken O Shea's first-minute goal gave Kilkenny a great start and they got to half-time level after playing against the breeze. They were well in control during the second half but Stephen McNamara knocked in a crucial goal for us. DJ hit back minutes later with an absolutely cracking goal and Kilkenny pulled away after that. It was our second All-Ireland semi-final defeat in two seasons and it was increasingly obvious that our powers were on the wane. Other teams had lifted themselves to the levels that had made us so successful.

2000 was Loughnane's final year in charge and he worked too hard on the physical side of our preparations. He pushed lads with too much mileage on the clock and it was the classic case of flogging a dead horse. Some players had no real appetite or buzz for the game and the zip was gone in training. Instead of realising this and working on mental attitudes, Loughnane decided to push us even harder in the physical stakes. It was a mistake on his part and it was no surprise that we were walloped by Tipperary in the Munster championship, 2-19 to 1-14. We didn't want Ger to leave, we still felt he was the man to revive our flagging spirits, but he felt that the time was right to step aside.

We all remember the glory days with fondness and when it came to match preparation, Loughnane was second to none. He was always scheming and plotting, all day long. There was nothing wrong with naming 'dummy' teams; the media made more out of it than it was worth. It was an easy excuse to launch another attack on Clare. Loughnane was one step ahead of everybody else and naming 'dummy' teams was a great idea. To his credit, he left a structure in place and stated publicly that he hoped his selectors, Louis Mulqueen and Cyril Lyons, would be given the opportunity to keep the show on the road, which they were. During his final year in charge, it had been clear to us that Loughnane had been grooming Lyons for the job.

I had a huge amount of respect for Cyril when he decided to take over because Loughnane was an unbelievably hard act to follow. Cyril didn't want Loughnane's shadow hanging over the panel and as a result, he was tough as a manager and made unpopular decisions.

As a panel of players we still trained in Crusheen but the dreaded Hill in Shannon was now a thing of the past. Training changed dramatically, it was not as long and tortuous as it had been in the past and was, in fact, much more enjoyable under Louis. We did a variety of eight-minute drills and, although an average session might only last an hour and ten minutes, it was quality stuff. Quality not quantity was the name of the game as far as Louis was concerned. Some of the lads gave out because Louis never stopped talking but that's just Louis, and the most important thing was that he knew exactly what he was doing.

Cyril wanted to be as ruthless as Loughnane but it didn't seem real. He should have acted naturally and when he acted tough, it seemed contrived. In Cyril's favour, I always felt that I could approach him and talk to him man to man. Loughnane wasn't like that; I never felt I could go to him with a problem. He wasn't an approachable man.

We were drawn to play Tipperary in the first round of the Munster championship on June 3, but less than a month before that titanic showdown we shadow-boxed at the Gaelic Grounds on May 6 in the league final. I am disappointed that I have never won a league title but we weren't unduly concerned losing to Tipperary that day. First blood to them, but we weren't mortally wounded. Their goalkeeper, Brendan Cummins, produced a man of the match performance so we had a feeling we would get at their defence when it really mattered in the championship. Brendan was brilliant in the league final and we were baffled not to have found a goal from somewhere.

When the sides met again four weeks later, Anthony Daly delivered the pre-match team talk in the dressing room. Dalo was still part of the panel but Cyril decided not to start him and we lined out without two-thirds of the half back line that had served us so well for years as Liam Doyle was injured. Dalo should have been brought on during that game but he still played a part in the dressing room, delivering one of the best speeches I ever heard before we hit the Páirc Uí Chaoimh sod. We nearly took the dressing room door off the hinges as we burst out, and one unfortunate steward who had told us to slow down took the full brunt of a shoulder as I charged on. He was just getting back to his feet when Colin Lynch ran straight into him, nailing him again. We were like men possessed and Daly had us wired.

Tipperary, who went on to win the All-Ireland, know they were lucky to win by a single point, 0-15 to 0-14, as Dickie Murphy produced the worst refereeing performance of his career. Ollie Baker chased an opponent before flicking the ball cleanly away but Murphy blew for a free for Tipp, which they converted. Colin Lynch was pulled for over-carrying, gifting Tipp another point, and I could not believe Dickie's attitude. Nicky English had got to him before the start, pointing out that the blue goalkeeper's jersey I was wearing clashed with Tipp's shirts and Dickie made me remove it. I ended up playing the game in a t-shirt, which I should not have agreed to.

I believe that referees' assessors review games but who do referees actually answer to? I can accept that they are only human and make mistakes, but when they do, they should be held accountable. I would like to see referees made answerable to a committee comprised of former players because the current standard of refereeing is just not good enough. I was very disappointed with Dickie, I still think he is a decent person but I disagree with some of his decisions in that match.

Before the 2002 championship, we lost the services of Liam Doyle and Anthony Daly through retirement. They were two fantastic warriors for us and, even though many of the players felt an acute sense of loss when the pair were absent from training, we had to plough on regardless. We were drawn against Tipperary in what was by now becoming an annual fixture. I have no quibbles about a 1-18 to 2-13 loss on May 19, because they were All-Ireland champions, full of confidence and we ran them to two points. We were drawn against Dublin in the first round of All-Ireland qualifiers on Saturday, June 15 and when I spotted the Dublin goalkeeper's jersey, I knew I had to have it. I never ask anybody to swap jerseys with me but Brendan McLoughlin's shirt was one I just had to add to my collection, it was a lovely jersey. Dublin weren't the worst draw in the world and we showed that we had plenty in the tank, running out comfortable 3-22 to 1-8 winners. We were drawn to play the losers of the Leinster final in our next round of qualifiers and we travelled to Croke Park to watch the Kilkenny v Wexford match. We trained at O'Moore Park in Portlaoise, our qualifier venue, on the way to the capital and I was blown away by the new look Croke Park. It was good for the team to travel together and we vowed to play in this magnificent arena before the year was out.

On July 14, we met a Wexford team on the rebound having narrowly lost to Kilkenny. We beat them well on the night but they were obviously on a downer after the Leinster final and we won much more comfortably than a 3-15 to 3-7 scoreline would suggest. We were back in Croke Park for an All-Ireland quarter final against Galway on July 28, a defining afternoon in our season. There was no more fitting reward for the efforts of Colin Lynch than when he surged forward in the dying seconds for the winning score at the Hill 16 end of the ground. Lynch was magnificent that afternoon, covering every blade of grass. We were that bit craftier than Galway on the day, and our greater experience seemed to swing it for us. It was a superb game, real end-to-end stuff. Brian Lohan was booked in the first half following an altercation with Eugene Cloonan, but the officials failed to spot Brian getting a dart in the balls from Cloonan. Brian obviously had had enough and hit back. There's not much love lost between the two.

It was just like old times as we celebrated wildly in the dressing room after the game. Loughnane, Mike Mac and Tony Considine made their way down to congratulate Cyril Lyons for the part he played, but they should have also congratulated Ollie Baker who issued a stirring team talk at half-time. He came on as a sub himself in the second half and showed that he had lost none of the drive that made him such a vital player for us. In 2002, John Reddan was playing great stuff for us and eyebrows were raised when he was taken off in the Tipperary match after scoring 0-3 from play. But the simple fact of the matter was that Ollie was going to replace John in every game. John, a club-mate of mine, knew himself that he was going to be taken off and, even though I thought that was very unfair, Ollie is vital to Clare. Wholehearted and a real leader in the dressing room, Baker will give you everything.

On Sunday, August 11, we contested our fifth All-Ireland semi-final in eight seasons. Our opponents were Munster champions Waterford, who started the game in sensational fashion. We were in big trouble until Alan Markham struck a crucial goal just before half time. We felt that if we could get close enough to Waterford, we would take them and myself and Colin Lynch took over at half-time, lifting the lads. Unfortunately that game won't be remembered for our 1-16 to 1-13 victory after Gerry Quinn sustained a nasty hand injury near the end. Gerry needed an operation on his hand that night after being injured in an incident off the ball that my father and several of our players spotted. I want to make a comparison here. In 1998, Colin Lynch was banned for three months for hitting nobody. Gerry Quinn was struck off the ball in a packed Croke Park and yet no action was taken, despite the fact that a man's hand was badly broken and everybody knew who the culprit was. I don't know what came over the Waterford player that day but he was lucky not to be suspended for three months. Even though the Clare county board was put under ferocious and unfair pressure to name and shame, we held firm. Gerry made a remarkable recovery to be ready for the final but he wasn't 100 per cent fit.

On September 8 2002, All-Ireland final day, Kilkenny were anxious to get back to winning ways after losing to Galway in the All-Ireland semi-final the previous year. We were in good shape and I was quietly confident until DJ popped up with an opportunist early goal. Henry Shefflin was shooting for a point and I followed the sliotar to my left hand post and watched it heading wide. DJ was on my right when I first looked out and there was nobody to my left, where a corner forward should have been. But DJ, the artist that he is, changed the direction of his run and arrived right on cue from my left hand side to bat the ball into the net. It was a well taken goal, an opportunist strike.

We hauled ourselves back into contention in the second half but Shefflin struck a killer goal when he deflected the ball into the corner of the net with a delicate flick for Kilkenny's second. I dived full-length, got my stick to the ball but it still trickled agonisingly over the line. Kilkenny certainly enjoyed the rub of the green and got the breaks at the vital times. Niall Gilligan had a great goal chance for us in the first half but he blazed the ball over the crossbar. Small things, but the small things make all the difference. I was gutted as we reflected on our defeat, but heartened the next day as we received a great reception after flying home to Shannon. It was a pity that we hadn't performed, we hadn't hit them and that annoyed me more than anything.

We were now without a trophy since 1998 but ahead of the 2003 campaign, we were adamant that we were not going to lose to Tipperary for a fourth successive season. It was time to put the record straight. We were so right for May 18 and Tipp felt that all they had to do was show up. It wouldn't have mattered who they had on the pitch against us that day, there was no way we were going to lose. Tipperary didn't rate us and that hurt. They weren't as fired up as they should have been either and we beat them quite comfortably, 2-17 to 0-14. It was a sweet feeling after being told that we had no forwards, no fewer than nine Clare players registered scores that day. Still, Tipperary bounced back to contest an All-Ireland semi-final; losing so heavily against us was the kick in the backside that they needed.

On June 8 we met Cork in the Munster semi-final. Cork had come through a winter of discontent and, with a new manager in charge, they were a completely new team. Donal O'Grady eventually led them to All-Ireland glory in 2004 but his work began from the moment he took over a disenchanted group of Cork players, disillusioned with their own county board. These players were right to demand what they did and I admire their stance, but now they were under serious pressure to perform. The winter of 2002 united them like nothing had ever done before and O'Grady unleashed a bright new star on the hurling landscape, Setanta Ó hAilpín. Setanta was an absolute gem of a hurler and a fiery player. We were shouting and roaring at each other all day long but even though this was his first taste of big-time Munster championship hurling, he stood up to the challenge and gave Frank Lohan his biggest test in years. Our supporters didn't like Setanta's antics as he grabbed his jersey and jumped in the air when he won frees, but I admired him. This wasn't for show, Setanta was seriously pumped up and we had to try to put him off his game. I couldn't and at one stage when we stood toe to toe, I was sure he was about to pulverise me! He was the difference between the two sides and enjoyed a fantastic senior hurling championship debut. Has any other player made such a huge impact in his first game?

Looking back, we were too carried away after beating Tipperary. We were in the comfort zone but we should have realised that Cork were a team on a mission. With less than ten minutes remaining, the Cork fans started to sing 'De Banks' and that was hard to listen to. I took a lot of stick from their supporters behind the goals in Semple Stadium but I am well used to that by now. Cork supporters started the personal abuse in 1998 so I would hardly expect them to stop now.

I do regret one particular incident during the game. An increasingly frustrated Frank Lohan went to have a go at Setanta before Alan Browne decided to act as mediator. I told Alan where to go because I remembered how he had blown a glorious goal chance for Blackrock against Sixmilebridge in the 2002 Munster club hurling championship. Alan was through one on one with me but blazed the ball over the bar when he should have been aiming for goal. In the heat of Munster championship battle, players do and say things they live to regret and I reminded Alan of his missed chance for Blackrock. I shouldn't have said it because I respected Alan Browne as a wholehearted player who gave his all for club and county. One thing you could never accuse Alan Browne of is bottling it on the big day.

Alan didn't shake hands with me after the game but Joe Deane, Setanta and his brother Seán Óg did, as they always do. Cyril Lyons was very dejected after a heavy 1-18 to 0-10 defeat and it seemed as if he had given up the ghost completely. We also knew that we would have to plan for Galway six days later without Colin Lynch who was sent off near the end of the game. Colin and Mickey O'Connell had been niggling all day and Colin finally snapped with five minutes to go and was handed a straight red card. His loss was a huge blow ahead of the Galway match but we had also overlooked the fact that it being a Saturday game meant that Seánie McMahon would miss out by a matter of hours. Seánie had been sent off against Tipp and his suspension didn't expire until twelve midnight on the Saturday of the game.

Our preparations were falling apart and a few lads decided to go on the beer on the Tuesday night, which was a shameful act. If you want to go on the beer, do so as a team. Six lads deciding to get drunk four days before an All-Ireland qualifier is a sorry state of affairs. I have nothing personal against the players in question, but Sunday night should have been enough. Did they really want to play for Clare or did they want to be on the social scene? In fairness, a few of those players have responded in the best possible fashion since that boozy evening. They have worked hard and shown their team-mates that they really do want to play for Clare. Hurling is not the be-all and end-all, but we needed to be right after losing to Cork. Somehow we managed to get things together for the meeting with Galway in Cusack Park and I had decided on an aggressive approach to the game. Damien Hayes proceeded to terrorise our full back line, winning frees for his team and I felt that the game was slipping away. In the second half I decided to have a go at him, he reacted and we started boxing. Hurls were flying and I got a nice welt on top of my head that needed a few stitches. TV viewers will have seen the aftermath of the incident with blood streaming down my face but I didn't care because I was so psyched up. People say that Davy Fitz loses the head but I knew exactly what I was doing. I wanted to lift Clare, and I wanted to put Hayes off his game. I succeeded in rising Clare but failed to distract Hayes. He is bold on the field and it's something I like about his play. He has the potential to become one of the game's top forwards if he continues to apply himself in the correct manner. Match referee Aodán MacSuibhne was criticised because he didn't order me off the pitch for treatment for the blood injury. But I refused to leave. 'Not a hope Aodán, not a hope.' Galway went on to win by a point, 1-15 to 2-11. I felt they deserved their victory. Now it was time for change in Clare again. Lyons stepped aside and a new leader emerged to drag us to our feet. We didn't have to look too far to find Anthony Daly.

6 OPENING OUR EYES AGAIN

Friendship improves happiness, and abates misery, by doubling our joys,
and dividing our grief.

Joseph Addison

When Cyril Lyons stepped down as team manager after the 2003 championship, Anthony Daly was the unanimous players' choice to take over the reins. Anthony, our former All-Ireland winning captain, had all the right credentials. He was a fearless leader, a passionate motivator and I felt that he would make a good coach too.

The senior players insisted that Anthony deserved the chance to make the step up from former player to manager, but at first he was reluctant to get involved. However, some gentle persuasion did the trick and Dalo relented. He let his name go forward and once he did, the end result was a formality.

I had great admiration for Anthony Daly as captain of the Clare hurling team but I recall a tension between us when I first broke onto the team back in 1990. I didn't have much time for him and I think he felt the same way about me. He was Clarecastle, I was from Sixmilebridge, and there was a great deal of division between the two clubs. However, when Clare started to come good, we made a big effort to get rid of the club rivalry that threatened to wreck our hopes of progressing. Anthony pulled us closer together than we had ever been and I have never played alongside a captain like him. He is the best skipper the game of hurling has ever seen, that is how highly I rate him as a leader of men. As a player, he was one of the cutest I ever came across and he had balls of steel. Before games, he was every bit as nervous as the rest of us but when the going got tough, Dalo was never found wanting. He may have been roasted in the 1993 Munster final against Tipperary, but who wasn't? And people forget that in the semi-final against Cork that year, he was man of the match.

Ger Loughnane deserves a huge chunk of praise for what he did, but Dalo had every bit as much to do with our success. Dalo knew how to pull lads together, when to talk to them and give them encouragement. When he decided to step up to the plate and run for the Clare job, it was time to put our differences to one side. In fairness to Anthony, he picked up the phone to ask for my opinion when he was in discussions with the county board. We had not spoken for almost a year because of personal differences and I had no real interest in breaking the ice, but when it came to Clare hurling, well there was no point in being selfish.

It didn't matter that Anthony and I had not been on good terms for a while, all that mattered was whether or not he would be good for the county. Because of his stature as former team captain, I felt that he would make a comfortable transition.

I met Anthony for a cup of tea in Ennis, we chatted and we aired our differences again. I went over one or two problems but I told him that I was willing to bury the hatchet and that he had my support. Dalo was one of the men I wanted to succeed Cyril Lyons, but Cyril Farrell is another figure who would do well for Clare. I have the height of respect for Cyril. Take a look at him on TV, he knows what he's talking about.

What really convinced me that Dalo was the right man was the make-up of his backroom team. When I heard that Fr Harry Bohan and Alan Cunningham were ready to come on board, I was happy. Alan coached Wolfe Tones when they won the county championship in 1996 and worked alongside me with the Clare U-21s in 2003. As a former manager of Clare, Fr Harry led the county to National League titles in 1977 and 1978. Those successes ushered in a new era for

Clare hurling and they were unlucky to lose two Munster finals against a Cork team that won three successive All-Ireland titles from 1976-78. Fr Harry had been around the block, he knew the players in the county and I knew that his experience would prove invaluable. Fr Harry listens to players; he's great to get inside a man's head and to read exactly what he's thinking. He is a fantastic man-manager and that takes the pressure off Dalo. Fellas get pissed off in training but all it takes is a quick word from Fr Harry and usually the problem is solved. His tenure in the late 1970s revolutionised Clare hurling in many respects. Back then, the club division was much worse than when I first linked up with the panel in the early 1990s. When Fr Harry was in charge, Newmarket and Clarecastle players used to tog out in separate dressing rooms, the rivalry was that deep-rooted. That all changed under Fr Harry and after one of his team talks, a united Clare team would eat the dressing room door to get out on the pitch. He broke the mould with training sessions on the Cratloe Hills at 6 a.m. and, although he was written off back then as a lunatic, all of his players turned up for training. For a spell, he operated with no selectors whatsoever, but he still turned the fortunes of Clare hurling around. And he came desperately close to a big championship breakthrough.

Johnny Glynn, a former soccer player with Galway United, arrived as our new physical trainer and he was present for that very first get together as a panel at the West County. Johnny also worked with the Galway footballers and I soon discovered that he was a very levelheaded guy who cared deeply about his job. I liked what he was trying to do because it was fresh and different. My father completed the team as liaison officer, that was no harm either and there was no hint of lingering ill feeling between my Dad and Dalo. In truth, my father was hurt by the comments from Clarecastle, but he's not one to bear a grudge.

We got down to business in November 2003 with a meeting at the West County Hotel where Dalo outlined his plans for the forthcoming campaign. Training would be tough, but he assured us that it wouldn't be a throwback to the Loughnane era when we were flogged. We soon knuckled down to gym and physical work and Dalo told me privately that he wanted me to take care of myself. That was good management because I have been playing for years, my residual fitness levels are high and I am still on top of my game. Dalo felt that he could get the best out of me without killing me and it made an awful lot of sense because I am no longer capable of training like the younger guys. There's no point even trying because I need to stay fresh. Dalo decided to look at every player on an individual basis and if a guy needed a kick in the ass, he got it. At the same time, if that guy needed a bit of freedom and flexibility, he got that too.

Before the 2004 league campaign began, I was part of the Vodafone Allstar hurling tour to Phoenix, Arizona, and Las Vegas in the United States. My Clare team-mate Tony Griffin was with me and we got to know players from other counties, lads you would normally be knocking lumps out of. I was sure that some players didn't like me, particularly John Hoyne and Eddie Brennan from Kilkenny. I cast my mind back to March 2002 when Kilkenny beat us in a league game at Cusack Park by 3-14 to 1-12. When Kilkenny scored their third goal, Hoyne roared at me and taunted me, telling me that I was useless. They were fired up for that game and some of their players later looked back on that victory as a significant turning point in their season. They went on to win the league title and later in the year we met them again when it mattered most – fighting it out for the Liam McCarthy Cup in September. We were running back onto the pitch for the second half of the All-Ireland final when I saw Hoyne in front of me. I spotted the chance for revenge and let fly with both barrels. 'You're fucking useless. Do you see that sideline? You'll be there in five minutes; you haven't hit a ball all day.'

But the Allstar tours are brilliant for breaking down barriers between players and I got on well with John and Eddie when we met socially for the first time. The tour took us to Las Vegas and we stayed at the New York, New York hotel. I like the odd game of blackjack and I decided to give it a lash in the downstairs casino. I hung in for hours but I was down a good few quid. I made my way to the roulette table for a shot at red or black. I put a few hundred dollars on red and

I remember that Eddie and John were more anxious than I was as the wheel turned. It finished on black and the lads could not believe that I had lost that kind of money. Meanwhile, I was still giving the blackjack a right rattle, spending as much time as possible at the tables. I was down $700 after 24 hours solid, running to the toilet now and again to throw water on my face as I tried to stay awake in the city that never sleeps. In the casino, I didn't know if it was night or day but I loved it there. Down a few quid, a couple of hours sleep, then back down to the tables again. But in Vegas, there's no point telling yourself that you're going to win thousands because it just doesn't happen.

During the trip I also got to know Kilkenny's Tommy Walsh, one of the real stars of hurling. When we met UCC in the Fitzgibbon Cup a few weeks later, Tommy embarked on a solo run from his own half-back line straight through to our full-forward line. I ran over to one of our players and roared, 'The next time he runs in like that, make sure he doesn't get up.' It may have been a bad thing to say but I wanted Tommy to hear it because he was breaking my heart that day and maybe he would think twice about another solo run. I get on well with Tommy, one of the finest hurlers in the country, and I sent him a text when Kilkenny beat us in the 2004 replay, wishing him the best for the remainder of the campaign.

Peter Barry is another great guy from Kilkenny and Henry Shefflin is as sound as a bell, despite our run-ins over the last couple of years. I thought the Waterford lads were priceless on tour. People can say what they like about them, but I enjoyed their company. Ken McGrath, Tony Browne, John Mullane, Eoin Kelly, they didn't give a feck. They went out to enjoy themselves and there was no badness in them whatsoever. People talk about the Clare and Waterford rivalry but I remember playing pool with the boys in a pub across the road from the hotel in Phoenix and we had great craic. The Tipperary lads were gents too, my goalkeeping rival Brendan Cummins, Benny Dunne, Eoin and Paul Kelly. You couldn't meet better. Apparently Clare lads are not supposed to get on with Waterford, Tipperary or Kilkenny lads? Give me a break. I played a game of tennis against Kilkenny's JJ Delaney and he is bloody competitive! I also went golfing with Waterford hurler Paul Flynn and my former team-mate and manager Cyril Lyons.

To captain the 2002 Allstar team in the exhibition match was also a great honour. I let in 13 goals against the 2003 selection but still picked up the winners' trophy. The game was played at Scottsdale Community College on what used to be an Indian reservation in Phoenix, Arizona. Players were shooting into readjusted soccer goals and there wasn't much respite for myself and Brendan Cummins. The final score was 11-20 to 13-10 but we still managed to pull off some top class saves. Allstar games are not hugely competitive but the lads tried hard to put on a show and displayed great skill. Eoin Kelly from Tipperary is a competitive young player, he wanted to win and he turned the game in our favour. Overall, it was a superb trip and Vodafone took great care of us. We were given fantastic gear and were well taken care of with money. Unfortunately, the flight home was a killer but myself and Henry Shefflin came up with a great idea. At the airport, we headed straight for the ticket desk to tell them we were injured and it worked a treat! We both ended up with lovely exit seats!

Tony Griffin and I were Manchester-bound when we got home from America to link up with the rest of the Clare lads who were on a team-bonding weekend. It was some comedown from the sunshine of Arizona and Las Vegas, to Manchester in the pissing rain. When we arrived, we discovered that the rest of the lads were off on a tour of Old Trafford. They met the Manchester United players at their training ground in Carrington. Stars like Roy Keane and Ruud Van Nistelrooy had no problems standing in for pictures. Myself and Tony were disappointed that we had missed out, we didn't like the hotel either but we cheered up on the Saturday when we went to the Manchester United v Southampton league match at Old Trafford. It was my first live experience of a Premiership game and we arrived well before kick-off. It was interesting to see the professional warm-up routines and it's a great idea to get out on the pitch beforehand, soak up the atmosphere and then return to the dressing rooms. I picked up a few training ideas myself just watching the players warm up. The atmosphere at the game was good but, as a spectacle, it just doesn't compare to hurling which is so fast and skilful. I have a soft spot for Arsenal but visiting Old Trafford for a game was a tremendous experience. We were lucky to get out of there alive when Diarmuid McMahon celebrated wildly after Southampton scored!

It was back to business when we arrived home from Manchester and Dalo laid out the ground-rules. It didn't matter how senior a player you were, everybody was treated equally. People thought Dalo might go easier on the older lads because he knew them so well but if he had to talk to them and tell them to cop on, he would. Dalo had a different style of management to Ger Loughnane. Anthony would talk instead of shouting your head off like Loughnane used to. Taking over the Clare job was a tough task for Anthony, but he is a born leader and having Fr Harry alongside him was a real bonus.

Training was good – Dalo and Alan Cunningham looked after the coaching side while Johnny Glynn pushed us hard with our physical preparations. I was really looking forward to another full season of hurling and I lined out in our opening two Allianz League victories against Laois and Dublin in February. But that was it until our Munster championship opener against Waterford on May 16. In Athlone, on March 5, my season took a desperate turn when I clashed with referee Pat Horan following LIT's Fitzgibbon Cup semi-final defeat against UCC.

The Higher Education Authority confirmed my two-month suspension on March 13. I attended the meeting in Carlow and I asked them to deal with it quickly because I was in danger of missing out on part of the championship. When the meeting ended, I waited outside in my car while they deliberated. Martin Meagher, chairman of the HEA, emerged to tell me the bad news and I was crushed. 'Martin, you've destroyed my hurling career,' I told him.

Don't get me wrong, I am not exempt from punishment but I had explained my situation and had asked the Committee to deal with me as a team manager, not as a player. 'If you have to ban me from college management for a year, go ahead and do that,' I told them. 'I'll take my punishment, but don't stop me playing hurling.' Two months was harsh in my opinion but it sent out a signal that verbal abuse of officials would not be tolerated. It made me so angry later in the year when Kilkenny manager Brian Cody got away scot-free after shouting at Diarmuid Kirwan and his officials during the All-Ireland qualifier against Galway in Thurles. As a manager, you have to do what it takes but if I had behaved like Brian Cody, I would have been banned for six months or a year. Brian roared and bawled on the sideline, ripping into the linesman before having a go at Kirwan as the officials trooped off at half-time. I saw Brian waving his finger at Kirwan and he was struggling to contain himself. In the second half of that game, Brian would not move from behind the goals as Eugene Cloonan lined up a free, despite repeated warnings form Kirwan.

During the year, our selector Alan Cunningham was warned by Croke Park that he was in danger of being suspended for running onto the pitch to issue instructions, so I have to ask the question: are there double standards? Myself and Tipperary selector Colm Bonnar were both banned for two months because of incidents in college hurling, and yet Brian Cody got no ban at all. Does it all depend on what county you hail from?

Now let me make this clear, I have nothing against Brian Cody, but the entire country knew that action should have been taken against him. The GAA suspended Colin Lynch in 1998 because of what some punter in the stand said. They were also quick to suspend me on a couple of occasions and I missed out on some serious matches. The GAA's President-elect Nicky Brennan was the Leinster Council chairman at the time and he ruled on my case. He was straight up, applied the rules and I deserved my two months, but the rules must be applied in the same manner right across the board. If Cody had been punished, it would have set a real precedent. All other managers would then think seriously before confronting an official.

My punishment was to miss league matches against Galway, Kilkenny, Waterford, Tipperary, Limerick and Cork: six savage games with in excess of 10,000 spectators at each of them. I missed out on getting match-sharp before the championship and it was a heavy price to pay. My understudy at the time, Ger O'Connell, gained some valuable experience and he wanted the shirt for the championship.

But my record speaks for itself and I will not step aside for anybody until I am ready to retire.

Pat Horan robbed me of two months of my playing career. He could have finished me as a hurler and I found sitting in the stands was a bitter pill to swallow. Match officials are not always right, as we have seen plenty of times.

I recall an incident during the 2002 All-Ireland quarter-final when one of Willie Barrett's umpires signalled for a Galway point at the Hill 16 end of the ground. Barrett booked me for protesting too much but because the game was so close, a single point looked like making all the difference. So it proved at the death when Colin Lynch fired the match winner and we won by the bare minimum. People thought I went over the top with my protests over the earlier incident but I was proved 100 per cent correct that night on *The Sunday Game*. I had been jeered off the pitch at half-time and branded as a lunatic, but do you take these decisions with a pinch of salt or stand up for yourself?

When I arrived home from the hearing in Carlow, I spent the entire evening in bed. Still, I couldn't sleep and even though I had 39 missed calls and 12 text messages on my mobile phone, I didn't reply to anybody. I hated the thought of missing two months of hurling but I travelled on the bus to Galway, with my playing gear. I still wanted to remain part of the Clare panel and do what I could for the team. I found it difficult togging out and warming up with Ger O'Connell, whose big chance had arrived, but I wanted to show that no matter how much disappointment I was feeling, I was still part of this Clare family.

Ironically, Horan was refereeing the game and, with me sitting in the stands, there was plenty of banter flying. I was my usual animated self during the game and when Colin Lynch put in a trademark challenge, I stood up and roared, 'That's the stuff Lynch! Sow it into 'em!' A Galway wag behind me in the stand offered the opinion that I didn't get half enough of a suspension, so from then on it was a running battle with a few good-natured supporters! I had detected a good spirit in our dressing room before the game and sure enough, the lads produced a good performance. Horan annoyed us again though when he sent off Brian O'Connell for an innocuous clash with Eugene Cloonan. Brian was very frustrated and he aimed a few choice words in Horan's direction as he left the field. Dalo had words too with Horan after the game. I'm sure Horan got a bit of a fright to see him approaching the changing room but Dalo wanted to get some things off his chest. He asked Horan what Clare had ever done to him and why he was treating us in this manner.

I was in the stand again for the league match against Kilkenny on March 21. Kilkenny had lost two out of their three opening league games and they were extremely fired up for this one. I had never before seen Cody so animated on the touchline but it was a sign of things to come. We should have beaten Kilkenny but we conceded two sloppy goals and ended up losing narrowly by 2-10 to 1-12. The most encouraging aspect from Clare's point of view was that the lads stood up to Kilkenny and there was real steel in our display. But it was another huge game I missed and it was eating me up inside.

I continued to train hard and I was part of a very happy Clare camp. Dalo liked to keep me involved as much as possible, encouraging me to take the warm-up and stretches on a number of occasions. That's Dalo for you, he tries to make each member of the squad feel important and players react in a positive manner if they are treated properly. He appointed my Sixmilebridge club-mate Niall Gilligan as vice-captain to Seánie McMahon. Some people didn't believe that 'Gilly' deserved it but it brought him on a long way because with the vice-captaincy came a real responsibility. As far as I am concerned, it doesn't matter who is captain or vice-captain of the Clare team but Gilly came of age and it was a great move on Daly's behalf.

We performed adequately enough in our remaining league matches, defeating Waterford by two points in the final game of the first phase. We followed up by beating Tipperary and losing to Limerick in our opening two fixtures in the second section. We now had to beat Cork in our final match and rely on results elsewhere going our way to qualify for the final. We took care of Cork under lights at Páirc Uí Rinn, winning a good game by 2-20 to 0-18. We thought we were safely through to a league final, but it was not to be, as on a Sunday of bizarre results, Galway and Waterford confirmed their spots in the May 9 decider.

I decided to travel to that match at the Gaelic Grounds in Limerick, a week before we were due to play Waterford in the championship. After witnessing a terrible Waterford performance, I felt sure that we would take them in Thurles. The entire county of Clare was thinking along the same lines, our supporters felt that it was a foregone conclusion. We had enjoyed a good league campaign, the feel-good factor was back and Waterford's supporters were pissed off and apprehensive. We wondered how Waterford would react and they were wired. We never got out of the blocks and it felt like the most disheartening day in Clare's history since the 18-point defeat against Tipperary in the 1993 Munster final.

We warmed up for half an hour in Cashel at midday and maybe that was a factor because it was a very hot day, but our attitude was the main thing. No matter how much Dalo had told us to be ready, and this was our big day, we weren't fully tuned in. When you hear supporters telling you over and over again that you're going to win, a certain amount of it seeps in. I don't believe that any team in the country would have competed with Waterford on the day because they were like men possessed. They were dead right to go in and mow us down when they got the chance; we've done exactly the same to other teams in the past.

So what if they were kissing their jerseys and playing to the crowd. John Mullane and Eoin Kelly had pride in their shirts, the single biggest ingredient for a championship Sunday. They did the business, played with that pride and heart and I took my hat off to them. I will fight with players on the field and bark at them but I had no problem shaking hands with the Waterford lads afterwards. In fact, a few of them looked for me. Kelly, Dan Shanahan and Ken McGrath will always come up and shake hands, no matter what has happened on the pitch, and Mullane asked me to swap jerseys.

On the day, I made no major mistakes but, with fifteen minutes to go, all I wanted to hear was the final whistle. I was disgusted with myself for quitting because I have never done that in my life. I was devastated and the scoreline said it all, 3-21 to 1-8, a 19-point demolition job. Spare a thought too for Anthony Daly, he stood up tall on the sideline for the entire game and that was a hard thing to do.

We didn't even go for a meal afterwards, it was straight onto the bus and we slipped in an appropriate manner down back roads into Tipperary town. We stopped in McGrath's pub on the way into Limerick, the place was fairly empty and the lads drank away, but we were ashamed of ourselves.

Myself, Tony Griffin, Colin Lynch and Diarmuid McMahon decided to head out in Ennis for an hour when we got back to Clare. We listened to a lot of negative comments, fellas roaring at us, telling us that we were useless and consigning us to the knacker's yard. I stayed indoors for a few days after that but each and every one of us needed that time alone to have a good think.

The day after the Waterford game, I made over twenty phone calls, getting in touch with the rest of the lads, asking them if they were prepared to up the ante. I also wanted to see who was still out on the beer because I was hurting inside and there was only one way to rectify the situation, to knuckle back down to business. I don't drink myself, and instead of drowning the sorrows, I thought it was time to pull together more than ever. I thumbed a text message to Dalo that read, 'Now, more than ever, we need you.' I told Dalo that I still believed in him, that we needed a leader and that he was still the man to turn us around. I had faith in him and what happened against Waterford was more our fault than his. He responded in the best possible fashion, sending every player a text, telling them to prepare for battle or get out.

We started to get it together, a few phone calls here and there did the trick and we lifted ourselves out of the gutter. Losing by 19 points to Waterford should have shattered our confidence but we had a few weeks to recover. We went to Milltown, back on the beach for 7 a.m. starts, which I hated. One morning, we warmed up with a game of rugby, followed by press-ups and sit-ups, before Johnny Glynn took off running up the beach, disappearing from view in the mist. We were told to complete six full runs as far as Johnny, as fast as we could. The runs were the length of Spanish Point beach and this was a good change of tactic. This felt refreshing! I love the sea water and there's nothing more therapeutic than a workout on the beach.

Rumours began to circulate that one of our greatest servants, Ollie Baker, had walked off the panel. It was a tough call by Dalo to substitute Ollie after 20 minutes against Waterford, but what people don't realise is that Ollie held his head high in the dressing room at half-time and kept encouraging us. I might not have been very close to Ollie during our successful period, but during the final years of his career he became a superb panel man. I often remember asking Ollie before games to get the rest of the lads going, and he was sorely missed in 2005.

Loughnane used to go very hard on Ollie, which I thought was unnecessary because Ollie is a sensitive chap behind it all. Loughnane might feel that he was vindicated by Ollie's performances and it is certainly true that Ollie was a powerhouse for us when he was playing well. People said his form dipped over the last few seasons but he trained harder than anybody and battled his way back after damaging his cruciate knee ligament. He went up an awful lot in my estimation and he continued to play a full role with Clare after the Waterford game.

Slowly the wounds started to heal and we drew Laois in our first qualifier on June 26. We treated them with the utmost respect but we wanted to bury them after what had happened to us. We beat Laois by 19 points, knocking 7-19 past them. The game was over as a contest very early as we banged in three early goals but we knew we had to win that game well. A week later, the entire squad and management team travelled to Dublin to take in the Leinster hurling final.

We left Clare on the Saturday destined for Dublin's Sunnybank Hotel, owned by my good friend Peter Garvey and situated not a million miles from Croke Park. We checked in before heading for the

National Aquatic Centre in Abbotstown. Myself and Jamesie O'Connor were petrified because neither of us can swim but it was a super buzz and I plucked up the courage to take on one of the water slides! We stayed there for an hour and a half before boarding the bus again for a trip to Leopardstown. I had never been to a race meeting before in my life but Dalo was mad to get us out there as a unit to enjoy the craic. Our team sponsors Vodafone had organised the tickets for the races and tips soon began to circulate. Dalo had one or two bits of information and Fr Harry had something up his sleeve, as usual! Myself and Brian Lynch decided to work as a double act, getting together for what turned out to be a very successful evening. We scored five winners from seven races and naturally, we thought we knew it all. Feeling cocky, we even ventured downstairs to Paddy Powers, looking at races in Limerick and betting on them. The buzz around the place that evening was brilliant and, having won five out of the first six on the track with Brian, I was in great form. I went bananas, placing €250 on the favourite for the last race. The horse lost of course but I still emerged from the evening handsomely in profit, as did my partner in crime.

Fair play to Dalo, I could not care less about the horses but I enjoyed mingling with the rest of the players, making a special effort to spend time with lads I might not often see. We got back to the Sunnybank and met for a few drinks in the bar but the lads took it easy. The next morning we trained in Na Fianna's grounds and it was a super session, I could tell that we were beginning to click. Later that day we went to Croke Park for the Leinster final, Wexford's goalkeeper Damien Fitzhenry had a great game and ultimately he was the difference between victory and defeat against Offaly.

Now we knew for certain who we would be facing in the next round of qualifiers and preparations for Offaly began immediately. Everything was going smoothly until ten days before the match when Dalo and Fr Harry decided to drop Gerry Quinn from the panel. I had lambasted Gerry at a team meeting before the Laois game because I thought his attitude was poor. Gerry didn't think it was the time or the place but I felt that something needed to be said. We chatted about it later, Gerry told me that he was not happy about what I had said but I didn't care. And I won't take back anything I said because I meant every word of it. Maybe I should have spoken to Gerry privately before I decided to let loose but I think he would have ignored me. Gerry was disciplined by our management team soon after, dropped for the Offaly game and told to get his house in order. The rest of the players were fully supportive of the action taken against Gerry but when he eventually returned to the panel, he was a new man. His hurling and appetite were at the required levels and when Gerry Quinn is properly focused, he is a super player and a real asset to Clare. There are one or two people close to him that probably took exception because I had been so blunt with Gerry, but I was calling it as I saw it. The management took a fair line with him and, even though he was out of sight, Fr Harry kept in touch with him on a daily basis.

I went to Thurles for the Kilkenny v Galway qualifier on July 11 and witnessed an awesome Kilkenny performance. Coming home in the car with my father, John Faul and Niall Considine, we heard the quarter final draw which pitted Kilkenny with the winners of Clare v Offaly. My first reaction was, 'Great, we'll have a go at them.' I was already thinking ahead to Kilkenny even though we still had to vault the Offaly hurdle. I couldn't get Kilkenny out of my head that night and I was restless sitting in my Lahinch apartment. At 11.30 p.m., I could take it no longer and I scrambled into my gear and headed down the beach for a hard run. This was completely out of character for me because I rarely run at night but I had to calm the thoughts that were running through my head. I pictured Henry Shefflin and DJ Carey in my mind. 'This is what hurling's all about,' I said to myself. 'We can have a go at the best team in the country.' Now and then, I still run the beach in Lahinch at night.

Gerry Quinn's punishment was to sit out the Offaly game, which promised to be an interesting encounter. I didn't care who we drew after beating Laois but Offaly, with our former selector Mike McNamara in charge, certainly made it interesting. I was genuinely worried because I rated Offaly and any team that Mike Mac is in charge of will battle until the final whistle. Offaly had enjoyed a two-week break since the Leinster final and we knew that Mike Mac was keen to get one over on us, but Clare needed a game like this against decent opposition to find out exactly where we stood. We beat them convincingly, 3-16 to 2-10, and I was surprised we received so little credit for that particular victory. We never let Offaly hurl. I have looked at the video a few times and I thought we went about our business in a very professional manner. Some of our hurling, blocking, tackling and chasing was top drawer and we felt good after the game.

We went for a pool session later that evening and crucially, no drink was consumed. I felt now was the right time to meet Kilkenny, considering that they had beaten Galway so convincingly. Everything had finally come right in our camp, the management were on top of their game, training was good and the players were taking a lot more responsibility for themselves. I sent a raft of text messages. 'If ever we were men and wanted to play for Clare,' I began, 'we have to stand up now and work even harder.'

On July 20, we travelled to Dublin for a look around Croke Park ahead of the game. A poker school was in full swing on the train journey up and that wily old fox Fr Harry was teaching us a few tricks. He sat innocently amongst us, staring vacantly at a hand of cards but we quickly discovered that he knew exactly what he was doing. Fr Harry pretended that he knew nothing about poker but he finished well up after the session. At one stage two tables were in operation – a 'Premiership' table and a First Division table. The Premiership table was serious stuff and the only way to get a place with the 'elite' was to gain promotion from the First Division. On the way home later that evening, we had a table from Dublin to Limerick Junction but after changing trains, we were out of luck. I suggested that we play in the narrow confines between carriages, using a gear bag as a cardtable. County board chairman Michael McDonagh got in on the act and it turned out he was a shark, just like Fr Harry.

The entire day was a complete success and some of the younger players who had never experienced Croke Park were simply blown away by the experience. I was tired but happy when I arrived home and headed for the homestead in Sixmilebridge. Normally I never answer the phone after I have hit the bed so my father was shocked that I took a call at one o'clock in the morning. Dr Padraig Quinn, a close family friend, phoned to inform me that my beloved friend and mentor, Kevin 'Trixie' Twomey, had died of heart failure.

Trixie, who spent his early years in Newmarket, was a huge asset to the Sixmilebridge club after moving to the area. He trained the 'Bridge to minor, U-21 and senior championships in 1979 and that was one hell of an achievement. Trixie and my father looked after teams together and I will be forever in Trixie's debt because he brought me onto the East Clare U-16 team that enjoyed so much success, and he made me captain in 1987. Trixie never questioned my ability, when I was just 15 years of age he felt that I was good enough for the Sixmilebridge U-21 panel and the Clare minor team.

I spent a few hours with Trixie the night before he died and we had a great chat. I always rang him three or four times a week, just to talk, but I am glad I went to see him in person before the visit to Dublin. We sat up until nearly three in the morning and it was one of the best conversations we ever had. Normally Trixie would not let his emotions bubble to the surface, but on this occasion he expressed his deep feelings. As the conversation ended, he rose to his feet the same as always, walked me to the door and said, 'Good luck Fitzy, I'll see you tomorrow.' I can still see him standing there waving what was a final goodbye.

After taking the phone call from Dr Quinn less than 24 hours later, I sat in stunned silence before finally deciding to head out to Twomey's house. I stayed until six o'clock and even though I find those situations difficult, it was the right thing to do. I even find it hard to go into a funeral home and the one exception I made was for Sheila Considine.

Trixie left behind his wife Marie and a young family: Kevin, Frances, Carol (mother of my godchild Kaci) and Trish. I really felt for them and it didn't seem right. Trixie was too young to die at just 57 years of age. A week before, Trixie had been doing what he did best, working hard in Clareabbey in preparation for the Offaly game with myself, Brian Colbert and Colin Lynch. Trixie was keeping a close eye on my footwork, my shot-stopping and virtually every aspect of my game.

'Davy, will you keep on the balls of your feet,' he roared. 'You're no good unless you keep on the balls of your feet.' I was cross because Lynch and Colbert, great friends off the pitch, were running to within 15 yards of goal and blowing the head off me. I was losing the rag but of course, Trixie loved every second of it. 'Are you any good? Can you stop anything?' Soon, we were all roaring at each other and I spotted two young lads crouched in the long grass at the edge of the field. They had been stunned into silence as they looked on. Trixie really drilled me that night, testing me with shots from all angles and winding me up to the hilt. He was the one man who knew how to press my buttons and I revelled in these private training sessions. I felt that I needed another one a few days before the Kilkenny game but it wasn't to be. I was struggling to get my head around it all – somebody I had spent so much time with was gone in an instant and I felt robbed.

Thoughts of Kilkenny vanished. I slept for maybe an hour when I got home from Twomey's house and when I woke up, I went back there again. I stayed with the family all day and it was impossible to think about the match until after the funeral on the Friday. I said to Maire, 'Listen, I have to go training and get my head right for Sunday.' She understood and wished me the best. I rang my personal trainer Darren Ward and did some work on the punchbag along with some sparring and skipping. Then I went to the alley for half an hour and headed to training after that. I needed those few sessions to get tuned into what lay ahead and I was ready to dedicate my performance against Kilkenny to Trixie.

On Sunday, July 25, we found ourselves back in Croke Park for the first time since the 2002 All-Ireland final. And once again, we were facing a challenge from the men in black and amber. In 2002, we felt that we let ourselves down and that left me very angry after the game. We had tried to beat Kilkenny with hurling but we forgot to really compete with them in the physical stakes.

I could picture Trixie as we ran out to face the reigning All-Ireland champions and I knew that his family would be looking on with heavy hearts and lumps in their throats. I wore a black armband for the game and standing for the national anthem, I closed my eyes, thinking about the special people in my life. I clutched the medals that I wear around my neck, medals that mean so much to me, given to me by people who really matter. I had visited my friend Sheila Considine's grave early that morning, as I do before every big championship match. I knew she was looking down on me and Trixie was too, still keeping a close eye on my game no doubt.

During those precious moments before throw-in, I thought of Sheila and how she fought to live despite debilitating illness and I thought about my son Colm and of what lies ahead of him. And of course, I thought about Trixie. I remember smiling to myself because he was always up to some sort of devilment.

Trixie's daughters Trish and Carol were at the game, they flew up with the Clare team and the county board made sure that they were well looked after. They travelled to Croke Park with the team and when the game was over my sister Helen drove them back to Clare. This was what Trixie would have wanted; he would not have wanted them sitting at home on a day like this. Young Kevin was at the game and he gave a perfect example of just how resourceful kids can be. After the game, he managed to find his way to the dressing rooms. The security guard tried to stop him getting in but Kevin was having none of it, he was there to see me and that was it.

We laid down a marker early, during the pre-match parade. Our captain Seánie McMahon ran to the outside for a march behind the Kilkenny flag and I nodded my approval. 'Great move, Seánie,' I thought. When the parade had run its course, I was psyched. Before the game, I had noted how Kilkenny's manager Brian Cody had acted on the sideline in their massive qualifier victory over Galway in Thurles. He was seriously wound up but there was no way he was going to get away with the same lark against Clare. I wasn't going to let him think that they were better than us. Brian Cody is one of the best managers I have ever seen, he does the business for Kilkenny, but

Accepting the U–16 Munster trophy from the late Brendan Vaughan, former chairman of the Munster council and a committed Clare man.

The victorious East Clare U–16 hurling team, Munster champions 1987.

Living the dream – The final whistle signals the end of the 1995 All–Ireland hurling final and Clare have put the curse of Biddy Earley to rest.

Tipperary's John Leahy strikes for goal in the closing stages of the 1997 All-Ireland final as Brian Lohan moves in to challenge.

But thankfully I was celebrating at the final whistle after saving Leahy's shot.

The smile says it all – collecting the trophy after winning the 1999 All-Ireland Poc Fada competition, Annaverna, Co. Louth.

First man sitting – I have just received my second Allstar award in 2002 from GAA President Sean McCague and Vodafone's Paul Donovan.

With my son Colm.

With my good friend Trixie, holding the McCarthy cup.

*My son Colm and I visit Sheila Considine, a young girl
who touched my heart.*

All the hard work pays off – Limerick Institute of Technology celebrate after winning the 2005 Datapac Fitzgibbon Cup hurling title.

Stretching to make a save during the National Hurling League Final against Kilkenny in Thurles in May 2005.
[Photograph by John Kelly]

Feeling the tension ... hand on heart with my colleagues during the national anthem before the All-Ireland semi-final against Cork in Croke Park, in July 2005. [Photograph by John Kelly]

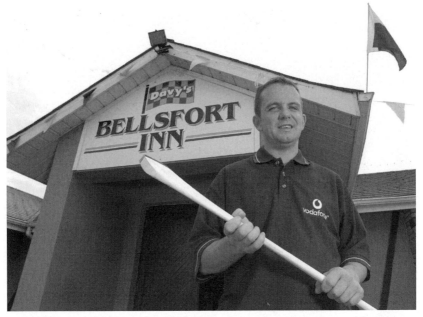

Standing outside my pub, the Bellsfort Inn, situated on the road between Newmarket and Shannon.

when I saw how he acted on the touchline during the Galway game, I said to myself, 'Jesus, the first chance I get, I'm going to have a go at him.' I found it galling that Brian had escaped a suspension after I had missed out on two months for something similar earlier in the year.

When the parade was almost complete, I stared at Cody and he coolly winked back at me. I wouldn't let it go and I started to jump and roar in front of their dugout. 'We're going to put them fellas in their place today!' I wanted Brian to hear that. There was going to be no backing down that day no matter what he threw at us, and Brian Cody knew his men were in for a tough time.

Anthony Daly deployed Alan Markham in a sweeper role behind the half-back line and it worked well as Kilkenny struggled to adapt. I gave it everything between the posts but I missed a second half penalty. I struck it well but it was at a nice height and Noel Hickey pulled off a great save on the line. My mind sometimes flashes back to that penalty and I think that if I had scored it, we would have won the game. Niall Gilligan took over when we were awarded a second penalty and, although my effort was a much cleaner strike, Gilly's was a real bouncing bomb and it roared up off the turf past the three Kilkenny lads on the line.

After missing my effort, I was absolutely furious with myself. I had used my puckout hurley to take the penalty and when I got back to my own goalmouth, I went to throw the stick into the corner of the net as hard as I could. But I miscalculated and ended up hitting one of the umpires on the leg. The hurley broke in two and I thought to myself, 'Jesus Christ, I'm going to get life for this.' The injured Brian Lohan, who was on hurley duty behind the goals, went to help the umpire to his feet and I was busy apologizing at the same time. It was purely unintentional and if anybody saw it in the stands, I am sure they were doubled over with laughter.

The umpire was in agony as he waved the next ball wide and he was pissed off with me for a few minutes. When he finally recovered he told me to forget about it and to concentrate on my game. He asked me for a hurley after the match and I was ready to hand one over when it was announced over the PA system that we were down to play extra-time. But when I saw Nicky Brennan rushing from his seat in the Hogan Stand, I knew that extra time was a non-runner. Kilkenny's county board chairman Ned Quinn must have broken the land speed record on his way from the stand to the pitch and here he was, waving his hands in the air. Kilkenny knew that they were in trouble, the momentum was with us and if the game had continued, we would have taken them out.

When the dust settled, I took a bit of stick because of my running battle with Kilkenny's star forward Henry Shefflin. I will admit that serious words were exchanged between us but I was ready for anything that he had to offer. Every time Henry had a sniff of goal, I was roaring him on to have a go. When John Hoyne scored Kilkenny's goal after half time, it was Henry's turn to hit back.

I raced from my goal to give him a piece of my mind and in my hotel room later that night, I reflected on the sheer futility of it all. Henry is at least a foot taller than I am but in the heat of battle, I feel very brave. On the pitch, I take shit from nobody. Henry was on my mind in the days leading up to the drawn game and I relished the challenge. Early on, he stood over a 21-yard free and I roared at him to go for glory because I knew I could keep it out. I was hoping he would go for goal again with Kilkenny's late penalty but he had to take the point. Jamesie O'Connor equalised at the Canal End soon after and it was no more than we deserved. We fought back from the brink, trailing by four points with 20 minutes to go, and at that stage I thought Kilkenny would step on the gas. They tried to but we kept coming back at them and, on the day, we were a much better team tactically.

The choice of venue and referee for the replay was a source of great anger in Clare. We did not want to play the game in Thurles because we felt that it was too close to Kilkenny and we certainly did not want Pat Horan as referee. Did we get any say in the matter? Of course not. We would have travelled to Cork, Limerick or back to Dublin but our wishes were ignored. Why not Limerick? It's the same distance from Kilkenny to Thurles as it is from Clare to Limerick.

I love playing in Semple Stadium, the pitch is first class but Kilkenny had played Galway there two weeks before and it was the venue they wanted for the replay. Many believed that we were upset because we had been hammered by Waterford in Thurles on May 16 but I can honestly say that was not a factor because we have had some great days in Thurles too. I have nothing against Cork or Kilkenny but if a tight decision has to be made, invariably they feel the benefit of it. It's not fair and the entire system should be re-examined. We need more people from different counties on more committees, let them in to have a say. Why did we have no say in this fixture? Surely if you object to playing at a particular venue, your objection should be taken into consideration.

Nevertheless, preparations for the replay were good. On Monday, we went to the Aquatic Centre in Abbotstown in Dublin, and on Tuesday, we trained on the beach in Milltown. After some badly-needed recovery work, the energy soon returned. It was a gamble to start our full-back Brian Lohan for the replay but Brian is an unbelievable player and he could have made a huge impact if he had been fully fit. Brian's hamstring went early and Dalo got stick that he didn't deserve. If I were in Dalo's shoes, I would have picked Brian too because he was keen to play. Unfortunately, the experiment didn't work out.

Kilkenny beat us by 1-11 to 0-9 in the replay and I took my fair share of stick from their supporters at the Town End of Semple Stadium during the first half. Henry hit me hard on the way out for a ball but I stood up and roared, 'Come on Henry if you want some more!'

What happens on the pitch should stay between the white lines and once the final whistle goes, players should respect each other and shake hands. Not one Kilkenny player shook my hand that day, and their management team stayed away from our dressing room afterwards.

That annoyed me because after the drawn game, Henry shook hands even though we had been at each other's throats all the way through. He even offered me his shirt at Croke Park because I had told him before that my son, Colm, thought he was a super hurler. 'Give that jersey to Colm,' it was a nice touch.

Now, Kilkenny refused to acknowledge our contribution to two savage battles. I have no bad feelings against any player once the game is over and I have always had good time for DJ Carey. Normally he would shake my hand after a game, but I didn't see him once over the two days against Kilkenny. I remember sending DJ a text message before the 2003 All-Ireland final when he was getting some stick from the media. I wouldn't normally do something like that that but, if I feel that somebody is getting a hard time, I will send a text. That's the way I operate.

Kilkenny have to accept getting hit hard and often. Maybe teams have stood off them in the last few years but we didn't hit them in a bad way, we just wanted to win the game. There wasn't a dirty stroke in the game but the post-match debate was dominated by the incident involving Shefflin and our own Gerry Quinn.

Henry sustained a nasty eye injury after tangling with Gerry in the final quarter of the game. The clash was scrutinised in great detail by the media but there was nothing in it. Gerry contests every high ball the very same way, he goes up guarding with his left hand, pushing over and back. If you study the video you can see Henry was moving his hurley just as much and the injury was purely accidental. Henry was understandably distressed after the incident and I hated to see him injured like that. I texted Tommy Walsh the next day, asking him to pass on my best wishes. I spoke to Peter Barry on the following Wednesday and sent more good wishes. I genuinely meant it because I wanted to see Henry Shefflin fit for the semi-final against Waterford. He is a great player, one of the best I have seen, and he is one of the real leaders on that Kilkenny team. The first day against us, when things were going wrong for Kilkenny, he stood up to be counted.

Gerry was upset by the one-sided coverage of the Shefflin incident and rightly so. I am the first to admit that Gerry is no angel but he was very badly injured himself during the 2002 All-Ireland semi-final against Waterford. How he recovered in time for the final, I will never know because Gerry had bones driven out through his hand. Nobody was charged, never mind suspended, for a cowardly blow but we knew full well who did it. We felt it was not our place to identify the culprit, the dogs on the street knew who he was, but the GAA didn't have the balls to name and shame. I was disappointed because it appeared as if Clare were being set up to blow the whistle on the offender, which was very unfair.

I thought the comments from the panellists on *The Sunday Game* on August 1, 2004 were despicable. They singled out very few other players during the year but they went in with studs up on Gerry. What about the blood on Niall Gilligan's face as he left the pitch? Niall required stitches in the wound later and he hardly hit himself. What about Jamesie and Peter Barry the week before? Nothing was said about that. I always had good time for former Wexford hurler Larry O'Gorman, but he should have thought about what he was saying before he put the boot in. Tomás Mulcahy went to town but there was no mention of the Cork minor footballers and their brawl with Laois on the same weekend. He conveniently decided to brush that one under the carpet, and I wonder if all the talk about Gerry Quinn was aimed at deflecting attention away from certain Cork officials.

A statement from the Clare county board backed Gerry and the GAA's Games Administration Committee's eventual decision to exonerate him was the correct course of action because there was no case to answer.

7 STEPPING UP

Management is doing things right; leadership is doing the right things.
                                                    Peter F Drucker

I didn't like doing it, but it had to be done. I didn't want to become manager of the Sixmilebridge senior hurling team but in December 2004, I ended up running for the post against a Sixmilebridge folk hero, Seán Stack. I was just unhappy with the direction in which the club was heading.

When we were hammered by Wolfe Tones in the 2003 county championship, Paddy Meehan stepped down. Paddy had won a Munster club title and enjoyed plenty of success on the Clare scene but things had gone a bit stale. Stack took over with selectors Corey Downes and Martin Corry for the 2004 campaign and deep down, I feared the worst.

We did win the Clare Cup, the league competition in the county, but who remembers the league at the end of the year? In Sixmilebridge and other top clubs, championship is all that matters. When it began, we beat Wolfe Tones, Crusheen and Tulla but it merely papered over some huge cracks. Te be honest, we could just as easily have lost all three matches. We ended up qualifying for a county quarter-final but in truth, we could have been fighting a relegation battle instead. That's how fine the line was …

Kilmaley hammered us in the last eight and that was a true indication of where we stood. In hindsight, we had it coming to us. Here is an example of how things were run: one player arrived twenty minutes late for a championship game and he was put on in the second half. That sent out a message to the entire panel that players could do what they wanted. Soon after Kilmaley beat us, a few people approached me and asked if I would consider managing the club. They had seen me training different teams and they wanted me to revive our flagging fortunes.

I weighed up the situation and thought, 'If we keep going the way we are, we could find ourselves in serious trouble.' If the club continued on its downward spiral, we could have ended up playing senior B or intermediate hurling, things were that bad. Deep down, I was itching to get involved and I also wanted to weed out a few troublemakers. There were a few lads acting the maggot in the club and, if we wanted to have a bright future, certain issues needed to be addressed.

The older members of the club felt that Stack should be left there, but in my view he wasn't good enough for the job. Now let me make this clear, Seán Stack was one of the best hurlers that I have ever seen and when I was a youngster honing my skills in the local Mill, I *was* Seán Stack. But that doesn't necessarily mean that I think he is the best trainer I have ever seen. I disagreed with his methods; they weren't good for Sixmilebridge and I am perfectly entitled to that opinion. I could have done without running for the job, it didn't sit easily with me, but in my heart I knew it was the right thing to do. He had been burned in the past, back in 1999 when Ger Loughnane let him go from the Clare backroom team. At that time, Stack felt that he was in line for the Clare job but Loughnane never rated him as a trainer or coach. I hated seeing that spat develop between the pair of them because Seán was a club-mate of mine, so I steered clear of the situation.

But now, here I was, running against Stack for a top job. I have never witnessed anything like the night we battled it out for the job in the Sixmilebridge clubhouse. It threatened to get nasty at one stage when one of Stack's selectors, who I was good friends with previously, questioned my commitment to the club. Yet, in sixteen years, I never missed one championship game. I even worked the dates of my honeymoon around Sixmilebridge matches. I have trained every team in the club from underage right through to intermediate. Is that a lack of commitment?

It was a very tense night. Stack had his say and then his selector got dirty. I was sitting by myself and I felt very isolated. Other gentlemen tried to kick to touch, they didn't want an election and that disappointed me. Eventually, it went to a vote by secret ballot and I got there. When the verdict was announced, Seán Stack stood up and said that he wanted nothing more to do with the Sixmilebridge club. He threw a few verbal digs at me on the way out and that was his prerogative. He said that he felt let down and betrayed by the club but in my view, he was being disrespectful. Before the vote, I had stated that no matter what the result, I would abide by the wishes of the club delegates.

My stance was vindicated by the presence of over 20 senior players at the AGM and that kind of representation was unheard of in the past. I picked my backroom team with Syl O'Connor and Flan McInerney as selectors. Noel Murphy and Eamon Fennessy were great back-up, true clubmen, as good as I have ever worked with. It was risky for some of those lads to come in because they were seen as taking sides against Seán Stack. But it wasn't like that, they were coming in to do a job for the 'Bridge. We were only interested in what was best for the club and if it didn't work out, I would have walked away and let somebody else have a go. Cyril Farrell agreed to act as a selector too but he didn't arrive until the club championship began in July.

The boys worked very hard for me and the commitment was first class all year long. I had to drop a few lads here and there, which was difficult because they are neighbours as well as team-mates. We carried a lot of injuries through the league and we ended up with our toughest championship draw in years. St Josephs, Clarecastle and Tubber were pulled out of the hat.

Off the field, I had no such worries. Discipline was back to where it should be – no drink the night before league games, no drink two weeks before a championship game. If you didn't train, you didn't play and lads were dropped for missing training. The worst turnout I had at training was 17 or 18 and they worked hard. The effort they put in from January was phenomenal. I put them through torture with those 6 a.m. starts and back again the same evening. Seven-mile runs, team bonding nights out, quiz nights, anything I could think of to get them closer together. No matter what happened in the championship, I knew we had achieved something. I verbally abused some of these boys, I even told some of them to go on diets. I dropped lads from the panel and told them that unless they met certain goals, they wouldn't be back. I only did that to get the best out of them and bring them on.

We won five and lost three of our league matches, but we were focused in on the championship. Our first opponents were Tubber on July 15, a week before Clare played Wexford in the All-Ireland quarter-final. We stormed out of the blocks and won by 5-14 to 1-7. But our other two group opponents, St Josephs and Clarecastle, didn't play each other because of county commitments and that proved to be a disadvantage to us. They eventually faced each other a week before our game with Clarecastle on September 3. So, before Clarecastle played us, they had a tough championship game under their belts. We were ring rusty, not having played for seven weeks. Clarecastle beat us well, 0-16 to 1-5, but we missed a penalty, hit the crossbar and had another great goal chance. If we had made those scores, it might have been a different story but Clarecastle were the better team on the night. We just didn't perform and I think that our boys might have been trying a bit too hard. We had trained so intensely, everything seemed perfect but perversely, that was our downfall. Lads got too tied up in themselves and failed to produce. It was a hugely frustrating defeat and I got loads of stick from the Clarecastle players on the pitch. There was pressure on Sixmilebridge to perform and I felt bad for the lads. I was very down and emotional in the dressing room afterwards. 'We'll bounce back from this lads,' I told them. 'We'll train tomorrow night and tear into Barefield next Saturday. No drink tonight, we have to knuckle down. We'll get a lot of stick in the 'Bridge after this.'

I went home and sat on the couch for the night, mulling over what had happened out on that pitch. And just when I thought that things couldn't get any worse, they did. At 2.15 a.m., a text message arrived on my mobile phone, telling me that some of the boys were out on the piss. I made a few phone calls the next day, trying to get in touch with the lads involved, but in vain. That night at training, four players were missing. I don't know why they went on the drink but they paid the price for it, I dropped them from the starting 15 for our crunch game against St Joseph's. The matter was well documented in the local media but we dealt with the situation in-house. Even though we made a definite decision that the four lads could not start the game, we had to think of our intermediate team from which the vast majority of our substitutes came. We asked the entire panel for their views, it was agreed that the four players would be kept on and used during the game so that the intermediate team would not be decimated. I felt bad because two of them are close friends of mine and we have hurled together for Clare. But no matter what, I wasn't going to fall out with them. One of the men involved stood up and gave the teamtalk before we went out to play St Joseph's and, even though I was still deeply hurt by the breach of discipline, I admired the perpetrators for the way they stood up, took their punishment and got behind the players ready to give their all for the club. As a management team, we had to be tough and leave them off from the start. Who knows what would have happened if they had lined out but there was no way we could pick them. We brought all of them on during the second half and nearly won the game. We were just a point behind with a minute to go but Ollie Baker hit 1-1 in injury time to secure a 1-11 to 0-9 win. The goal Ollie scored, he'll never hit a better one again. But I didn't feel too bad after losing because we fought on our backs. The year before, I hadn't seen any future for the club, but I see one now and, after we laid down the law, there will be no problems with discipline from now on.

I might not have won titles this year, but we trained hard and became closer as a unit. We didn't hide from anything or anybody. I have taken criticism locally, some individuals have even said that I can't be a player-manager, but I didn't play badly. I let in two goals in three championship matches, blameless for both. Everything was done professionally and in a straight manner, my backroom team did a top class job, but you will always have the knockers. I gave everything that I had to the 'Bridge and I have no regrets about standing up for my principles, taking on the job and doing my bit for my parish. A journalist with *The Clare People* had a pop at me a few days later. It was a very personal attack but *The Clare Champion* set the record straight the following Thursday. A journalist like that would have annoyed me in the past but now I just laugh and shrug it off. It's like water off a duck's back at this stage.

****

I have been lucky enough to win All-Ireland medals for both club and county. I am often asked how these successes compare but I find it impossible to choose and could not possibly place one above the other. To win an All Ireland club title is a serious achievement and March 17, 1996 was one of the best days of my entire life. On that St Patrick's Day, I finally realised my dream of winning an All-Ireland club medal with my beloved Sixmilebridge. It marked the end of a long journey to the top of the club game that had begun years before as a hungry teenager.

Paddy Collins and Brendan Flynn were the two goalkeepers ahead of me in the Sixmilebridge pecking order, but I was ambitious.

The competition was tough, Paddy had kept goal for Clare for a couple of years but he packed it in, leaving the country for Australia. Brendan had been pretty successful with the county and played at various grades. He had U-16, minor and U-21 experience, and he also enjoyed a brief flirtation with the senior panel. These two men had serious credentials and I was third in line for the number 1 shirt in 1989. But when Paddy left the country, it was a straight shootout between Brendan and I.

I was Clare's minor goalkeeper at the time and, although I had played in a couple of league games for the club, I didn't expect to make the step up to championship level so quickly. Lady Luck smiled down on me again when Brendan did his knee in before the championship opener against Tulla and I was lobbed into goals. I played my first senior club hurling championship match for Sixmilebridge just short of my 18th birthday – I was learning fast.

I came through without any major problems but the selectors still wondered if I was up to the challenge. Before we played Ruan, I heard that the selectors had told Gerry Corry to be ready to come in because they were afraid that I would have a nightmare between the sticks. They need not have worried because I stopped a penalty and kept out two other point-blank efforts as we drew the game. From that game on, I never looked back. Victory against my uncle John's O'Callaghan's Mills set us up for a crack at Kilmaley in the county quarter-final.

A day before the Kilmaley match, I played in a minor final against Éire Óg and let in a silly goal at the end of the game. We lost narrowly and it dented my confidence. We had a meeting later that night and our manager Jim Faul told me not to worry, that he had total faith in me. I felt good against Kilmaley and I stopped another penalty. I played reasonably well and we emerged to face our arch rivals Feakle in the semi-final.

Feakle had the great Tommy Guilfoyle in their side but we had John O'Connell. At the time, Guilfoyle was Clare's main man but O'Connell was the best club hurler I have ever seen or played with, the Brian Lohan of Sixmilebridge. Kieran O'Shea was another hard man in the full back line along with Jamesie Keogh so I had plenty of protection in front of me. I was still only a teenager and every time I togged out with these men, I was in awe. There they were: Seán Stack, Flan Quilligan, Noel Earley, Pat Morey, Danny and John Chaplin, John Lynch, Leo Quinlan, and my all-time idol, Gerry McInerney, the best forward the 'Bridge has ever produced. They were getting ready to represent Sixmilebridge in a county semi-final and I was sharing the same dressing room. Sometimes, I was so starstruck that I could hardly speak so most of the time, I kept the head down. I knew my place in the Sixmilebridge hierarchy but as a team player, I was their equal and I had my own very important patch to take care of.

These were inspirational men seated beside me, men capable of producing amazing feats in adversity. Danny Chaplin, a close friend of mine, played on that team. John Lynch, my old buddy who pucked around with me in the local Mill, was another. He had peppered me with shots during my childhood days and here I was now, aiming the ball out to him. We beat Feakle that day and we went on to beat Clarecastle in the 1989 county final. Clarecastle had Anthony Daly in their team and they also had Ger 'Sparrow' O'Loughlin, who would go on to become a deadly finisher for Clare and a key component of our great teams. Sparrow would also become a business partner of mine.

When a shamozzle broke out around the goal during the county final, somebody hit Sparrow on his bad knee. He got up and started roaring at me even though I hadn't touched him. Two men of similar stature, face to face, shouting at each other. It must have been some sight.

We went on to Munster and beat Glen Rovers from Cork to qualify for the 1989 provincial club final against Limerick's Ballybrown at the Gaelic Grounds. The pitch was in terrible shape and for one of their goals, I was buried into the net along with the sliotar. I was badly winded but Kieran O'Shea was screaming at me to get up and to get back into goals. I will admit that there have been a few occasions during my career when I stayed down when I shouldn't have, but this was genuine.

Of course, the pain of defeat was desperate but in hindsight, 1989 was a super year for me. St. Flannan's contested an All-Ireland final, beaten by a DJ Carey inspired St Kieran's from Kilkenny. I had a Munster minor hurling medal in my back pocket, I played in an All-Ireland minor final, played senior for the county, won a county championship with the club and played in a Munster club final. I had achieved so much in such a short space of time.

In 1990, Éire Óg beat us in the county semi-final and we felt as far away as ever from the Munster club title that I yearned for. One of my heroes, Seamus Durack, was in charge of Éire Óg and I am sure the old master had told their full-forward Peter Barry to stand on my toes because he was at it for the entire match.

In 1991 we suffered a championship defeat at the hands of Kilmaley, 0-8 to 0-7, in the Cratloe field opened by the late, great GAA commentator, Micháel O'Hehir. But in 1992 we were county champions again and we got back to a Munster club final where we met Kilmallock. This would turn out to be one of the worst weeks of my life. We were eight points up against Kilmallock with 14 minutes to go, but they went on to score three goals. Paddy Kelly buried a 21-yard free into my top right hand corner and there was nothing I could do to stop it. Then Paddy soloed all the way through and buried the ball in the same corner. With two minutes remaining, a speculative ball in took a deflection off one of our defenders and I was left wrong-footed as the ball dropped over the line.

Just days later, Tom O'Halloran, a man I had worked with at Seasky Express in Shannon, was killed in a car accident. The very next day, an old school-mate at St Flannan's, Padraig McNamara, died. The Sixmilebridge players were still out drowning their sorrows when the news came through about Padraig. The shock news created a huge stir in Sixmilebridge. I admired Padraig because he was a superb athlete with so much talent. The lad could turn his hand to anything – soccer, rugby, hurling, football or athletics. His death put everything into perspective for me and he will always be remembered fondly.

The 'Bridge retained the county championship in 1993, defeating O'Callaghan's Mills in the final. We went on to contest the Munster club final against Tipperary club side Toomevara and, in a remarkable twist of fate, Seán Stack found himself in an impossible situation as a Sixmilebridge player and Toomevara's coach. Seán lined out in his customary centre back position for the 'Bridge, but on the day the pupils beat the master as Toome took the title 0-15 to 0-7. That was a real killer, the one final we were well beaten in. We had lost three Munster finals in five years and I was starting to despair of ever winning one.

I was appointed club captain in 1994, the year we went gunning for a third successive county title. We beat Kilnamona in the first round before facing a clash with our old rivals, Clarecastle. It was a game we should have won, five points ahead approaching the closing stages, but Fergie Tuohy inspired a Clarecastle comeback for a draw. They beat us in the replay before going on to win the county title.

Finally, it all came right in 1995. We played Tulla in the first round of the Clare championship and they gave us a real battle. We were lucky to emerge one-point winners but it was the launchpad for a run to the final and a showdown with Scarriff. We fancied our chances going into the game but we were in for some shock. Everybody in the ground was shouting for Scarriff; the neutrals had seen enough of us winning county titles. I made a double save with 15 minutes to go that rates up there with the very best in my career. Picture the scene. Barry Murphy gets possession, gets past the full-back and finds himself one on one with me, ten yards from goal. I stop it but the ball rebounds off my stick to another Scarriff player five yards from goal. Somehow, I manage to keep them out again. We were blessed that day but seasons can turn on such games. A couple of minutes after the double save, I lobbed a puckout to Gerry McInerney who won a free. Gerry hit the post but the rebound dropped to Davy Chaplin and he rattled the back of the net.

Scarriff might not have progressed very far outside the county but we felt that it was now or never in our pursuit of a Munster club title. We took the Kerry champions Ballyheigue on their home patch in Kerry but it was one hell of a tough game on a windy day. Our semi-final opponents were Ballygunner from Waterford and we had to travel to Walsh Park to play them. From start to finish, myself and Paul Flynn were mouthing off at each other, it was relentless. I stopped a penalty from Flynn during the first half and that drove him mad completely. We played well to beat Ballygunner and we were down to meet Tipperary opponents once again in the final, Éire Óg from Nenagh. It was a milestone day for me as I scored a goal from 100 yards, a huge delivery dropping all the way into their net. We won that game in Limerick in convincing fashion, 2-18 to 1-7, and it was great to get the Munster monkey off our backs. It capped a great year personally for me after Clare had won the 1995 All-Ireland title, everything was going right.

The club had won the Munster title just once prior to 1995. That was back in 1984 and at the time, they probably thought they might not see another one. We now decided to push on for more and we worked even harder. Jim Faul came up with the idea of a double diamond run in training. A player leaves the middle of the 21-yard line, sprints to the sideline at the halfway mark, from there to the middle of the other 21 and back to the opposite sideline again. We ran double diamonds, sometimes ten in a row, and we suffered. We did weeks of that type of work during the winter months but there was real method to our madness. As a result, fitness was not a problem for our All-Ireland club semi-final against Galway outfit, Sarsfields, early in the New Year. Pat Hayes hit Sarsfields' star man Joe Cooney with a shoulder early in the game and knocked Cooney's collarbone out. That was the end of their challenge and, on a chilly afternoon at Semple Stadium, we ran out comfortable 5-11 to 1-12 winners.

It was some feeling approaching the very first All-Ireland club final in the long history of Sixmilebridge. We were on a high, benefiting from the feelgood factor in the county. Wearing the very same saffron and blue colours of Clare, the club just kept on going, carrying on from where the county had left off. We prepared in a professional manner for our St Patrick's Day showdown with Antrim side Dunloy, but there was hassle within the club because of the amount of money being spent. The players were treated very well but some club members did not want to see us pampered. We received new suits, new gear and we flew up to Dublin for the match, which was unpopular with some people in the club. I think it was important that everything was done in the proper manner, and the more progressive club officials had also organised a team holiday.

Dunloy had contested the previous year's final against Birr and, although they had been well beaten in the replay, we knew we were in for a tough challenge as they had comprehensively beaten Kilkenny champions Glenmore in the semi-final. But we were on a roll and felt invincible. We bagged two early goals and, even though Dunloy made a fight of it in the second half, we were well worth our 5-10 to 2-6 victory. It was an unbelievable achievement and now I had an All-Ireland club hurling medal to add to the Celtic cross I had collected with Clare six months earlier. It was a fairytale end to a fairytale season. And finally, Sixmilebridge GAA club had reched the summit. It was fantastic really when I look back on it, the culmination of so much hard work down through the years. Tom Sheehan had been a major influence on me when I was just an U-12 player learning the ropes. Gerry Meehan, Willie Chaplin (RIP), father of my good friends Danny, John and Christy, Noel Murphy and Johnny Flynn (RIP) touched my career at different stages. Then there is the great Johnny Moroney – you tread on the local hurling pitch at your peril after it has been groomed by his loving hands! Noel Casey was one of the finest Clare hurlers in history, John Corbett, Paddy Meehan, PJ Fitzpatrick, Mickey Quinn, Tony Downes, Tom Reidy, our former physio Marty Murray – it's a who's who of Sixmilebridge GAA. I cannot forget our great team sponsor of many years, the late Dominick Murphy of Shannon Precision, who paid for a well-earned ten-day holiday in Spain when we won the All-Ireland club title.

Naturally enough, Sixmilebridge hurling club has struggled to reach those heady heights ever since. We were brought right back down to earth with a thump by Wolfe Tones in the 1996 county senior hurling championship but I was relieved. I had been on the go with club and county from September 1994 until August 1996 and now it was time for a well-earned break.

Our All-Ireland success inspired other clubs in Clare and our conquerors Wolfe Tones went on to contest the 1997 club hurling final, beaten by Athenry of Galway. A year later Clarecastle lost a semi-final to the great Birr team from Offaly. St Joseph's/Doora-Barefield won the 1999 All-Ireland club title against Wexford's Rathnure, before losing the 2000 decider against Athenry.

It was brilliant for Clare hurling and as a club, Sixmilebridge were right behind Wolfe Tones, Clarecastle and St Joseph's as they competed on the national stage. But I would often travel to their matches and listen to some supporters from Clare roaring against those clubs. I couldn't believe that they were shouting against men from their own county, and it saddened me. The club rivalry in Clare is very intense but the club that represents the county should receive 100 per cent support in Munster and beyond.

That great run by Clare clubs shows what can be done when a group of players strive for a common goal. Unfortunately, in Clare social lives now seem more important than playing the game. I do not understand why some players can't wait for the months when they can socialise without interfering with their game. After all, a club player can live it up for six months if he wants to.

A dominant St Joseph's team beat us in three successive county championships from 1997-1999 before we regained the county championship in 2000, beating Éire Óg in the final. It was a memorable day for me as I saved a penalty and scored one in the same match. We went on to win a Munster club hurling final later that year, defeating Mount Sion, but I should have sat that game out as I was suffering from the effects of glandular fever.

During the semi-final victory against Patrickswell, I had suffered a fit of shaking and I knew that something was badly wrong. But this was our first appearance in the Munster club series since 1995 and I was determined to battle on. We met Mount Sion on the first day in December, two weeks after the Patrickswell game, and as we warmed up in Boherlahan, I felt unwell. Sitting in the dressing room beside Danny Chaplin, I started to shake and the tears streamed down my cheeks. I had known during the week that I was in bad form but, as the match drew ever closer, excitement got the better of me. I never felt as bad as I did in Thurles that afternoon and if I had been in my right mind, I would not have hurled. I was diagnosed with glandular fever later in the week by Dr Padraig Quinn but still, I travelled to London the following Saturday for the All-Ireland club hurling quarter-final.

I was recovering from the after effects of the illness when we took on Kilkenny's Graigue-Ballycallan in the All-Ireland club hurling semi-final on February 25, 2001. We racked up a good tally, 2-13, but Ballycallan matched that with 1-16. It was a game we should have won but we gave away a lot of silly frees. The following Saturday, our All-Ireland dreams died as we lost by a point. I was the pivotal figure in the game, producing a number of great saves but missing the target at crucial stages in the second half with a 21-yard free and a penalty. The penalty, three minutes into injury time, would have won the game for us had I goaled it, but I blazed the ball over the bar and with that, our chance was gone. I was devastated in the dressing room afterwards and I apologised to my team-mates. They placed comforting arms around me and reminded me that if I hadn't made those first-half saves, we would have been out of contention in any event.

Later that year we were beaten in the county final by our bogey team, St Joseph's, and we had to wait until the 2002 campaign to register a first victory against them in five attempts. We went on to defeat Clarecastle in the county final before qualifying for another Munster club final after a fantastic semi-final victory over Cork's Blackrock at Cusack Park. Blackrock had a very good team, sprinkled with inter-county players, and it was one of the best matches Sixmilebridge has ever been involved in. Mount Sion got the better of us in the Munster club final but that was a game we should have won instead of losing by two points.

In 2003 we had the upper hand on St Joseph's once more and amazingly, I scored a goal. I launched a massive free from 120 yards that went all the way to the net and it proved to be the crucial score. Our campaign ended prematurely at the quarter-final stage, beaten by Wolfe Tones, and an emerging Kilmaley side put paid to our hopes in the last eight of the competition last September, 2004. But Sixmilebridge remains a club capable of doing the business, we have been the most dominant team in Clare over the last 25 years.

There is a great spirit attached to the club team and going to big Munster club matches a few years ago, I really enjoyed the card games on the back of the bus. Myself, Danny Chaplin and Niall Gilligan against John Reddan, Christy Chaplin and John O'Meara. As a group of players, we get on very well together and we have had some great nights together in my pub, the Bellsfort Inn, with our stalwart full-back Pat Hayes providing the musical entertainment.

When I was team captain in 2001, I organised three fundraisers for a team holiday to the Canaries. It was a fantastic week and brought the club players even closer together. I am very close to the Chaplins, Danny and Christy were county panellists in 1995 and 1997 when Clare won our All-Ireland titles. Craig, Danny's son, is the man who looks after my hurleys at Sixmilebridge matches. Before I take a puckout, Craig will hand me the correct hurley for the job before replacing it with my 'shot-stopping' hurley. I get lads to help me with my hurleys because I don't like to take my eye off the game for a second. In hurling, as in life, you should rarely look back.

8 KEEP HER LIT

A college education should equip one to entertain three things: a friend, an idea and oneself.

Thomas Ehrlich

A new and unexpected name was added to the Datapac Fitzgibbon Cup roll of honour in 2005 – Limerick Institute of Technology. March 5 was certainly a red-letter day as LIT created history and simultaneously avenged a hiding at the hands of University of Limerick in 2003. When the wheel turned full circle, the feeling was very sweet and helped to erase many bitter memories. Our captain Eoin Kelly lifted the trophy at the Gaelic Grounds and it only struck me later that it was exactly twelve months to the day since UCC had knocked us out of the competition at the semi-final stage the previous season. On that occasion, I ended up with a two-month suspension for my criticism of match referee Pat Horan.

Now all that was forgotten because we had achieved what we had set out to do, to put LIT on the hurling map. It seemed a far-fetched plan in September 2002, when I first set foot in LIT, with hurling there in dire straits. But with plenty of hard work, dedication, belief and a bit of luck, we got there. Trixie would have loved this unique rollercoaster ride and I am sure he was looking down on us. He was a huge inspiration behind the team's victory and he was in my thoughts right through the historic Fitzgibbon weekend. It was a massive couple of days for LIT as the college was hosting the Fitzgibbon, Ryan and Fergal Maher Cup competitions for the very first time. No stone was left unturned by the visionary Jimmy Browne, GAA club Chairman Liam Kelly, and their team in ensuring that the weekend was a tremendous success.

A couple of days of top-class hurling like that was the stuff of fantasy eighteen months before, when I got involved with LIT. Not long after Clare lost the 2002 All-Ireland final against Kilkenny, Jimmy Browne approached me with his vision for hurling in the college. Jimmy, a distant cousin of mine, is a hugely influential figure in LIT and he had decided that it was time to get serious with hurling. Jimmy wanted to see LIT really competing at the highest level and he invited me in to have a look. I was shocked by what I saw; there wasn't even a set of jerseys to work with. There were rugby jerseys all right but only twelve of them, not even enough for a team. Still, I decided to have a go with LIT. I like these challenges and turning the underdog into a winner is far more satisfying than continuing to feed the fatted calf.

I used to sponsor the Liscannor senior football team and for the 2003 tournaments, LIT wore the Liscannor jerseys. Before that, we had to find players to fill the shirts and we pinned notices around the campus letting students know that we were in business. That move had the desired effect and for our first day of training, we needed two buses to ferry over 100 players to Sixmilebridge. We had to use the pitch in the 'Bridge because LIT had no pitch to call its own, things were that bad. I was in control of two teams, the Freshers (first years) and the seniors, and my first year in charge proved to be a huge learning curve.

In February, the Freshers were defeated by Dublin IT but the loss that hurt the most was a humiliating 2-21 to 0-10 defeat against University of Limerick (UL) in the Fitzgibbon Cup quarter-final. I hadn't seen it coming but I should have. Throughout the league, we had made steady progress but training had not been hard enough. I was preparing the players as if they were to peak in June or July, but Fitzgibbon hurling is totally different to summer hurling. It is tougher, stickier, more of a dogfight and the ball moves slower than it does on the harder ground.

We beat Dublin IT in the first round of the competition and that victory set up a home tie against our keen rivals from UL on February 15. That Saturday afternoon, and its consequences, fuelled me with the motivation to succeed with LIT.

Before the game, there was one obvious problem – we had no pitch. So we plumped for Sixmilebridge. That was a major motivating factor for UL, the reigning champions, and they took full advantage. Playing LIT in Davy Fitz's back yard, they pulverised us. I will never forget their attitude on the field. They were UL, we were only LIT, and they were going to destroy us. With five minutes remaining and leading by 14 points, their coach Davy Clarke told them to go for goal from a 21-yard free. That was a valuable lesson for me and it showed how ruthless Fitzgibbon Cup hurling can be. The standard in this competition is extremely high, almost on a par with senior inter-county hurling, and arguably better than U-21. I was gutted that UL had run out such convincing winners because we had been level four times in the first half. No way were UL seventeen points better than us but we had not performed in the second half. I had to question the attitude of some our players who threw in the towel early in the second half but overall, I had no complaints. We were beaten by a better team on the day.

I was angrier with myself because I hadn't trained the players properly. I had been too lenient with them, letting them come and go as they pleased, but I swore that would not happen again in 2004. I pride myself on the fact that the players in any team I am over always give 100 per cent, but those players came up short and they knew it themselves.

One of my selectors John O'Meara, a trusted friend, told me he had had enough but Trixie, John Faul and Jimmy decided to tough it out. Trixie was a fantastic character. I knew him since I was nine years old and as each day goes by I miss him more and more. He will always be a part of me, a unique character in so many ways. Back in 1967, Bridge United was founded to promote soccer in the Sixmilebridge area following England's 1966 World Cup success. Kevin 'Trixie' Twomey was the man who scored the club's opening goal in their very first game against Milltown-Malbay all those years ago. He taught me everything I know about hurling and here he was, deciding to soldier on with me for what could have been another disastrous year with LIT. But Trixie didn't mind what happened to us, loyalty was far more important to him. Behind the scenes in LIT there was something of a structure in place and Seoirse Bulfin had been appointed as Sports Development Officer, a very shrewd move. In 2004, LIT turned out eight GAA teams, double the 2003 total, so we knew we were making progress.

I had learned some valuable lessons in 2003 so I decided that we would have a serious crack at winning the 2004 Division 2 league title.

Our pre-Christmas campaign brought victories against Mary Immaculate College (coached by Eamonn Cregan), Carlow IT and Tipperary Institute. Our good form continued after the winter break when we beat Maynooth in the semi-final of the league and DIT in the final. Finally, we were getting somewhere. Winning the league was a massive step forward but we needed to improve further for the bigger tests that would come our way in the Fitzgibbon Cup.

I decided to change direction and introduced the players to Darren Ward, my personal trainer. Twice a week, Darren came to the gym in LIT to work with the players on their upper bodies. I was conscious of how we had lost out to UL in the physical stakes a year before and it was clear to me that we needed to train harder and play serious challenge matches. I arranged games against Garda, GMIT (twice), the Clare seniors, Limerick seniors and UCD. The team won every single game they played, but I felt they were getting a bit too cocky and I certainly did not want that. The night before we played NUIG in our next challenge, I took the lads for an hour and a half of physical work and an extra 35 minutes before the game itself. I wanted them absolutely wrecked by the final whistle and, true to form, after building up a good first half lead they fell flat in the second half and ended up losing by two points. It gave me a stick to beat them with ahead of our first round Fitzgibbon Cup showdown with Cork IT, finalists in 2003. I knew that CIT's coach John Meyler would have them well prepared and playing them away from home was a tall order for our players. I was meticulous in my preparation and one night, less than two weeks before the game, I spent six hours going through every aspect of our preparation in extreme detail. I examined the team; I thought of what I wanted to say to every fella the week before the game and what I wanted to say to the lads on the day of the match itself.

I organised the bus we wanted, the driver we wanted and the schedule for the week leading up to the game. The night before, the lads met in my pub, the Bellsfort Inn, between Newmarket and Shannon. We met at six o'clock on the dot and whatever they wanted was ready for them, sandwiches, biscuits and drinks, non-alcoholic of course! Then we had a pool competition, something I always find great for team spirit. Afterwards, we went to the Shannon Shamrock Hotel for a massage and a swim before they retired to bed.

I insist on the same ritual for every game. We meet up early in the morning and eat breakfast together in LIT. Darren looks after the lads' diet, what they eat, what they drink and how much they consume. I had a huge backroom team including hurley carriers, five on statistics, four selectors, a doctor and a masseuse.

After the hiding we took from UL, which was still in my mind, nothing was left to chance. When we arrived at CIT, we were informed that we could not warm up on the main field. We were sent to a soccer pitch and that gave me the ammunition to wind up our lads to the hilt, especially as CIT were warming up where we had been ejected from. I played *The Wolfe Tones* in the dressing room, just to see what kind of an effect it would have on the players. I don't want the players uptight before a match and I like to create an atmosphere where they feel good going out onto the pitch. There is no point in being wound up for an hour and twenty minutes beforehand so, for forty minutes, I let *The Wolfe Tones* do their thing. It seemed to work.

As I expected, CIT were well prepared and the tackling was some of the manliest stuff I have ever seen. We took it, gave back as good as we got and came through to set up a meeting with Queens University Belfast in the quarter-finals. We were told that we had a home game but a rule had been introduced that if a Northern team was involved, they didn't have to travel. That annoyed me greatly but a compromise was reached and the match was switched to Athlone. That was fair enough because it was the venue for the Fitzgibbon finals weekend. We started slowly against Queens but once we went into overdrive, we won very comfortably to set up a titanic showdown with UCC.

****

I do not actively court controversy but nevertheless, it seems to follow me around. On March 5 2004, I found myself up to my neck in it again. As usual, the entire panel ate breakfast in LIT on the morning of the game before boarding the coach bound for Athlone. We arrived with plenty of time to spare and, as the lads warmed up for the game, I decided to have a quick word with referee Pat Horan. Normally a person would look me straight in the eye while shaking my hand but Horan was different. 'Pat, best of luck,' I said. He neither looked at me nor said a word to me. I was suspicious and after that meeting with Horan, I went to speak with Trixie. I was spooked and I felt there was something wrong

Before the throw-in, I reminded Horan that we were due to observe a minute's silence for Cormac McAnallen, the Tyrone football captain who had passed away so suddenly. Horan snapped back 'I know nothing about that.' 'But Pat, there has to be a minute's silence, it's only right,' I replied. I could see I was getting nowhere so I asked Jimmy Browne if he would talk to Horan, who eventually relented.

Horan seemed paranoid to me and I could sense that we might be in for a long afternoon. The vibes weren't good. Two minutes into the game, as I was patrolling the touchline, I took one hell of a shoulder from the UCC sports officer. I had expected something like that; I knew they would try to needle me so I let it go. The game itself was tough and hard but punctuated by passages of good hurling. The main thing was that we were able to compete. We knocked the stuffing out of UCC and I was very proud of the lads. The newspapers later described the game as a high-octane affair and it certainly was. We lost by 0-19 to 1-11, but the game was much closer than the final score suggests.

We could have won it but didn't due to a couple of second half incidents. Our goalkeeper Seán Hawes hit a short puckout to Brian O'Connell who failed to control it, the ball went loose and we conceded a point. Then, Shane Tierney stumbled on our own 50-yard line just as he was about to clear the ball. Shane said that in releasing the ball, he hand-passed it but Horan said that he threw it and that cost us another vital score.

With five minutes to go, there was only a point between the sides but a point each from Mark O'Leary, Eamon Collins and two from Kilkenny's James 'Cha' Fitzpatrick saw them pull clear. I had been convinced that we would beat them and I was absolutely gutted to lose. I went into the dressing room and sat down beside our full back John Coen. I picked up a hurley and broke it in two pieces off the seat. I did not know or care that it was John's good stick. Looking back on the game itself, former Cork manager Bertie Óg Murphy and his sidekick John Considine had their homework done and they conducted themselves well on the line. The sports officer had a go but we shook hands afterwards. He had tried to upset me and I accept that they would think I am a hothead and might have been wound up by such tactics.

After the game I told reporters that I thought Pat Horan was 'an absolute disgrace' after his refereeing performance. There were a number of reasons why I did so. During the first half, our right corner back Micky Cahill went down injured. Micky's shoulder had popped out and he was on the ground, roaring in pain. Still, Horan didn't stop the play. I was infuriated but in the second half, it got worse. Maurice O'Brien went out to a ball on the sideline and a UCC player pulled across his ankle. The clatter could be heard all over the field, it was a terrible blow, but Pat Horan never even checked if Maurice was ok. I was furious and Horan told me to calm down. Maurice eventually rose to his feet, only to hobble about for two minutes before we had to take him off. Incredibly Horan did not award a free for that incident and the Cork mentors were roaring at Maurice to get up. I told them where to go.

Near the end, UCC introduced a sub but Horan allowed play to continue as the corner forward who was being replaced left the field. As UCC took a free the player being substituted clearly interfered with the play while running towards the touchline. He may not have touched the ball but he impaired the vision of one of our players who lost the ball, resulting in another UCC point. When UCC scored, they had 16 men on the pitch but Horan did not call back the play. Those reasons alone were enough to make my blood boil. I approached Horan as he was walking off the pitch, a good distance from where I was situated.

Horan sensed that I was approaching so he stopped and turned to face me. 'Pat, you're only a f*****g c**t after what you did today, and I'll do you if I get a chance,' I told him. Those were the comments that landed me in hot water.

I knew that Horan would report me for my comments so I decided to take action a couple of days after the game, when the dust had settled. I picked up the phone to contact a good friend of mine in Horan's home county of Offaly. The man at the other end of the line was former Offaly goalkeeper Damien Martin, an Allstar back in 1971. Damien promised that he would speak with Horan who, as it transpired, had already submitted his match report. Pat told Damien that he was very hurt by my comments in the newspapers and had reported me for verbal abuse. When I found out about this, I asked one of my father's good friends to organise a meeting with Horan and I met him on the following Monday. I did not want to be suspended and I knew that I had been out of order to publicly verbally abuse Horan, but I just could not hide my feelings. I apologised to Horan and I also apologised for the fact that his family had seen what I had said about him in the paper. But I also told him straight out that I thought some of his decisions on the day were terrible. Horan decided that he would send a note to the disciplinary authorities stating that he accepted my apology. Unfortunately, it made no difference but at least it was a gesture on his behalf. Horan reminded me that during the UCC game, there was an incident involving one of our players, Conor Plunkett, where he could have sent him off. He let Conor stay on and I accept that, but the flipside was that two Cork players should also have got the line. Horan then said something that totally unnerved me. 'I took stick from Mattie Murphy (former Galway senior hurling manager) back in 1999,' he recalled. 'Because when you ran 40 yards from your goal to shout abuse at me, I did nothing.' That particular incident, which had happened almost five years before, was still in Horan's mind. I believe he felt he had been undermined back then so, perhaps to prove a point to Mattie Murphy, he made up for it in Athlone.

People thought my suspension might teach me a lesson but it didn't change me. I do not regret a thing that I said and I told my LIT players that we would never let each other down. I had simply made my feelings known.

Naturally, we felt aggrieved but the 2004 campaign ended on a high note as LIT won the division 1 Freshers All-Ireland title for the first time on April 21 in Emly, Tipperary. I remember that we were seven points down at half-time and I pressed one of our players, Donal O'Reilly, to give it a bit more in the second half. Even though Donal was playing with a broken finger, I knew there was plenty left in the tank and I wanted to see him perform. Fittingly, our first attack of the second half ended with Donal finding the back of the net. It was heart-stopping, end-to-end stuff after that but we had great performances all over the field and we came through by a single point, 2-15 to 3-11. Our Galway star, Niall Healy, held his nerve a minute from the end to convert the winning free.

That was a massive lift after all that had happened but by then, I was already plotting our 2005 assault on the Fitzgibbon Cup. A week after losing the UCC game, I was back out to Trixie's house, scheming. We sat down together and came up with a detailed blueprint for success. We knew that we had been hard done by but the best possible response was to come back even stronger the next year. Referee or no referee, we were going to win the competition. In fact we wanted more than to win it, we wanted to hammer everybody in sight and finish streets ahead of the opposition.

We sat for four hours drinking tea, going through the team and analysing the players we had. Sadly, Trixie died before our successful campaign but he was certainly there in spirit. His death was a massive incentive for me to win that competition because his heart and soul were in it. And the players had massive time and respect for him.

****

As preparation for the 2005 Fitzgibbon Cup, I was anxious that we reached at least the semi-final stage of the league competition. Before the Christmas break, we beat GMIT, NUIG and UL to qualify for a semi-final against, ironically enough, UCC. There were no thoughts of revenge on my mind though, due to the form we had shown in our league games to date. People were already starting to talk us up as serious contenders for the Fitzgibbon Cup. I wanted to keep some powder dry for the New Year and certainly did not want the players listening to those sort of whispers. On the eve of the UCC game I warned Jimmy Browne that we might be well beaten. I knew that we were going well and did not want to show them my cards. I burned the lads for the two nights before the game. Sure, I wanted them to battle but I also wanted them to run out of steam. I knew we were going to lose the game and, true to form, the lads were sluggish. Once again I had the ideal stick to beat them with. By now, our preparations for the Fitzgibbon Cup were in full swing. We had been doing three nights a week physical work from October onwards and, after the UCC defeat, I did one more physical session before giving them a month off. In early January, they were back in for a specially designed training camp. It was a three-day job, Friday, Saturday and Sunday with the aim being that the lads would not be able to walk properly by the Sunday. Looking back, it was the making of us. I put the lads through the wringer but for the most part, they enjoyed it. We trained three or four times a day but we didn't ignore tactics and, to keep them amused, we laid on activities for them. We had pool competitions and indoor soccer competitions to break up the heavy training.

It was gruelling stuff for all concerned. We started at 5.30 a.m. on Saturday and 6 a.m. on Sunday. With LIT, 'team' was everything and I can't thank my backroom boys enough. We put a huge amount of thought into the weekend and it ran like clockwork. Darren Ward organised the activity side of things and both Seoirse Bulfin and Jimmy Browne gave a hand. I brought in John Carey to work with the lads on psychology and our Cork senior player, Kieran Murphy, was so impressed that he got John down to Cork this year. John specialises in focusing the mind and getting the best out of oneself, and he went down a treat with the players.

The three days were intense but I can only stress how important it is to keep things varied for players. The typical timetable included hurling, physical training, stretching, pool session, and activity session. As promised, they were barely able to walk on Sunday evening. Seven one-mile runs in Cratloe Woods might have had something to do with that. We split them up into four teams of seven and the run ended when the last man of the seven crossed the line. The idea was that a man was never running for himself, it was for the team. It's the same on the hurling field; you should never be playing for yourself. Over the weekend, the lads stayed in nearby student accommodation at Thomond Village and for that, I have to thank Lily Goggin at LIT, a great friend who helped the team so much.

After the training camp, we kept up the intensity of training. We were at it three times a day for the next three weeks and it was heavy going: 6 a.m. to 7 a.m. weights; 7.30 a.m. to 8 a.m. speed training; 12 p.m. to 1 p.m. hurling. Darren Ward supervised the weight-training and I looked after the speed work and the hurling. It was all geared towards having the body right, having good stamina and speed bases while also ensuring that our hurling and tactics were spot on. We knew that the first match of the Fitzgibbon Cup campaign against Cork IT in Shannon was going to be a tough one. I felt that we were only starting to come together but we had to put serious pressure on ourselves. The Fitzgibbon Cup finals weekend, the culmination of the competition, was being held in our very own LIT and we had to get there.

In the end, we ensured that we would have more than just a passing interest in the competition, but only just. On February 19, we edged through by 2-12 to 2-10 against CIT. We were coasting in the first half but we gifted them a goal before half-time and they got close to us and went in front in the second half. Things went against us but we still won late on with my Clare team-mate Barry Nugent managing a crucial goal. The defining moment for me came towards the end of normal time. We were a point down and our captain, Eoin Kelly from Tipperary, lined up a free 50 yards out. I will never forget it, I was right beside him on the touchline. Cool as a breeze, Eoin looked at the posts, lifted the ball and stuck it over the black spot. 'There's a man that eats pressure,' I thought to myself. Eoin scored 0-9 and even though CIT got all the breaks, I never had any doubts about us.

Following that scare, it was down to more heavy duty stuff ahead of the Fitzgibbon. I held a two-day camp where we pushed the lads to the limit. We started early on a Tuesday and by Wednesday evening, we were approaching our last hurling session. We had done so much work over the two days but the lads were still buzzing. Looking at them hurl, I knew they were ready even though they were so tired. Their touch was in big-time and I knew that we would not be beaten over the Fitzgibbon weekend. A friend of mine phoned and asked if he should put a few quid on LIT for the Fitzgibbon. 'Don't have any doubts,' I said. 'We'll win it.' I knew we were on fire.

On and off the pitch, we were brilliantly prepared for our semi-final against NUIG on Friday, March 4. I had written 15 pages of notes in preparation for the game and it was a detailed rundown of how I wanted things done. There were notes about each player, instructions on how I wanted our dressing room kitted out and even what music I wanted playing when they arrived. I had everything down to the last-minute detail – how long it would take the lads to get from the dressing room to the pitch. Everything was timed to the last second and each member of my backroom team played a part.

Former Galway manager Cyril Farrell, a hurling man I respect, joined me on the touchline as he promised he would, to run the rule over our Fitzgibbon Cup matches. I would take some of Cyril's views on board but I am very much my own man. Cyril was there for games only but psychologically, it was good to have him on board. I first got to know Cyril through Clare physiotherapist Colm Flynn. Cyril came to my wedding to Colm's daughter Ciara in 1997 and we have kept in touch ever since. I have heard people in Galway saying that Cyril knows nothing about hurling but they have short memories. He delivered three All-Ireland titles in the 1980s for Galway so he knows plenty. I respect Cyril's point of view but we don't always agree on things. Despite our occasional difference of opinion he had no problem coming in to help me out with LIT and Ennistymon's junior hurlers last year.

Before the Fitzgibbon Cup, I made a vow to myself that I would not get involved in running touchline battles with opposition managers and selectors. When the game against NUIG began, former Galway captain, Joe Connolly came over and stood close to me. He was very much wound up and I felt that he was trying to get to me but I just walked away from him. I had other things on my mind. The hardest thing that I had to do that day was to drop our goalkeeper, Seán Hawes, a fellow Clare man. Having analysed the CIT game in detail we weren't happy with Seán's form, we felt that his game wasn't up to scratch. It had been a toss-up for the goalkeeping position even before the CIT game with Seánie getting the nod on that occasion, but this time we decided to go with Aidan Ryan between the sticks.

We also decided that we had to start Kilkenny's Jackie Tyrell against NUIG. Jackie had been left out of the CIT game because he hadn't done enough training with us, but we felt he had to start now. Shane Tierney lost out and it was an incredibly tough call for me. I would have Tierney on any panel but I had to tell him an hour before the game that he was dropped, and he was devastated. I asked him to take a leading role in the dressing room and through the pain, he did that. It showed me the calibre of the man. They were difficult decisions, but no matter how close I was to certain lads, I had to do what I felt was best for the team. Shane gave a good team talk before we went out and we hit the field hopping. I knew we were in business and after fifteen minutes, the writing was on the wall. NUIG were disappointed with their performance, they felt they had under-performed but we never let them play. They had a nice team but I had learned a lot about them in their previous game against UCC. It is important to do the homework and certain things I saw in that game worked to our advantage when we came up against them.

Time and time again, we drilled it home to the players how we wanted to play NUIG and it worked out. Tactically, we got it spot on but we had some help from above too. Straight after the game, we got the players into ice-baths, they had a bite to eat and then we went to visit Trixie's grave in Bunratty. Before every Fitzgibbon Cup game, we visited Trixie and we needed his help again. The lads were still on an almighty high after beating NUIG, but there was still a job to finish. I asked Trixie's daughter Carol to join us at her father's graveside that night. My big worry was getting the players switched on and balanced mentally for the final the next day. A few words at the graveside and Carol's presence had the desired effect.

Cork's Kieran Murphy spoke too. Kieran is an intelligent lad, he spoke well and he's a great team player. He has a winner's attitude and he doesn't care about personal accolades once the team gets the result. For LIT he tackled, passed, blocked and hooked and that's what impressed me most; he did the donkey work. I asked him to play a role that many people would be unable to fulfil but he did everything that was required.

After visiting Trixie, we went straight back to the Shannon Shamrock Hotel for another ice-bath, some pool work and massages, before the players got an early night. I left at 10 p.m. and spun by LIT to pick up a copy of UL's victory against Waterford IT. I watched the video three times and didn't get to bed until 5 a.m. I made six pages of notes, sometimes they might not be worth a damn but small things about UL's performance had stood out.

After what had happened against them in 2003, when we were annihilated, I really wanted another crack at UL. I remember going into their dressing room after they hammered us on my own club field in Sixmilebridge and I vowed there and then that I would get one over on them some day. There were incentives everywhere I looked. Waterford IT had been unfair to us earlier in the year. Tipperary's sub goalkeeper Damien Young, the WIT sports officer, took a walkover against us in the Freshers tournament. We were unable to play the game because of fixtures congestion but there was no room for leeway as far as Young was concerned. WIT had a super team and probably would have beaten us anyway, but that was not the point; you don't take a walkover unless the circumstances are extreme.

In the end, our 2-13 to 3-6 victory against UL in the Fitzgibbon Cup final was much more comfortable than the scoreline suggests. To achieve what we did was brilliant and it certainly was not all down to me. This was very much a collective effort and I was just part of the jigsaw. The best moment for me that day was watching Eoin Kelly, our leader on the pitch, lifting the trophy. Kelly epitomised what LIT was all about. It didn't matter whether you were from Clare, Limerick, Tipperary, Cork, Kilkenny or Galway. County rivalries didn't come into the equation and it was something I was anxious to get a handle on when I first walked through the gates of LIT. If I had to cross a Clare man to win for LIT, I would do it. And if Eoin Kelly had to cross a Tipperary man, he was going to do it because he was the captain and leader. This success wouldn't have been possible without so many other great people, my backroom team of Jimmy Browne, Cyril Farrell, John Faul, Darren Ward, Seán Chaplin, Bertie Sherlock and Seoirse Bulfin. There was one man who certainly wasn't forgotten amid the celebrations. As we hugged each other on the pitch after the final whistle, I heard the familiar 'beep beep' as a text message came through on my mobile phone. It was congratulations from Trixie's wife Marie. She knew what this would have meant to her husband … so did I.

The lads celebrated well in Limerick that night. I let them at it and took it upon myself to act as chauffeur for the night. We organised a reception in the College soon after and that same night, we brought the cup out to Trixie's grave for a visit. For a woman that didn't have any understanding of hurling, LIT director Dr Maria Hinfelaar made a great acknowledgement of the significance of our victory. She was 100 per cent behind our idea to hold a victory reception and she recognised the profile for LIT that naturally went hand in hand with our success. The awards night that followed was very special. I hired comedian Brendan Grace for a set and we had some Riverdance thrown into the mix! We did things a bit differently at the Radisson Hotel in Limerick and Marie Twomey presented the medals. I decided that the function itself would be a black-tie affair and that capped it all off. That's how I wanted LIT to do things – better than anybody else.

When the dust settled, there was talk about the eligibility of a few of our players. Niall Healy from Galway, Clare's John Reddan, Jackie Tyrell and Kieran Murphy were the targets. I know for a fact that two other colleges tried to dig up evidence that some of our players were not qualified to play for us to belittle our great success. I can sleep at night safe in the knowledge that LIT will always abide by the rules, and has done in the past. We should have beaten UL by ten or twelve points on the day and it makes my blood boil when the opposition go to any lengths to try and drag up excuses. We were within the rules and we had only one apprentice on our team, a fella learning a trade, even though we could have had more. We were entitled to have apprentices on our team but we usually avoided them because they may have difficulty getting to training. Neither did we have anybody on night courses, all our players were full-time students. Jackie Tyrrell, Kieran Murphy and Shane Tierney were out on co-op. This means that even though these lads were on work experience, they were still registered players with LIT and perfectly entitled to play with us. If we had been illegal, we would not have been allowed to take that Fitzgibbon Cup.

We were the new kids on the block and we weren't wanted there. The other colleges should have been prepared, after all we had won the Freshers tournament the previous year so it wasn't as if we came unannounced. I am sure some institutions wanted the status quo to remain the same but the balance of power shifts, that's the nature of sport. No other college worked as hard as us last year and that's why we won the Fitzgibbon Cup.

The training we did was phenomenal. We worked from the panel of players available to us. Guys like Jackie Tyrell and Kieran Murphy came to us. They needed to come to LIT to further their studies. I was not made aware that Clare man Fergus Flynn, who used to play with WIT, was even studying at LIT until he was in the place a week or two. Fergus got an awful lot of stick after one of our games but he did nothing wrong.

Now, other colleges are carrying a huge resentment against LIT because of our success. It is this kind of success, which we worked so bloody hard for, that gives me a real buzz. I was told that I would never win anything in charge of Ennistymon's junior hurlers but they won a county 'A' title last year. I was also told that I was wasting my time with LIT. It is nice to prove the critics wrong, and to do it with teams that have no tradition and, apparently, no hope is ten times more satisfying than taking the best team under the sun and leading them to glory. That's where the real challenges are, and I have always liked challenges.

****

I started training teams when I was 18 years of age and a fresh-faced Niall Gilligan was on the first team I ever took charge of, the Sixmilebridge U-15s. I had seen Gilly as a young fella and his mother, God rest her, hailed from an area close to where my father grew up in Truagh. Gilly is a player I have kept a close eye on ever since and as a person, I have had the height of respect for him from day one. At times we don't see eye to eye because I tell him things he may not like to hear, but that's aimed at driving him on to better himself. There is an awful lot more to Niall Gilligan than he even realises himself.

For me, there is a great buzz in looking after teams and I like to get involved with the so-called no-hopers, to see how far I can go with them. As a coach, it's about helping out and giving something back because hurling has been very good to me. In Sixmilebridge, I have coached minor and U-21 teams to county titles but some of my most treasured memories are with the Clare U-14 team in 1993. I was 21 years of age and my first inter-county management team was completed by Trixie, Kevin Kennedy and Tom Hogan. I was delighted to get my hands on that particular crop of players because I had seen vast potential in them. I worked on them three nights a week, two hours at a time. No physical work, just speed work and hurling, hurling and more hurling.

The annual Tony Forrestal U-14 tournament is a breeding ground for the inter-county stars of the future. My team included the likes of Ger O'Connell, my former Clare understudy who transferred to Limerick, former county panellist Kenneth Kennedy and my club-mates John O'Meara and John Reddan. We played Cork on Waterford club side Mount Sion's pitch and, despite playing the first half with the aid of a stiff breeze, we found ourselves eight points down. I called the lads together at one corner of the pitch and let rip, managing to somehow convince them that the game was still there to be won. I could not see us being beaten and in the second half we pulled 3-1 out of the fire. Our team captain Stiofán Fitzpatrick broke his finger ten minutes into the second half but still completed the match. The lads were out on their feet but they came through, and it was a huge boost to beat Cork in an All-Ireland semi-final.

The energy that match took out of us ultimately told in the final, when Tipperary beat us. Stiofán couldn't start the game but, even with the broken finger, he came on as substitute and kicked two points over the bar. It told me something about the character of Stiofán and that particular team, character that would see them crowned All-Ireland minor champions in 1997. I knew there was something special in the lads and I stayed with them at U-15 and U-16 level, only going as far as a Munster semi-final. Loughnane would not let me take over as minor manager under any circumstances and that disappointed me. It was a shame because we did a lot of hard work with that group of players. We built a lot of steel into them and I pushed them very hard. They were thick enough with me because of that but the stuff I did with them at U-14, U-15 and U-16 levels definitely paid off. It was identical to the Clare senior training, fast, fast, fast hurling training.

Blocking, tackling and never giving up. I think it was worthwhile because you don't see a minor team winning an All-Ireland overnight. The groundwork is done in the earlier years.

As it transpired, looking after the minors in 1997 wouldn't have been feasible. It was a huge year for the Clare seniors and I got married too. But I remember every game the minors played, listening out for them on the radio. On All-Ireland final day, I ran out onto the touchline to see how they were doing against Galway because my heart was still with them. They were heroes all, my club-mate John Reddan captained the team, Ger O'Connell was between the sticks and Diarmuid McMahon's brother Brian played too.

Adding the senior All-Ireland title to the minor success put the seal on a fantastic day. I played a significant role in both successes and I felt very proud. Coaching has always been a massive part of my life and someday I hope to manage the Clare senior hurling team. I am still learning the ropes as a manager and some of the stuff that goes on at club level has certainly hardened me mentally for the bigger jobs that lie in store.

****

In 2001, local referee Tom Stackpool contacted me and asked if I would help out with the Ennistymon junior hurling team. Although Tom probably receives abuse from me more than anything else, I have great time for him and decided to muck in without hesitation. The fact that Ennistymon are the neighbouring hurling club to Liscannor, a senior football parish, was an attraction because I like the somewhat perverse jobs. I trained the team for five weeks before Tulla ended the team's interest in the county championship. Even so, I was hooked.

I decided to train the team full-time in 2002, even though I knew that that they had not contested a junior county final since the 1980s. The normal Ennistymon approach was to train like dogs in January and February, peaking for the league instead of the championship, when it really mattered.

I saw no reason in them training that hard at that time of the year so we ambled through the league, struggling to win matches, and the lads found it hard to adapt to this new approach. The championship began soon after Clare's All-Ireland final defeat against Kilkenny and looking after Ennistymon was a welcome distraction. The lads gained revenge on Tulla for the previous year's defeat and victory against O'Callaghan's Mills in the semi-final sent the club into a first county final for many years. There, we met Éire Óg, a very young and fast team. We made a few mistakes on the day and it cost us as we lost 3-4 to 1-7. I was still hurting after Clare's loss to Kilkenny but I felt even more gutted for the Ennistymon lads. More than anything, I wanted to see them win something and it stiffened my resolve to have another real cut at it in 2003.

We got back to another county final but stage fright got the better of us again and we ended up beaten by Newmarket. The knives were out and I took a fair bit of criticism around Ennistymon.

My training methods were called into question and I got wind of it one night. I rang Trixie and John Faul and told them to prepare for a battle. We met with the Ennistymon committee and I had my entire backroom team with me, John, Trixie, Phil Fahy and Tom Stackpool. We all sat together and took the committee on point by point. I explained my reasons behind everything because I hate people cutting me down behind my back. To put things into perspective, Ennistymon were a junior 'B' club until they won a county title at that grade in 1983. Now, here they were enjoying some belated success and yet the knives were out. Ok, we were beaten in two successive county finals but Newmarket and Éire Óg are two strong clubs and we were making progress.

The meeting was stormy enough but I made my feelings perfectly clear. Some local people thought that I was making a few bob from Ennistymon but I did not take a single cent from the club. Other managers that were there before me squirreled away a few quid all right, but I have no interest in that. I had actually sponsored t-shirts and paid for breakfast for the players on more than one occasion.

'Where's all this stuff coming from?' I asked. 'Here ye are talking about not having enough hurling done but we have contested two county finals in the last two years.'

I was hurt and felt that perhaps I had stayed on a year too long. I should probably have walked away but I wanted to help these lads across the finishing line. I wanted to leave but the players wouldn't let me. I stayed for them, I thought it was against my better judgement but it turned out to be the right decision.

We got things sorted and the air was cleared. Some people were wondering why we didn't start training in January. The answer was simple: because the championship did not start until August. The league was of no concern to me so I felt we were better off getting down to proper training in March or April. I wanted us to peak at the right time. We made slow progress, up and down during the league but I was confident that we would come right.

Training was going well and it was all fast-paced stuff, hurling, hurling, hurling with 50 sliotars at training. But one night, I had a huge run-in with one of my players. He had obviously been listening to the lads outside the camp who were criticising the management team. I walked away towards the dressing room and in my mind, this was it, I was never coming back. The two of us were equally pig-headed but he gave me some sort of an apology and we backed down. 90 per cent of the lads were behind me and I knew that.

Looking back, that night was the making of us. It gave me a bit of a shake, I upped training and worked even harder myself.

We lost our first two championship matches and that left us with a do-or-die game against Tulla. Our lads were up for it and we had timed our run to perfection. The players were in good shape and their hurling was coming together.

We beat Tulla, O'Callaghan's Mills and Crusheen to set up a county final against Wolfe Tones at Clareabbey on October 18. We weren't given a prayer but I had my homework done. I could nearly have told you how much each of the Wolfe Tones players weighed. Our players knew who they were marking, how to play their opponents and the gameplan was mapped out a week before the final.

The boys were ready to die for each other on that pitch and, although I knew that we were a better team than Wolfe Tones, I had a feeling that they might take us for granted. Our captain, Jason Buckley, had missed the semi-final against Crusheen through injury. Now, I was faced with an agonising decision. Michael Anthony Devitt came in for the semi-final and played very well but Jason was available again for selection.

We decided to leave Jason on the sideline and that was a hard call to make. Jason was one of my best friends in Ennistymon and his leadership qualities made him an ideal team captain. I relayed the bad news to Jason on the Thursday evening before the game and he was not happy. The night before the match, I attended a dinner dance in Ballymena, County Antrim. I left at ten past two in the morning and it was close to six o'clock before I got back to Sixmilebridge. On the way home, I sent Jason a text message from my mobile phone. 'Jason, tomorrow you will be needed more than ever even though you're not playing. I need you strong in the dressing room and I need you to show the lads that the only thing that matters is Ennistymon.' I received no reply but Jason told me later that he got the text. The reason he decided not to reply was because he wanted me to think he was asleep, not up all night anticipating the game.

True to form, Jason played a key role in the dressing room before the match. 'I don't matter, all that matters is Ennistymon winning,' he roared. All week, I had been wondering what I could do differently to relax the lads because I didn't want them too uptight. I knew which dressing room I wanted so I arrived at Clareabbey two hours before everybody else.

I decided to play some music and chose *The Wolfe Tones*, how appropriate! The lads walked in and they were flabbergasted. They were looking at each other but they were relaxed and I knew that they would give me everything. Tactically, they did everything we asked of them. We won by three points, 1-13 to 2-7, but we should have won by more. I was so happy for all my team, names that come to mind are 'Mobile', 'the Dog', 'Booboo', Martin Greene, Robbie, Martin

Looney, Joe, Ciaran, Tommy and the great Mick Malone. GAA followers all over the county were delighted to see Ennistymon win a county junior A title for the first time ever. Coming from a football hotbed, this was a serious achievement. On the way home, we made three stops before arriving in Ennistymon. We were part of a convoy of 60 or 70 cars and the buzz was incredible with bonfires blazing along the way. I enjoyed it every bit as much as anything I have achieved during my playing career. Ennistymon had been successful at junior B level before but this was the one they wanted. They are now an intermediate hurling club and for me, there is nothing like being part of something for the first time. It took me right back to 1995 with Clare.

I was delighted for club chairman Tony Slattery and my selectors, John Faul, Tom Stackpool and Phil Fahy. Ciara, Phil's daughter, was physio with us and she was brilliant. I asked Cyril Farrell to come down for the day of the final and to his credit, he did. He didn't have too much work to do because things ran fairly smoothly. Cyril kept an eye on things from the back wall and I only got one message from him. I don't know it all about hurling and it's nice to have other people there to help me along. My Dad still attends all of my matches and my uncle John is never far away, and those two lads always make sure I listen to what they have to say.

I would like to go into full-time management when the curtain finally comes down on my playing career and the first men I'll turn to for advice are Tyrone manager, Mickey Harte and Armagh boss, Joe Kernan. These are two men who have brought Gaelic games to new levels. I compete annually in the Poc Fada competition on the Cooley Mountains in Co Louth and I stay in the Carrickdale Hotel outside Dundalk. In 2002, I was lucky enough to meet the Armagh team on their way home from Dublin after winning the All-Ireland quarter-final. I have never met such a level-headed bunch of lads and they were always looking for the extra edge, interested in little things we might have done with Clare. Normally after playing a big match like that, certain lads would rather not reflect too much and I didn't want to interfere with the Armagh boys. So, I was pleasantly surprised when they came over to chat to me in the hotel. I discovered that all they were thinking about was success and what they could do in the future. I have a huge amount of respect for the Armagh players after what they have achieved and how they have handled themselves. They are thorough professionals and that is why they have reached and stayed at the top.

Joe is a good friend of mine and he will do whatever it takes to achieve success. He leaves no stone unturned, he's a good guy and I am looking forward to keeping in touch with him for many years. I may need his advice in the not too distant future because I will always be involved with teams. I will continue to take the no-hopers of course, but managing the Clare senior hurling team is one of my burning ambitions and, please God, it will materialise. I have invested the time, my track record is good and I think I deserve a go. Ideally, it won't be for a few years yet and, looking at the job from close quarters, there are certain aspects that do not appeal to me. When my playing career comes to an end, I will do anything to help Clare win another All-Ireland title. The county has to remain successful and if there is anything I can do to help, I will do it. Just because I have won things as a player will not necessarily mould me into a good manager but I have certain strengths. The one thing I can guarantee the Clare county board is that when I eventually step into the role, I will give it everything I have, and the teams I put out on the pitch will reflect that.

Still, I will try not to overdo the management side of things because I have learned my lesson with health scares. At the height of it in 2001, I was totally immersed. I remember the timetable of one particular Saturday. At 6.20 a.m. I left home for training at seven in Ennis with the Clare senior hurlers. We trained until nine o'clock and then I headed for Sixmilebride for an hour-long training session with the camogie team from eleven o'clock until midday. I drove to Whitegate to play with the Sixmilebridge senior team at one o'clock and from Whitegate I made my way to Liscannor to train the ladies football team at four o'clock. It was back to Ennis for six o'clock for a training session with the Clare U-21s before I fulfilled an engagement in Shannon at 8.30 p.m., presenting medals. In hindsight, what I was doing was crazy but at the time, I thought I could take on the world. And sometimes, I still do.

9 THE REAL LIFE

Learn as if you were going to live forever. Live as if you were going to die tomorrow.

Mahatma Gandhi

Sometimes life offers a sharp reminder that hurling is not everything. In March 2004, it seemed to me that the Grim Reaper had me in his sights. Sunday, March 14 was a bleak day as I sat out my first game under suspension when Clare travelled to Salthill to play Galway in the National Hurling League. I was suffering mentally because of not playing, and I was no great shakes physically either. In the hotel after the game, I suffered a dizzy spell. I was sitting beside Dalo and I could feel myself becoming very weak. I told Dalo to call the doctor; I thought I was a goner. I was taken outside for air and I firmly believed that there was something wrong with my head.

On Monday, I decided to go the Regional Hospital in Limerick to undergo a brain scan. My sister Helen accompanied me to the hospital, the scan was completed and I was told that they would be in touch within ten days. A diagnosis arrived the very next day. I was at Trixie's house when the mobile phone rang. It was the Regional Hospital and I was informed that a three-centimetre cyst on the wall of my brain had been detected. I had to return to the hospital as soon as possible for an MRI scan, and naturally I feared the worst.

'This is it, I'm finished,' I thought to myself. When the phone call ended, I told Trixie I had to go. I was too shocked to even tell him what was wrong. I was spooked and speechless and had to get out of the house immediately. I rang my father trembling; I couldn't get the words out of my mouth. It took me five minutes to explain the situation and he too became upset as the story finally unravelled. I was engulfed by extreme paranoia and convinced that something terrible in my head was trying to kill me. That same night, I met this book's publisher at the Clare Inn Hotel but I found it impossible to take in anything of what was said. My mind was elsewhere. When I got home I was in hell and couldn't sleep for hours as the prophets of doom chattered incessantly in my head.

The next day, I went for the MRI scan and that was an uncomfortable experience. Helen was brilliant again; there was no way she was letting me go to the hospital by myself. In the chamber, I found it difficult to breathe. I am claustrophobic and inside, I was full of fear and panic. I was told to stay there for 25 minutes but there were moments when I came desperately close to pushing the buzzer to ask for help. Instead, I closed my eyes and tried to concentrate. I thought about the good things in life, my son Colm and playing in big hurling matches. The waiting game began after the scan and it was the toughest game I was ever involved in. 15 weeks passed before I got the results and during that time the weight of the possible consequences was almost unbearable. The chances were that I would be ok but until this was officially clarified, I could not relax. All I wanted was a specialist to sit down with me, to go through the scans and tell me that everything was going to be fine.

I found it difficult to concentrate on training and I was afraid to close my eyes at night in case I would develop a pain in my head and never wake up. The smallest pain would keep me awake all night long and this could happen up to four times a week. I was living on my own in Lahinch and that made it even more difficult, even though I knew that family members and friends were just a phone call away. Therapy arrived from an unlikely source, pop group *The Corrs* of all people. Seeing them live in concert in Dublin's Point Theatre on Tuesday, June 29 was the perfect pick-me-up after weeks of worry. I managed to secure a ticket from a contact in Ticketmaster for the concert. Amazingly, it was scheduled for the night before I was due into the Blackrock Clinic for my results.

The concert was first class and the seats were fantastic. I was three rows back from the stage and I had a perfect view. I always liked *The Corrs* and I have a particular soft spot for the lead singer, Andrea, a great looking woman. She looked even better in the flesh and turned in a dazzling performance on stage. I allowed myself to relax, time flew and I came away from the gig on a complete high. Instead of taking public transport back to the Burlington, I decided to walk. I was floating on air and deep down, I had a good feeling that my results would be positive the next morning.

I slept deeply that night but I was nervous on the taxi journey from the Burlington Hotel to Blackrock. I arrived at 11.30 a.m. and, thankfully, didn't have to wait long. I presume that when patients are awaiting results of this nature, they are not kept in suspense. The less drama, the better. The moment of truth had arrived and I celebrated wildly inside when the doctor gave me the all clear. He said that the cyst would do no harm and not to worry about it. I felt a blissful relief running through my veins and I was mad for training when I got back to Clare that evening.

Generally I have been lucky with my health, but that scared me. It took me right back to when I took an awful turn after playing a club match for Sixmilebridge against Wolfe Tones in August 2003. At the time I was pushing myself hard, training seven nights a week with various teams. It was all go and Dr Padraig Quinn, a good friend of mine, told me to slow down and take it easy. I had seen the doc on the Thursday night before the Wolfe Tones game and had told him that I wasn't feeling well. I had been experiencing pains across my chest and, in the dressing room before the match, I felt an awful tightness in that area. It was difficult to breathe properly and it was an unnerving experience. I convinced myself that I would get over it, but during the game, I didn't feel well at all.

After the match, we heard that Danny Chaplin's son had been knocked down crossing the road so Danny was in a rush to get to the hospital. I offered him a lift, quickly changed and made my way to my car. As I was walking, I felt a sharp pain across my chest and the doc, thankfully on the scene, told me to get myself into hospital immediately. So, instead of me ferrying Danny to see his injured son, he ended up driving me to the hospital at 100 miles per hour! I can look back on the situation now and smile but when I arrived in hospital, they immediately shifted me to the emergency unit. I received a few morphine injections for the pain and I was very worried. Two of my uncles on my mother's side died young from heart attacks and a third, Conor, underwent a triple heart bypass operation when he was 38. This stuff was going through my head as I lay in silence.

The matron of my ward was the mother of Niall Dunne, who plays for Clarecastle, and she was very good to me. I was sent for an angiogram, a necessary procedure because of the history of heart problems in the family. I was under Dr Meaney and I hated the 6 a.m. blood tests every morning. Although I had one done before, the angiogram still frightened me, and being in hospital was a lonely experience. Fr Michael McNamara, the former Clare county board chairman, spent twenty minutes with me before I went for the procedure and he was a great help. I felt more relaxed after his visit and I will never forget it.

In simple terms, an angiogram consists of opening one of the patient's legs, inserting a tube that travels up through the groin, through the middle of the stomach and finally arrives at the heart. The tube pumps dye through the arteries looking for problem spots, and while this is happening, the patient is wide awake under local anaesthetic. It is not too uncomfortable but then again, it is not something you would choose to do for pleasure. Thankfully, I got the all clear but I was sent for another test two days later to get to the root of my problem. The doctors sent a tube down my throat with a tiny camera attached to look into my stomach. They discovered that the tube entering my gut had narrowed to half its normal size. Substances going down were coming straight back up and that was where the pain was coming from.

At first I had no idea how long I would be kept in hospital so I felt in limbo. In the end I spent a total of ten days in there, after which I was delighted to make my escape. As a result of this health scare, I took stock of my hectic schedule. At the time, I was training hard with

Clare but also looking after a variety of different teams: Limerick IT, the Clare U-21s, Liscannor's senior footballers, the Sixmilebridge hurlers and Ennistymon's junior hurlers. Throw day to day business dealings into the mix and I had concocted a recipe for possible disaster.

****

So many people say that modern-day GAA is a game for single men and I would have to agree with that when I reflect on my marriage to Ciara Flynn. I was 24 when I met Ciara and before that, I had been involved in two pretty serious relationships. I find it amazing to think then that I have a reputation for being a womanizer!

It was difficult when the speculation about my private life reached its peak a few years back. If you believe some people, I have been with every woman under the sun, I never work and I am an arrogant, ignorant bollocks. Look, I am human, just the same as anybody else and if I see a good-looking woman, naturally I will take notice. Plenty of women chat to me, I chat back and I see nothing wrong with that.

Of course I'm not squeaky clean but if I had been with even a quarter of the women I am supposed to have been with, I'd be some man. When I tell people the truth they still refuse to believe me. One night in Ennistymon, one of my friends stupidly tapped a girl on the shoulder and asked, 'Do you not know who this fella is?' She turned around and replied, 'Oh I know who he is. Stay away from me; I don't want anything to do with you.' I had never met this girl in my life and yet she had cut me to ribbons. I told her what I thought of her fairly quickly and we left it at that. As far as I am concerned, that kind of behaviour is unacceptable.

The first time I saw Ciara was in the Queen's Hotel in her hometown of Ennis. It was August 13 1995, the night we beat Galway in the All-Ireland semi-final. I can still see her standing there at the far corner of the dancefloor; it is an image that has never left my mind. I thought she looked absolutely beautiful. I was captivated but far too shy to approach her. She was wearing an Offaly headband around her neck and I thought to myself, 'Oh my God, who is she? She's unbelievable, out of my league.' I remember promising myself to find out more about Ciara. I soon discovered that she was involved in a relationship but I was prepared to wait.

I recall chatting to Fergal Hegarty about her on a team holiday to the US in December, after we had won the All-Ireland. 'That Ciara Flynn, I'd love to get a chance with her, maybe the fella she is with might mess up,' I said to Fergal, more in hope than expectation.

No matter how I tried, I could not get Ciara out of my mind but I accepted she was with somebody else and I wasn't going to annoy her or jeopardize her relationship. However, I did not have to wait long for my opportunity as Ciara's previous suitor was sent packing. Shortly after, I heard she was going to spend a night in the Queen's and I made it my business to be there too. The place was packed but eventually, we found time to chat, alone. I was nervous as hell but I managed to keep the conversation flowing and towards the end of the night, I plucked up the courage to ask her to a dinner dance in Milltown. She was somewhat taken aback but she agreed to accompany me. I was on cloud nine.

Naturally, I felt a bit awkward approaching Colm Flynn's house to pick up his daughter on a frosty night. It was freezing mad, the roads were icy and you would have been arrested by animal rights police for putting a cat outside the door. The speedometer needle of my snazzy Nissan Primera never ventured above 20 miles per hour as we made our way to the dinner dance. The car had all the extras, electrics included, and it was a pretty up to date model. I thought so anyway, and I am pretty sure Ciara was impressed! Of course I was taking my life into my own hands driving in such treacherous conditions but I badly wanted this to work out.

We had a good night at the Spanish Armada and I was the special guest, along with Jim Gavin, the former Dublin footballer. It was my first official function with Ciara and I asked her on the way home if she would like to see me again. 'No, I don't think so,' she replied and the impact was like taking a shoulder from a 15 stone full forward. I was completely taken aback. 'Give me one good reason. I'm not taking no for an answer.' I was prepared to dig the heels in and persist until she eventually relented, which she did. I wore her down and very soon, Davy Fitzgerald and Ciara Flynn were an item.

Ciara was working for Aer Lingus at the time and her job as an Air Hostess took her all across the globe. New York, Boston, Chicago, the life of a jetsetter was the life Ciara loved but I hated it when she went away for days on end because we spent every spare second with each other. The return flights would arrive into Shannon airport at six o'clock in the morning and who was there to pick her up, beaming from ear to ear? You guessed it.

Ciara has a special family who mean the world to her. She has an older brother Padraig and twin sisters, Katie and Ailish, both younger than Ciara and the most affectionate pair you could ever wish to meet. Her other two sisters, Sorcha and Aoife, were always very good to me and her parents, Colm and Kay, could not do enough. I loved everything about Ciara, she was fiery and independent and that was really attractive because I have similar qualities. She showed a slight interest in hurling but nothing major and that ensured that she was a great release from the game for me. When I was with Ciara, the extra-curricular activities apart from hurling ceased to exist. I even cut out golf, which I loved. Now I had something very special to occupy my time.

Less than eight months after speaking to Ciara for the very first time, I decided to propose to her. From a very early stage in our relationship, I knew instinctively that she was the girl I wanted to marry. I planned the proposal down to the very last detail, purchasing the engagement ring in Limerick before giving it to Kevin Corry to look after. I told Kevin, my best man, to make sure he met me in the tunnel straight after the 1996 All-Ireland club final at Croke Park. That was where I intended to pop the question. 'Make sure you're on time, Kevin,' I pleaded, but Kevin missed the train from Ennis and ended up forking out a small fortune on a taxi from Sixmilebridge to Dublin.

Ciara was one of the air hostesses on the Sixmilebridge flight from Shannon and I proposed to her at the back of the Cusack Stand after

Sixmilebridge beat Dunloy on St Patrick's Day to capture the title. So many supporters were approaching me to offer congratulations and I was struggling to get the words out. I blurted out a proposal but I would have to wait for an answer. Ciara didn't say 'yes' immediately, like in the movies.

The rest of the team could really unwind and celebrate but I had to get back to Ennis early the next morning for a Railway Cup tie against Ulster at Cusack Park. Ciara and I took the train home instead of travelling with the team so I would be in time for the match.

I was on fire for Munster against Ulster that afternoon, still buzzing from the previous day's events both on and off the field! After the Munster match I met the rest of the Sixmilebridge lads back at the West County Hotel before heading back to the 'Bridge. We were afforded the mother and father of all welcomes, the entire village roaring its approval as we greeted our people from a hastily-erected stage. Arriving home was an emotional moment, the square was full and Clare FM radio was in the middle of a live outside broadcast. I thought things couldn't get much better after the 1995 season with Clare but this was something else. This was club, this was special and to see an All-Ireland club title in Sixmilebridge was an indescribable feeling. Later that night, Ciara said to me, 'Listen, I just knew when I saw you on that stage.' She uttered the magic word 'yes' and I jumped for joy.

Ciara and I were inseparable and nothing was going to stop us walking up the aisle. Clare were caught on the hop in 1996 following our Munster championship and All-Ireland title winning exploits of the previous year. We ended up losing both crowns on June 16 against Limerick at the Gaelic Grounds.

I was feeling very down after the game so Ciara and I got away from it all. We went to one of my favourite spots on earth, the beach in Lahinch, and we sat and talked. Ciara could always cheer me up.

In August, Ciara discovered that she was pregnant. She rang me from the US and calmly asked me if I was sitting down. When she told me, I wasn't worried because we were so wrapped up in each other. We knew the risks we had taken, but things were so good we felt we could get through anything.

Ciara and I were engaged for months at this stage but of course there were people who said the only reason we were was because of Colm. What a load of rubbish! The lad was conceived three months after Ciara agreed to marry me. She became very frustrated when she was pregnant, she had to stop flying and as a result she felt unhappy. Ciara is a very independent person but Trixie decided to help out and offered her some part-time bookkeeping, which was great to tide her over for the few months. At night, with Ciara by now heavily pregnant, she would tell me when Colm was kicking. I used to love laying my hand on her stomach and feeling my baby inside, that was something very special. She was unhappy due to her work situation and I could sense that but, as a couple, we were still very much united. She was used to flying all over the world and she was pissed off with Aer Lingus because they could have looked after her much better and offered her some office work.

On March 10 1997 we trained on the Hill in Shannon, one of those tortuous nights. I was wrecked when I got home, but late that night Ciara said, 'I think I'm in trouble.' We went straight to the Regional Maternity Hospital in Limerick and they decided to keep her in overnight. I stayed with her and she went into labour the next day.

Initially I had decided that I would not accompany her through the birth but I just couldn't pull myself away; I knew that I wanted to be with her. I held Ciara's hand throughout and Colm was born later that evening. It was some experience being present for the birth of my son, although it was difficult to see Ciara in pain. March 11 was a special day in my life, the day my beautiful son entered the world. At this time, things could not have been better. I was madly in love with Ciara and, to raise our son together, we moved into the old Fitzgerald base in Thomond Terrace, where I had grown up. Now, I had everything I ever wanted: a woman I adored and a new-born son. I was happy that Ciara had agreed to move to Sixmilebridge but looking back, she missed her home and friends in Ennis. It was also the first time I had moved out of the family home and I found that this was a huge change, just a week after Colm was born. Previous to this, I had never lived with anybody except my family and now, I was moving in with my fiancée and our baby. I had too much going on in my life at the time and soon, the problems started between us. I suddenly had much more responsibility than I could ever have imagined and I struggled. We began to fight and some of the rows were terrible. We were both left feeling really low afterwards.

In spite of all this we still loved each other and we were married on July 11 1997 in Ennis. The day itself was good but we were at loggerheads for the entire build-up. I suppose it begs the question – why did we get married? We just hoped that things would work out.

I tried not to let what was happening at home affect my hurling but when we beat Tipperary in the All-Ireland final in September, I was in tears in the dressing room. Anybody looking at me would have mistaken my tears for tears of joy after winning an All-Ireland medal but I was breaking up inside because Ciara and myself were fighting.

In March 1998, the time was right for an amicable split. That is, if there can ever be a right time to split up with somebody you have shared such a close bond with.

Even though we are not a couple anymore, we still fight the odd time! But I have to say that Ciara is a fantastic mother. We can still talk openly to each other and I have told her that no matter what, I will always be there for herself and Colm. I have a lot of respect for Ciara and she has done a great job raising our son.

I look back on my relationship with Ciara in a number of ways. I will always remember the love we felt for each other and I wish that feeling had continued for ever. It is a shame that things didn't work out. Hurling was a major part of my life when I was with Ciara, she wanted to spend more time with me but I wanted to do different things. I started to play golf again after the honeymoon period and I became more interested in the coaching side of hurling. I can see now that I did not devote enough time to her, but I was blind to it then. I will never, ever forget the fights we had and the way I felt when we did fight.

Rumours began to circulate in 1997 and 1998 that I was seeing other people, and that Ciara was too. I was never once unfaithful to her and she assures me that she never strayed either. When I was with Ciara, nobody else mattered. It was said that certain members of the Clare hurling team were with Ciara, but that's absolute rubbish. Ciara did go out with one member of the Clare team but that was before I even met her. Maybe that was how the rumours started.

Once the Chinese whispers start, they gather momentum and can be extremely difficult to stop. It never bothered me because I knew that she was never with any of the players but I was shocked when the 'stories' began to rumble down from the terraces.

I became a victim of terrace abuse for the first time during the 1998 Munster semi-final against Cork at Semple Stadium. We produced one of our finest ever performances but I was bowled over by what some Cork people shouted at me. I was horrified but the only way I could answer them was in my hurling, and I managed to stop Joe Deane in his tracks in the early stages. Soon I could hear the taunts. 'You couldn't keep your wife happy.' 'Who's with your wife now?' 'Who's she jumping now, Davy?' Stuff like that, and it wasn't just coming from one person, hundreds were having a go at me. I had never before been subjected to verbal abuse on such a grand scale and it took me a long time to get over it. After the game a letter from a Cork person landed through my letterbox, apologising for what had been said about me on the Semple Stadium terraces. Ciara stopped going to Clare matches for a long time after that and I would not let her or Colm go to any Munster championship games until recent years, when I felt comfortable that the yobs might have found fresh targets. Colm is at the age now where he loves to go to matches, but I do not want him to hear people shouting lies about Ciara and myself. The young lad eats, sleeps and breathes hurling and I am very upset that he has to listen to certain people spreading these vicious and unfounded rumours about him. The same morons may inadvertently shout and roar abuse at me while Colm sits right beside them in the stands. It is not something I like to dwell on.

Unfortunately, modern day inter-county hurlers and footballers are seen as public property for some supporters who have no idea of what might be going on behind the scenes. Out on the pitch, we are easy targets for lads with a few jars on them; people who like to deflect the attention away from their own problems and take everything out on us. Fans can be fickle, so I always find it useful to remember how short a distance it is between a clap on the back and a kick in the arse!

What can I do when I hear the abuse? I have to bite my lip because I can't turn around and tell them to fuck off or flick a v-sign in their direction. If I do it on the pitch, I'll get suspended, and if I do it on the streets at night-time, I'll get abused. I go into my own little world and take them on. As well as playing Tipperary, I have to compete against their supporters. The reason they don't like me is because I saved John Leahy's goal-bound shot in the dying stages of the 1997 All-Ireland final, and I scored a penalty at Páirc Uí Chaoimh in 1999 which broke their hearts again. I love playing against Tipperary, I love beating them even more but there are many Tipperary people who I would class as really good friends of mine.

But of course, it is impossible to change thousands of minds. I became very depressed towards the end of 2002 and, heading into the New Year, I felt even worse. I should not have let the abuse affect me, people are going to talk anyway and they probably slag me off to make themselves feel better. If I was seen talking to a woman in the Queens, I had people staring at me. I have become accustomed to the stares down through the years. They look at me as if I have two heads, but in 2003 I became so paranoid that I stopped going out for months, afraid to go near Ennis. What really bothers me is that people think that just because I am a Clare hurler, I think I am some sort of God and above everybody else. What a load of rubbish. I would love to go out for a night and NOT be Davy Fitzgerald the Clare hurler. I would like to go out as Davy Fitzgerald from Sixmilebridge, a regular guy. If somebody genuinely wants to approach me and talk about hurling, I will talk all night but not for the slaps on the back. I just want to be normal and appreciated on a human level like everybody else. People say I overreact and I have a chip on my shoulder, but maybe I found the bad times much too difficult to deal with. Now I get on with my life and say to myself, 'If somebody wants to talk about you David, let them off.' I am not going to judge anybody until I meet them and talk to them myself.

For a long time I was not involved in a steady relationship, but recently I have found happiness with a new partner. Olivia and I are really good for each other, she makes me feel special. I just hope that she can cope with my hectic hurling schedule.

I make mistakes the same as everybody else, I am not innocent but I am not all I am made out to be either. I hate it when I am out for a night with my sister Helen and some gobshite walks past mouthing obscenities. One night in the Queens, a lad approached me with plenty of drink on board. As always, I was stone cold sober because I don't drink, but he was not to know this as he launched into his foul-mouthed tirade. 'You never picked my brother on the under 21 team – you're a stupid fucker.' I do the best I can and pick teams as I see fit. I have no personal vendetta against anybody and I wish certain people would get that into their thick heads. Helen gets terribly upset when somebody has a go at me, I am sorry that she has to listen to it but I wish she could detach herself from it. I found it very hard to cope with when it first began to surface, but I am doing much better over the last couple of years, mellowing in many ways. A lot of the abuse can be traced back to my attitude on the pitch because people think I am a cocky git who thinks he can act how he likes and get away with what he wants. I do not care what they think about me anymore because I feel free. Nothing and nobody will ever stop me running out in that Clare jersey, hitting that crossbar a leather and hearing the Clare crowd roaring me on. I don't think I am better than anybody else just because I play for Clare. In life we are all equal, whether you have €10m or 10 cents. To me, the guy with €10m is the exact same as the guy with 10 cents, I will view them both the same and make up my own mind.

Since 1998 I have developed my own style, which is to be more aggressive in my play during the Munster championship. The only reason I am more aggressive is because it seems to be the only way I can combat what they say to me behind the goals. There is no point in turning around and saying, 'You don't have a clue; you're talking through your arse.' So what's the best way to get back at them? By frustrating the life out of them.

The way I act on the pitch is my way of getting back at them. It might spur them on too, but that is what I want to do. I want to show the opposition that Clare are not going to be walked on any longer, that we are here to stay, that I am not going to take any shit and that I want respect. I will never draw a bad blow on the hurling field, I never have, but I will stand up for myself and for my county because I love Clare. I am passionate, I want Clare to win and I will do everything to try to make that happen. I express myself and let myself go a lot more on the field now; I get the abuse and take it in my stride. I will not let the crowd get to me. I will stand up and do what I want to do. I will be bold. And why shouldn't I? That's my arena out there ...

10 PREPARED

People who never get carried away should be.

Malcolm Forbes

Where business is concerned, I tell friends that I am destined for Millionaire's Row or Mountjoy Prison. I tell them that they will visit me at my Spanish villa or in the cells. I am a risk-taker, but I am also pretty confident that I'll be rolling out the welcome mat somewhere in sunny Spain.

I have done well in business but I have been prepared to gamble. I admit that the material rewards are nice, the house, the car, the money, but I don't let them dominate my life because there are more important things to worry about. After all that I have been through, the old saying that 'health is wealth' certainly holds true. Still, I am satisfied with my achievements in the business world. I set goals for myself and I achieved them. It has been a rollercoaster ride in so many respects but I am now in a position where I can afford to sit back a bit. It's a far cry from the early days when I was hungry for success but struggling to even get some pocket money together.

My young business mind cranked into life during my school days. I spent the summer months working at Trixie's filling station in Shannon and they were great times. As a young boy, the few bob that came my way was greatly appreciated and Trixie always looked after me.

I took my first major step into the world of business in December 1989 when I got a job with MSAS Cassin International, a freight company based in Shannon. My official title was 'filing clerk' but they neglected to inform me that 'filing' also included cleaning the canteen!

I was a general dogsbody, earning £90 per week into the hand, and that was just fine for me starting off. I wanted to work hard, get promoted quickly and to start earning some serious cash. To do that, I had to show my employers what I was all about. I remember the room that housed the company files because it resembled a bombsite. Boxes were strewn everywhere and the filing cabinets were there merely for decoration it seemed. In this room, 'filing' was a misnomer.

In my second week in the job, I spent three nights in that room until midnight, bringing some order to the filing system. My work paid off and after two and a half months at MSAS Cassin, I was promoted to a higher department. Now, I was part of CID. It sounds like something from a James Bond movie but it actually stands for Cassin International Distribution. Aer Rianta International regularly distributes merchandise to Russia, cities like Moscow and Leningrad, and I was in charge of loading containers for export. I was working alongside Angela Donnellan and the pair of us soon discovered that we were related, third cousins. Angela was a great help to me and I enjoyed the work with CID.

I spent two and a half years there but we lost the contract to Walsh Western. That was a political decision because I had ensured that everything ran smoothly for MSAS. I soon moved on to another department, air exports, and became friendly with Mike Guilfoyle, a former Clare hurler who was involved with another freight company, Sea Sky Express. Sea Sky was a much smaller operation than MSAS but Mike's van driver was leaving and he asked me if I was interested in coming on board. The prospect of a company van was too good to ignore and I jumped at the new challenge. The work with Sea Sky was pretty varied. I was involved in importing, which I had never experienced before, as well as the collection and delivery of freight. I spent much of my time in Shannon at Aer Lingus imports where the lads never missed a chance for some good-natured banter. On Friday nights, I would sometimes work until 11 p.m. but the craic was brilliant in the airport. Once, the lads got their hands on a huge piece of timber and on it, they sketched the rough outline of a hurley with black marker. 'Maybe you might stop something if you had this, Davy!' read the inscription beneath.

The part of the job that I did not like was driving to Cork and other places with freight, because the long journeys affected my hurling. Mike and I clashed on this issue and I thought he could have been a bit more understanding, especially as he came from a hurling background himself.

It was summer 1993 when I finally decided that I had enough of Sea Sky Express. I walked into Mike's office, placed the keys on the table and told him that I was leaving. Mike and I were very friendly once upon a time but the friendship cooled after that. Still, we salute each other today when our paths cross.

It felt like a huge weight had lifted from my shoulders when I left Sea Sky because I hated my last year there. After that, I was unemployed for four months before Pat Keogh offered me a job in his filling station on Limerick City's Tipperary Road. People had told me that Pat was straight but a hard taskmaster. Looking back, he is one of the most honest men that I ever worked for and we never fell out.

Pat handed me the responsibility of managing the filling station but it was virtually impossible to get good, reliable staff. A particular employee decided to pack in his job at four o'clock one morning and I had to get out of bed to pick up the pieces. Anybody that works, or has worked, in a filling station will tell you that job satisfaction is not part of the package but Pat was very supportive to me when it came to hurling. He gave me plenty of time off for training and matches. But I got itchy feet after Clare won the All-Ireland in 1995 and I decided to leave.

My next port of call was as a sales rep for Martin Donnelly, a very efficient businessman. Martin is well known in GAA circles and he currently sponsors the annual Poc Fada competition which I enter every year. In recent times, he has thrown his financial weight behind the interprovincial hurling and football competitions. A great supporter of Clare football, Martin taught me some valuable business lessons and crucially, he instilled in me a desire to branch out on my own. As a result, Martin understood when the urge to go into business for myself became too strong.

I decided to take a chance on the cleaning business. Hand towels, soaps, cleaning detergents, toilet rolls - you name it, I planned to supply it. I wanted to nail down as many businesses as possible, from hotels to schools to workplaces. I saw a genuine opportunity and decided to wade in as fast as I could. I bought a Volkswagen van and knuckled down to serious work immediately. I was based from the family home on the Castlecrine Road and the garage was full to capacity with the tools of my new trade. The business went very well initially and I was turning over in excess of £8,000 per week. Soon, I found that I couldn't manage by myself and I hired a unit in Shannon, equipped with a proper office and phone. I kept the merchandise in a warehouse in Sixmilebridge, which I rented. I was flying but neglected to pay enough attention to the paperwork, and pound signs clouded my vision. Before long, I took over a big warehouse in Shannon and employed a driver, a sales rep and a secretary for the office. Having started from nothing, I now had three company cars to keep on the road and everything was happening much too quickly. In theory, my idea was good and the market was there to be exploited, but I made mistakes in taking on too many people and too much debt. I made basic business errors and ended up in a massive hole. Invoicing was a major problem and I panicked when I tried to recall whether or not I had invoiced customers. Paying wages was becoming more and more difficult and I came under massive pressure in early 1998. The business folded after two years. I had a personal guarantee to the bank to the tune of £50,000, a substantial sum of money for me at the time. After taking that kind of hit, many people would consider bailing out completely but I was lucky.

A few months before the cleaning business wound up, I took over the lease of a pub in Ennis along with my former Clare team-mate, Ger 'Sparrow' O'Loughlin. The Usual Place was my first venture into the pub business and we got in there at the perfect time. Winning the All-Ireland in 1997 was my saving grace as the cleaning business folded. We had a fantastic end to the year with Clare's success and, in tandem, the pub's takings rocketed.

After the final against Tipperary, the place was thronged. I estimated at the time that three times the amount of people inside in the pub had congregated on the street outside. It was sheer bedlam. That was a lucky break for me, the first of many, and a nice pick-me-up as the pressure of the cleaning business began to take its toll.

When we arrived home from Dublin on the Monday after winning the All-Ireland final, I went straight to work in The Usual Place. I did the same again the night after. I should have been out enjoying myself but I had to work. It was hectic stuff, but enjoyable.

In the pub business, I have been surrounded by drink but thankfully, I don't have a problem with alcohol. I can take it or leave it and I very rarely take it. I am just not a drinker and never have been, which is just as well in this business.

Less than a year after taking the lease on The Usual Place, Sparrow and I had the chance to buy a famous pub in Liscannor – Joseph McHugh's. Many of the locals were unhappy when we got our hands on that pub and we were lucky to make the purchase after sticky negotiations. It is a popular haunt and there was plenty of interest in it when Susan McHugh, Joe's sister, intimated that she might be interested in selling. Sparrow got the early tip-off and immediately, we went to meet Susan. After plenty of haggling, we eventually brokered a deal and toasted our good luck. We shelled out a pretty penny for the pub but it was the first one we owned ourselves and I was anxious to make a real go of it.

Towards the end of 1998, I was itching again. I was looking at the Bellsfort Inn, a pub situated on the back road between Newmarket and Shannon, just five minutes from the airport. I mentioned it to Sparrow but he was happy with his lot and I decided to go it alone. It was a huge purchase and cost a lot more than Joseph McHugh's. But the Bellsfort was a much bigger premises and it just felt right to me. I approached the owner, Tom White, and we discussed a possible fee. We eventually came to an amicable agreement and I wrote Tom a cheque as a deposit. Tom had a change of heart soon after but, when it came to the crunch, he decided to go with the original deal. Finally, I had my hands on my very own pub. I thought to myself, 'Fitzy, where are you going to find the money for this?' Still naïve, I didn't realise that I needed a ten per cent down payment for the premises. I have never had as much trouble trying to come up with money and the deal would not have gone through without the help of one special man, Fr Harry Bohan, who was unbelievable. I was sure 'friends' of mine would have helped me out but they chose not to. They were unconvinced that I would be a success. Another good friend of mine, Syl Adley from Killaloe, decided he would take a chance on me. Syl was anxious to see me doing well and I owe him so much for his help and support. A huge Clare supporter, Syl is one of the main reasons why I am in business right now. He believed in me at a time when others didn't.

The Bellsfort deal was tied up at the end of November 1999, a year after I had first scratched the itch. I was sick at the time and I decided to let the pub run for a few months ahead of an official opening in February. I hired a band, *One September*, for opening night, which was a roaring success. One of the tills was so full of money at one point that I couldn't open it. It was absolute mayhem, up to 800 punters packed the place and it was a perfect start. I ran the Bellsfort for the first six months but once it was up on its feet, I decided that it was time to put somebody else in charge. My mother has been at the controls since and she is first class. Some great characters enjoy a pint in the Bellsfort and my mother enjoys the company and the craic during the day. I like the fact that she works because it gets her out of the house, which is lonely each day when it is vacant. I am always on the go, and Dad and Helen are at work in Shannon.

When I first arrived in Liscannor to take on the famous Joseph McHugh's, I made it my business to mix with the local people from the very start. More than anything, I wanted to be known as Davy Fitz the landlord, not Davy Fitz the hurler.

I am also involved in a venture in Portugal with three local Clare businessmen, Martin Hanbury and Dermot and John O'Sullivan. Investing abroad was something I always wanted to do and we took the plunge on a pub in Praia da Rocha, down in the marina. As four of us are involved, the risk is minimal and it is nice to have a free place to stay on trips to Portugal. The three lads are great to deal with and they have become good friends over time. I know Dermot since 1997, he gave me a Citroën Xsara for six months and we became very close friends. John is a fantastic lad to be involved with and Martin has always helped me out when required, most notably when I needed a hand starting up in Portugal. No matter what Dermot has achieved in business, the one thing that impresses me about him is that he has kept his head. He is forever giving out to me, but in a good way, telling me what I'm doing wrong and offering words of encouragement, for both business and sport. The three lads are well known from their work with O'Sullivan & Hanbury motors, and they are the kind of people I like to deal with.

In my pubs, I want people to be comfortable and I have enjoyed good support. I paint the Bellsfort every year and put in new carpets regularly. I am very particular about cleanliness. As well as dabbling with the pubs, I own various other properties at home and abroad. I recently completed my new house on the Castlecrine Road, beside my parents. One of my favourite places in the world is my apartment in Lahinch, overlooking the beach. I don't have a nine to five job, wheeling and dealing on the property market is my main occupation because I find it so difficult to sit down, relax and spend some time by myself; I like to keep the mind active. Luckily in recent years, I have become much better at taking some time out for myself. My health scares have put everything into perspective.

I decided to sell Joseph McHugh's last April because I just didn't have the time to devote to the pub business. I wasn't in McHugh's enough and I got a bit of hassle for that because when your name is associated with a licensed premises, you are expected to be there. People don't understand that I have other things to do and, after a few great years, I just felt the time was right to go. I will always have regrets about selling McHugh's because I loved the pub and I thought I would never sell it, but it was a business decision, not a sentimental one. If I had searched my heart, I would never have sold the place because I did not want to, but I made a business call and it was good one that turned a handsome profit.

The Bellsfort Inn is still up for sale – it failed to go at auction on the same day that I sold Joseph McHugh's. In hindsight, that might have been a good thing. The Bellsfort is situated on a valuable piece of property just minutes from Shannon, and property will start to develop on that road because development is at breaking point on the other side of Shannon. In time, the property may turn out to be very profitable. There is serious restaurant potential, which I thought about investing in myself and might do yet.

I have been hungry in business but I am hungry in all aspects of my life. I was struck by Roy Keane's World Cup mantra, 'Fail to Prepare, Prepare to Fail'. It struck a chord with me in so many ways.

Some people believe that I am fanatical in my match preparation, and they are right to a certain extent. A few weeks before the championship, I normally take time off to train at least twice a day. I started working with my own personal trainer, Darren Ward, a few years back and he has been brilliant for me. I work on a number of key areas with Darren to make me a more powerful proposition on the field of play and this new approach has paid dividends for me. I have often sparred with Darren and it is no holds barred stuff. He is a former boxing coach who worked with Chris Eubank, so he knows what he's doing in the ring.

Trixie was the man who taught me everything I knew since I was a teenager and his death left a gaping void that will never be filled. Trixie knew my game inside out and I trusted him. When he told me to work on something, I didn't query it, I just worked on it.

Within reason, I will do anything to get an edge. Back in 1990, when I was first breaking through onto the Clare team, my main rival for the goalkeeping position was Leo Doyle from Bodyke. Leo worked in Shannon and I knew the road he drove to work every morning. So, every day he passed by, I was there banging a sliotar against a wall on the side of the road. I got out of bed early and cycled down the road to do this but it was worth the effort.

On the pitch, shot-stopping is my forte but I have a very complete game and puckouts are a massive challenge for a goalkeeper. I feel that I can do anything with a puckout and will hit a fly on the wall from anywhere between 50 and 90 yards. If I can't do that, there's no point in my keeping goal for Clare. I have to hit my spot from that distance or pick out a player on the run. If I feel that I am weak on a certain part of my game, I won't rest until I have it rectified. For goalkeeping alone, I practice ten different drills dealing with all aspects of my game: how I'm covering my angles, the movement of my feet, my timing, sharpness and touch. On championship day, my touch has to be spot on. One mistake and I am history. Anthony Daly and Cyril Lyons gave me the licence to do my own individual work in training and that makes sense. Team training is good but it does not benefit me because I need to prepare for what I will face on match day and I need to ensure that the work I am doing will stand to me. I work on my speed and my handling, the stuff Trixie used to help me with. The pressure playing in goal is massive because if I fuck up, it's one of the first things in a journalist's match report the following day. Observers take the saves and the difficult balls a goalkeeper deals with very much for granted, and the goalie doesn't get the credit he often deserves. A shot that bounces two yards in front of my stick before I kill the sliotar might look like a routine save, but believe me, that is the one that can bobble over the line. That's the one that makes me look like an ass and wish the ground would open up and swallow me whole. That's Michael Duignan's shot in the 1995 All-Ireland final. Now you understand …

Goalkeepers are undervalued because if a team has a bad one, that team is going nowhere. Between the sticks is the one position on a team that a manager cannot afford to take chances with under any circumstances. A wing-back hits ten balls, his direct opponent hits the same amount but the wing-back might get away with it because of the five massive clearances he has completed. If a goalkeeper makes four great saves but lets one trickle through his legs, there is no chance of forgiveness.

I spend ten days on mental preparation for a big championship game if time allows. I will take time out during the day and picture every possible situation that could occur during the match. I might be driving along a road and suddenly I see Henry Shefflin striking a shot, standing over a 21-yard free or hitting me with a shoulder. I picture myself diving to my right, diving to my left, lining up alongside two of my defenders to face a penalty with a sliotar approaching me at speeds of up to 100 miles per hour. If I have gone over those situations in my head, they won't bother me on the big day when faced with them for real. That is why I will put myself under so much pressure during those ten days. The physical training takes a back seat in the days leading up to a match, I prefer to prepare in my head. I convince myself that nothing will faze me and that is the reason I am so built up.

My family don't talk to me for three days before a game. They realise it is a futile exercise because I am away in my own world. They grant me solitude in the family home on the day before a game when I find it hard to sit down. I do try, pulling the same three videos from the cabinet beneath the television. They are films that make me feel good, make me smile and the adrenaline starts to flow. They're not videos of hurling matches or anything to do with the game but a sporting theme runs through each one. *Hoosiers*, also known as *Best Shot*, stars Gene Hackman as a washed-up coach who takes over the 'Hickory Huskers', an American high school basketball team from Indiana. Hackman is Norman Dale, who takes over a hopeless team because it is the only one that will have him after his dodgy past. In true Hollywood style, they go all the way to the top and to me; the story mirrors that of the Clare hurling team, real rags to riches stuff. Hackman is Loughnane, we are the Hickory Huskers. They came from nothing, so did we. I pick out *Chariots of Fire*, one of the most famous films of all time and *The Cutting Edge* starring Moira Kelly, who I used to think was a bit of all right! Kelly and DB Sweeney play a former hockey player and a skater who compete together in figure skating at the Winter Olympics. Before I settle down to watch those three videos, I close the curtains and make myself comfortable on the couch. They all make me feel good but I leave *Best Shot* until last. It has a certain resonance to it.

After the championship game against Waterford in 2004, I developed a habit of going down to the beach in Lahinch shortly after midnight, togging out and running up and down. I love the sea and it is an exhilarating experience in the dead of night. I feel refreshed afterwards, the head totally clear, the way it should be. Other little things can help too. We had our own team song last year, which was written by Kieran McDermott. Each member of the panel had his own CD.

On the morning of any match I feel perfect because I am ready, I have left absolutely nothing to chance. Some players hide away and try not to think about the game and then when it comes, it hits them straight between the eyes – bang! And they crumple like a deck of cards. They suffer with nerves just as I do, but when I hit that field, I am perfect. Instead of hiding from my environment, the cauldrons of Semple Stadium, Páirc Uí Chaoimh or Croke Park, I will absorb everything. I will run out of that tunnel and hit that crossbar a flake of my hurl. It is my way of letting off steam but often, it can take up to five minutes to recover from my feverish dash from the dressing room to the goalmouth. I am usually wrecked but, after getting my second wind, I am ready for action.

When Clare are involved in the championship, I might only go out socially once or twice in six months. The GAA is for young, single men these days, men with time on their hands. The game is professional now in all but name, with management teams adopting a scientific approach to preparation. Some players visit Michael O'Doherty, who runs a successful business in Ennis, the Plexus Bio-Energy Clinic. Michael attempts to re-balance the energy within the body and I find that his treatment works well to relax the mind and get focused.

Nutritionists outline diets and players are told to consume only specific foods and drinks. I find it hard to stick to diets and I reckon I will be forming my own little fellowship quite soon, Junkaholics Anonymous. I eat too much junk food but I have admitted my problem, which is half the battle. I picture myself standing up at my imaginary JA meetings and addressing the floor. 'My name's David, and I am a junkaholic.' It is a humbling experience, I can tell you. I just never seem to find time to sit down and eat a healthy, nutritious meal. Far too often, I pick up food on the run but I do scale back before big matches and I try to drink plenty of water and consume lots of fruit. Johnny Glynn tests the body mass index of the Clare players and analyses the levels of fat in their bodies but I managed to avoid all of these tests. He went to put the clampers on me during the year but I told him to get lost! I don't know how he took it but Dalo was laughing. Before every championship game, I take a cold shower before running out on the pitch. I complete my warm-up and then take the cold shower, just minutes before hitting the tunnel. I did this in 2002 but I stopped for a couple of years before taking it up again this year. It makes me feel fresh and good just before I hit the field. Ice baths are good too after training or matches but I avoid them. I prefer a cold shower when I get home. Sleep is another vital aspect of preparation but, when I am under pressure mentally, I find it very difficult to come by.

Modern hurling is a fulltime occupation because the game is practically professional now. Frank Lohan travels from Cork to training and Ollie Baker used to make the trip from Ballinasloe in Galway. I am fortunate because I am not tied down to a nine to five job, five days a week, and what is even better is the fact that I am based locally. Frank and Ollie lost five hours out of a typical day purely through travel. Repeat the roundtrip four nights a week and twenty hours are gone, on travel alone! People in top jobs work 40-hour weeks and get well paid for it, but we don't earn a single penny.

Hurling and gaelic football are great games, but soccer and rugby are much more attractive financially for the average young player who will turn to them if there is a chance to make some money. In my opinion, it is only a matter of time before the GAA turns semi-professional, and it has to happen if the GAA wants to survive. We have the best field games in the world but they should be marketed much better and with more vigour outside our own country. Who would have thought that we would get to the stage where watching Australian rules football is considered an attractive proposition for the armchair sporting enthusiast in Ireland?

When I was Clare's U-21 hurling manger, I was entitled to travelling expenses but, hand on heart, I never claimed them. That's why the penny pinchers in the GAA really make me sick. The penny pinchers exist in every county and they take the piss, claiming much more than they are entitled to. Then you have the 'know it alls' looking in from the outside, discussing the massive amounts of money we make from the game. My family has never made a red cent from the GAA, but I don't want to sound like a martyr because monetary reward or compensation for perceived loss of earnings doesn't interest me. I get pleasure from hurling and I cannot put a price on that. Some cynics will invariably point out that I am doing quite well for myself in business, but that was not always the case and yet I still never claimed from the GAA.

Incidentally, I am not a member of the Gaelic Players Association. I joined at the beginning but I didn't receive much correspondence and the appeal quickly wore off. I felt that I was not fully informed of the workings of the GPA and, although it may be a better-run organisation now, I have lost all interest. Where is the GPA when players get hit with harsh suspensions during the championship? I will admit that the GPA has accomplished some good things but I am my own person and if something needs taking care of, I will take care of it myself. It seems to me that the GPA only looks after an elite group of players and I see few benefits to the average inter-county player. The big names seem to be creaming it all from the top. In September 2004, I announced a two-year sponsorship deal with Umbro, which I secured without any help from the GPA. And, for at least another season, I will wear and promote the entire range of Umbro playing gear. How's that for product placement?

11 YOU GOTTA
HAVE FAITH

The grand essentials of happiness are: something to do, something to love and something to hope for.

Allan K Chalmers

Let's stick together. That is my message to Anthony Daly and the Clare hurlers as we look ahead to 2006. The obituaries have been written before every season for as long as I can remember, so let's delay them by one more year.

I can promise you that I will be around for at least one more season. When I feel that I can no longer do the business for Clare, then I will walk way. But in 2005, I believe that I played as well as ever.

At 34 years of age, I feel proud that I can still mix it with the best on the hurling fields of Ireland. Since 1990, a host of top goalkeepers have competed with me for a Clare jersey but I managed to hold them all off. Leo Doyle, Noel Considine, Eoin McMahon, John O'Brien, Stephen O'Hara, Damien Garrahy, Brendan McNamara, Christy O'Connor, Ger O'Connell and Philip Brennan have all tried and failed to take my precious jersey down through the years.

There is no reason why goalkeepers cannot play until they are 35 or 36 years of age and I believe that I have been playing well enough over the last couple of years to hold on to my position. But there is no point in just holding on, I want to do the job and I want to be the best that I can be. I had a special relationship with Ger O'Connell when he was sub goalie with Clare. I coached him at U-14, U-16, minor and U-21 levels and, of all the other goalkeepers that have been on Clare panels, he is the one I could relate to best.

At the same time, I had no intention of stepping aside for Ger and letting him take over my position. He got a good run of games in the 2004 league but when my suspension was up, I was straight back in. Ger couldn't see himself breaking through for a few years so he decided to leave Clare and chance his arm with Limerick in 2005. I was sorry to see him go but I didn't go chasing him either. In hurling, there is no room for sentiment.

Before every season, I ask myself one question. Do I still have the drive and ability to play in goal for Clare? The answer is always 'yes' and I know that I still have plenty to contribute. Top goalkeepers in the Premiership can play until they are 40 and that is a professional code, seven days a week. I take care of myself and, as long as my reflexes are good, which they seem to be at the moment, I will play on. I have shown over the last few seasons that I am still on top of my game, I won an Allstar award in 2002, and I am still capable of keeping out the game's top forwards. Every goalkeeper will make mistakes but I am not letting in shots from 20 or 25 yards out. I will do the right thing for myself, my team and my county; and I will never let my heart rule my head.

I am never happy with what I have achieved in the game. There are players out there with no medals who might think I am happy with my haul but I have yet to meet a successful player who is happy to rest on his laurels. Two All-Ireland senior hurling medals, three Munster titles, one All-Ireland club championship, two Munster club medals, six county titles, two Allstars and four Railway Cups is a decent return but I want as much as I can get my hands on for as long as I can. When it is all over, it will be nice to sit back and reflect but I still maintain that hunger for glory.

This is a new Clare team, it is great to be a part of it and we are very close to getting it right. Winning another All Ireland would be massive and it is driving me on because I firmly believe that we can do it. We were so close in 2005 but, to take it to the next level, we must make some serious sacrifices and stick together. A final message to the hurlers of Clare: give up the social life and get the best out of yourselves mentally and physically. We can come even closer together as a unit. We can win that All-Ireland title.

The vast majority of our players are in their mid-twenties so the future is bright. We are not that far off the pace and this is without question, the most dedicated bunch of Clare hurlers that I have ever seen. All you have to do is look at their bodies; they are in superb physical condition.

In 15 years of senior hurling, I have played 54 championship games for the county. There have been the severe lows, Tipperary in the 1993 Munster final, Limerick in 1994 and Waterford in 2004, but for me, the worst of all was losing to Cork this year. Of course, we have enjoyed incredible highs too. Munster and All-Ireland champions in 1995 and 1997, Munster champions again in 1998. We were awesome against Tipperary in the 1997 Munster final, and we annihilated Cork in 1998. We beat Waterford that same year in the Munster final replay with our most powerful display ever; we blew them away with brute force and skill.

It is lovely to be able to sit back and reflect on those great days and we should never, ever forget where we came from before the big breakthrough. When Clare were down, we were looked upon as nothing. That will never happen again. We are staying up there and we have managed to survive better than most. I find it incredible how opinion can change in this game. When we were successful, the big counties hated us. But now, a lot of people want to see us victorious again and we won back the hearts of the neutrals with that performance against Cork.

I would love to have a go at the Clare team, and sooner rather than later. I have been managing teams since I was 18 and in the last couple of years, I have started to achieve a lot. I don't think I would ever be able to manage another county against Clare. If I were to take charge of another county, one of the conditions would have to be that if I came across Clare, I would step aside for the match. I would like to try to bring Antrim on a bit, there is a lot more in them. They are passionate hurling people in the Glens but they are somewhat detached from the rest of Ireland's hurling fraternity.

I am lucky to be a Clare man and I am lucky to have come across some of the greatest figures ever to have played this great game. Kilkenny's Christy Heffernan, Tipperary pair Pat Fox and Nicky English, and Cork's Ger Manley were super forwards. In Kilkenny, DJ Carey has taken a lot of stick over his personal life and I can relate to him on that level. DJ will be fine because he has a good head on his shoulders. What bothers me is that people judge DJ even though they don't know him and I often hear lads telling me stories they have heard about him, false stories. I think DJ is a class act, one of the best players the game has ever seen, and people need to get off his back. Carey's Young Irelands club-mate Charlie Carter was another fantastic Kilkenny forward. Towards the end of his playing days with the county, I felt that he was hard done by as he was ignored by manager Brian Cody. Charlie is one of the best forwards that I ever played against and I believe that his inter-county career ended long before it should have.

Cork forward Joe Deane is another great lad, an absolute gentleman and the same goes for Brian Corcoran and the Ó hAilpín brothers, Seán Óg and Setanta. Seán Óg oozes talent while Setanta has been a massive loss to the GAA since he decided to pursue a professional career in Australia. Setanta was a huge player for Cork in 2003, a driven man who played with a real determination. When we played Cork in the Munster championship we gave each other plenty of stick but when the game was over, it was an honour to shake his hand.

People look at Waterford's John Mullane and they say that he is arrogant but I admire his passion and heart. I have also been on tour with John and he is not the bad boy that people make out. In fact, he was one of the most popular figures in Phoenix and Las Vegas in January 2004.

I work with Tipperary forward Eoin Kelly in Limerick Institute of Technology and he is a lad I have great time for. Eoin was one of the real cornerstones of our Fitzgibbon Cup win in 2005. He is already renowned as a class forward but he is not the finished article yet. He is on his way to being a great player but there is a lot more in him. It is up to Eoin himself to decide how much he wants to achieve in this game and how he wants to be remembered. He could go down in the history books as one of the best of all time, but only time will tell with Eoin because he can be a bit lazy sometimes. If he continues at his current steady rate, he will be remembered as a good forward but he has the potential to be one of the best that ever lived. That is how highly I rate the lad and that is how much potential I see in him. Eoin is as cute as a fox too and nobody will buy or sell him. Eoin, my advice is this: work as hard as you can on your game, and ignore the lads who want to put their arm around you and lead you down the wrong paths.

From Galway, you couldn't meet nicer fellas than Kevin Broderick and Ollie Canning, two relaxed chaps who I have also toured with. Down goalkeeper Graham Clarke is a fantastic player and I have a special relationship with the Dunloy club in Antrim. I first got to know the Dunloy players after Sixmilebridge beat them in the 1996 All-Ireland club final and when our club went up there for a weekend, we were treated like royalty. The Dunloy people are unbelievable hurling people, they know the game inside out but they also know how to enjoy themselves.

Our club travelled up in November 1998, it was a special weekend. We played Dunloy in a challenge and I have never seen as many sick bodies in my life on a Sunday afternoon! We had had a great time the previous night and when I asked one lad what time the bar closed at, he replied, 'Some time in December!'

The O'Kanes, the Elliotts and the Richmonds are great people to socialise with. Seamus Elliott used to manage Dunloy's senior team and he remains a tower of strength for both club and county. Seamus is now Antrim's hurling development officer and one of the men responsible for Dunloy's great youth policy, which has paid dividends for over a decade. He is becoming increasingly alarmed by the state of the game in Antrim and I like to help out by travelling up to coach young kids. I love it up there, the people are first class and they treat me with respect.

The state of hurling in Antrim is not bad but the county badly needs a big championship victory. It is difficult to keep the game alive but they keep plugging away. Seamus McMullan, 'Mushy', is my best friend in Antrim and he got married earlier this year. His brother Frankie passed away tragically in April 2004 and he was a smashing lad and a fine hurler too. Frankie was a quiet man and he preferred to let his hurling do the talking.

He was one of seven brothers who have worn the Dunloy jersey in both hurling and football and the McMullan family have been great to me. Mushy always phones me before a big Clare game to wish me luck and he will never let me forget the day he stuck a penalty past me in a league match. He still takes great pleasure in recreating the moment, mimicking my head turning to one side when the ball crashed into the net. It always brings a smile to my face. In 1998, Seamus and I won the Comórtas Beirte, the pairs contest at the annual Poc Fada competition in the Cooley Mountains in County Louth. Seamus will always be a good friend of mine.

***

The norm in other books is for a player to pick out the best 15 players that he has ever seen but that would be too difficult for me because who would I leave out? Instead, I have decided to give a brief run-down on some of the greatest Clare hurlers that I have soldiered with over the last 15 years.

Michael O'Halloran – A club-mate of mine in Sixmilebridge. Growing up he wouldn't have been the greatest hurler in the world and for a long time, I didn't even think he was related to one! He never made any of our underage teams, even up to minor level, but as he grew older, I could see how determined he was to make it. He was a dogged player as a senior, tight and hard and a player I really admired. He was one of those guys who made up for his lack of natural ability with a willingness to work his socks off. You wouldn't get an inch off

Michael during a match because he used to stick to an opponent's shirt. He would attack the ball brilliantly and when he was beside the two Lohans, he was at home; the three of them were like a family in that great full-back line. Michael might not have stood out in our team but he was very effective and you would do well to score off him.

Brian Lohan – A tough man who is tough on himself. A lot of people find it hard to figure him out. There are times when people find it hard to talk to him but I would still regard Brian as a really good friend. Sometimes I ring Brian for a chat and I find it hard to get words out of him and then there are other days when he would chat away for ages. He has Clare running through his veins and Brian is unquestionably one of the best full-backs ever to grace the game of hurling. When Brian decides to go forward and play the game, there is no better full-back in the country. He has done it consistently and I don't see too many full backs playing at the top level for over a decade. We had one run-in a few years back when we played Waterford in a challenge game in Newport. A ball dropped in the goalmouth, we got our wires crossed and the full-forward knocked it into the net. Brian lambasted me but I hit back, roaring, 'Brian, I've covered your ass so many times, don't be giving out to me because that was your ball.' In the dressing room we apologised to each other and we never looked back after that. I find it great that he feels comfortable enough to allow the ball to drift back to me when he could take it on himself. It shows great faith in me and, for a goalkeeper, it is a great boost of confidence. Brian bounced back well this year after his run-in with Tipperary's Michael Webster in the Munster semi-final but Brian always has that stuff in him. In my opinion, Brian Lohan is fit enough to go again for another year but it is up to the man himself if he wants it and if he is prepared to put the same work in again. He is under no obligation to keep hurling for Clare; he has already done so much and given so much to the county. If he wants to retire today, I can't say a word to him because he is a legend in my eyes.

Frank Lohan – Much different to his brother. Frank wouldn't be as dour as Brian and would talk to anybody. Brian might not like me saying this but he is not as naturally talented as Frank, who can turn his hand to anything. Brian is driven but Frank has talent coming out his ears, he could play any sport. Not once have I seen Frank getting carried away by success and in all the years he has been a member of the Clare senior hurling panel, he hasn't changed one bit. He drives up and down from Cork for training and when he was in Edenderry in Offaly, he did the same thing. He loves the game, he will have his few pints and loves the craic, but he is a straight, down to earth guy. He still has so much to offer the Clare senior hurling team.

Liam Doyle – I reckon Liam was the best stickman on our successful teams but he never got much praise or stood out like myself, Brian Lohan or Anthony Daly did. He had skill to burn but he could mix it too. I got on well with Liam.

Seán McMahon – When he was young Seán was told he would never make it, that he had no legs. But Seán had the talent, desire and temperament to make it. Seánie can hurl and he has won matches for us with vital contributions both from play and from placed balls. The one that stands out of course is the 1995 Munster semi-final against Cork when he won the crucial line ball which led to our winning goal, despite playing with a broken collarbone. I know that my own clubman Seán Stack was an excellent centre-back but Seánie Mac has everything. He can rally the lads around him and you can always have a good heart to heart with Seánie.

Anthony Daly – I have said plenty about Dalo and I am sure that he has come across as a great leader. I would like to let him know that I plan to stick around with Clare for at least one more season and he knows that I will always give everything for Clare. I fully believe that Dalo is the man to bring us forward and who knows, maybe there is another All-Ireland title in us.

Ollie Baker – I wasn't close to Ollie for the first number of years on the panel and I honestly didn't think that he had much skill. But Ollie worked terribly hard on his game and his hurling began to improve as a result. We would not have won matches but for Ollie Baker, he threw himself around, hit fellas and delivered good ball. He was more of an asset to Clare hurling than I realised at the time. A big, dour man but he is a lad I have great time for. His heart and soul are in Clare hurling and even though he was written off, he worked harder than anybody to get back playing. He was not happy when he was substituted against Waterford in 2004 but he is a team man, and in the dressing room and the dugout, he was full of encouragement. In 2002 he issued many of our half-time teamtalks and he was a superb motivator.

Colin Lynch – Colin is one of my best friends. Honest, hard-working and a real family man who adores Edel and their son Barry. Colin would not let me down if I ever needed him and it is great to have people like that to rely on. He has listened to all the rubbish that was said about him down through the years and many people don't realise that Colin had it tough growing up. He used to bag coal and deliver it to make a few bob before coming to training in the evening. We have had our battles down through the years and if Colin has something to say, he will say it. He is a great Clare man, a great hurler and one of the greatest midfielders of the last 10-15 years. He possesses an incredible engine, he can score, he can pass, he can do it all.

Fergal Hegarty – He was a good hurler and Loughnane rated him highly. He played a lot of good games for us, didn't get much credit but always used his head. He was in and out of the team but in the 1995 Munster final, he threw over a few great scores. Not a guy I was very close to, he had his own crew but I would respect that. I always salute him and most important of all, he did the business for Clare.

Conor Clancy – He was invaluable to Clare. I always knew I could hit a puckout to Clancy and he would win it. We didn't realise until he was gone just how big a loss he was. The amount of possession he laid off was phenomenal and he was one of the best target men I have ever hit the ball to, he could catch anything. I went to school with him, we often had run-ins at club level but I respect him as a hurler.

Fergie Tuohy – Scored four excellent points in the 1995 All-Ireland final win over Offaly. We used to slag the life out of each other. A more confident guy you would never meet, he had confidence in abundance and he delivered on the big days. Before we played

Offaly he was giving out to me about puckouts. 'Just give me the ball, I'll do the business.' 'Go away; you'll do nothing with it!' He ended up playing a blinder and he gave me an awful time over it! He is always good for a dig and he was the life and soul of the Clare team, constantly having the craic with Loughnane or Mike Mac. He was a great man to have around and I do miss him since he retired.

PJ O'Connell – He possessed great speed and he was good at the basics of hurling: pulling, blocking and hassling. We have missed the likes of himself and Conor Clancy, real workers. A very effective player, 'Fingers' was a good target man and I knew that if I landed a puckout in his general direction, the ball would not come back too easily.

Jamesie O'Connor – Jamesie has unbelievable skill. I was with him in Flannan's and we got on well, we always ended up rooming together on holidays, playing golf or having the craic. He is a genuine guy and I like him a lot. He was as good a forward as I have ever seen. He had the skill, he was able to get stuck in and he had great vision. He scored a great point in the 1997 All-Ireland final to win the game. He took a bit of unwarranted criticism in his later years but he went out in style with the equaliser against Kilkenny in 2004 and a couple of classy points in the replay.

Ger O'Loughlin – Myself and 'Sparrow' were very close and the first time we met was during the 1989 county final between Sixmilebridge and Clarecastle. He had come through an operation on his knee and when he received a clatter during the game, he thought it was me. He told me that he would break my neck and drive me into the back of the net, but we got on ok after that! He was an exceptional forward with a great brain, one of Clare's greatest ever attackers. He wasn't the fastest but he was always in the right place and he poached some great scores. We went into business together and he was a straight guy. He liked to do things his way but I couldn't say a bad word about him.

Cyril Lyons – Great skill and a great fella to have around the team. A genuine lad and anybody could talk to him. It was great to see him getting his All-Ireland medal in 1995.

Jim McInerney – 'The Bulldog' had so much power. During a training session before the 1995 Munster final, he got a ball five yards out and stuck it into my puss, knocking me to the ground. That was Jim, no half measures. Another man I was delighted to see getting his hands on a Celtic cross.

Eamonn Taaffe – Came on, scored the goal in the 1995 All-Ireland final and was taken off again. Some contribution! He had serious skill and although he wasn't the quickest, he made up for that with the other parts of his game.

Niall Gilligan – I trained Gilly as an underage player and, although he never made it on to many teams, I recognised serious potential. In 1998 he had a good year but the two of us ended up bickering at the Allstars. I felt he had much more in him and we exchanged serious words, it was harsh stuff. The only reason I was telling it straight was because I wanted Gilly to make it. Sure enough, he picked up an Allstar in 1999. Gilly's mother died when he was young, she grew up near my father in Truagh and I regard Dad as a close link between myself and Gilly. I think he has time for me but he thinks I am very hard on him. He had a tough time as a youngster, renowned as a messer who could be easily led. Gilly likes a good time and likes the attention but I want him to be the best he can be.

Brian Quinn – A straight guy who loves Clare hurling. One of the brainiest players I have ever seen on a pitch. He might not be the quickest but he can read the game so well. He has been exceptional at corner back for Clare, his heart and soul is in it and he is a great trainer. He is a quiet guy but when he has something to say, you listen. I get on well with his brother Andrew too, I have coached him since he was a young player and he possesses great skill. I hope he fulfils his potential but it is up to Andy himself. If he puts his mind to it, he can be massive.

Daithi O'Connell – Hard to keep him under control at times because he has a tendency to fly off the handle but, if he settles down, he can make the grade. A lovely young fella, there isn't a bad bone in his body, and Daithi's brother Brian is one of the best young hurlers I have ever seen in Clare. Brian will be a mainstay on the Clare senior team for many years to come and I like the two O'Connells who are very good to train.

John and Christy Chaplin – the most dedicated brothers I have ever seen playing the game. Great clubmen and great with the county, they both won two All Ireland medals and three Munster championships.

David Forde – Supersub in 1997 and one of the main reasons we won the All-Ireland. I do not think he realises his own potential and ability and if he ever does, he will be some player because he is still young. Always good for a goal, there is more to come from David.

Barry Murphy – The most easygoing guy you could meet, he cracks me up. He gives out to me about being lazy but he is the laziest of the lot. A super hurler when he puts his mind to it. That is what kills me about him, sometimes he wants to do it, sometimes he doesn't. Barry has great talent and I hope he fulfils his potential because he deserves to.

John Reddan – John has been very unlucky, he has come on a few times and done well but he never got the breaks. In 2002 he felt he was always going to be taken off because Cyril Lyons wanted to bring on Ollie Baker in every game, which was unfair on John. John is still good enough to make it, he gets on well with everybody and he works like a dog at training. His future is in his own hands.

Alan Markham – An exceptional talent. One of the most skilful players on the team, left and right. It is hard to get to know him because he is a quiet chap unless you are really friendly with him. A tremendous talent and he will be a big player for us in years to come.

Tony Griffin – Tony would train night and day. A great lad to talk to and he is a good friend. If Tony could help you out or do you a favour, he would and he has bags of potential as a hurler. He went to Canada to pursue his studies last year and we missed him when he was away. His hurling suffered too with the lack of matches and quality training. But with his never-say-die attitude, big things lie ahead for Tony.

In recent years, a host of top players have broken through. David Hoey has been around for a while. He is a solid wing back and has bounced back well from a broken leg. Then there is Gerry O'Grady, a tough corner back who looks like being a mainstay on the Clare team for years to come. Diarmuid McMahon is a forceful, direct young player who can play at midfield or in the half forward line. And, in my opinion, Tony Carmody will only get better. He discovered some top form in 2005 and took four points off Cork's Ronan Curran in the All-Ireland semi-final. Tony put in a serious effort before the championship and it paid off. Like so many talented young hurlers, it is up to Tony to see how good he wants to be. Barry Nugent, one of my LIT men, will only improve after his debut season at senior level for Clare. If he had scored a couple of goals with the chances he had in the Munster semi-final against Tipperary, he would have been man of the match. But he was taken off injured in the second half – that's how cruel hurling can be sometimes.

***

Some players are admired for their skill but the player I look to is the one that never gives in. He might not have been blessed with natural ability but he will battle and fight until the final whistle. PJ O'Connell, Conor Clancy and Ollie Baker are players of that ilk and they were invaluable to Clare when we were successful. The perfect example in modern day hurling is Cork's centre forward, Niall McCarthy. He might not score enough at times but Niall would go through a brick wall for you and he would be first choice on any of my teams. Kilkenny's Henry Shefflin is the complete player, blessed with serious talent but when the going gets tough, he wants to be involved. His team-mates Peter Barry and JJ Delaney are men of steel, those lads would fight on their backs for you. Wexford's Rory McCarthy is another with that special never say die attitude. That's what I like about hurling because it's not all about skill. We all admire the forward who dummies a defender and arcs over a beautiful score, but what about the lad in the half-back line who hooked or blocked seconds earlier to win back possession? What about the quick puckout that is an ever-increasing part of the modern game? On the hurling field, every man has a part to play.

I am not afraid to stand up for myself. People might not like my attitude but I play as I feel. One of the best compliments I ever received was from John O'Mahony, the former Galway football manager. At the 2002 Allstars ceremony he came up to me and said, 'Davy, never change the way you play, never change.' I was taken aback; it was a nice compliment to receive from a man of John's stature who has achieved great things in football.

When I finally hang up that hurl, I will give the golf a good lash and see where it takes me. I have been playing the game since I was 16 and, although I didn't take it too seriously at first, in recent years I decided to get my handicap down. When I started to work on my game I was playing off 13 and I have come down steadily from that mark. In recent times I have been hovering around the three, two and one area and this is my first year playing off one. I am almost a scratch golfer now and, when I am playing regularly, I have no problem with my handicap.

When I started playing the game, I was right hand over left but I changed it to left over right, the right way. The main reason I took up golf was because of Trixie. We loved going out having the craic and playing with Trixie was brilliant. He was handy enough himself and known as a bandit on the golf course. He played off 18 and he was comfortable with that. When the pressure came on, Trixie could really perform. All he wanted was a bit of fun and when he died, I lost a lot of enthusiasm that I had for the game. He always took me for a round the day after a big championship match. I might have been feeling terrible but, after 18 holes with Trixie, I always felt good again.

If you are serious about golf, you need to play and practice the game an awful lot. At certain times during the year, I might get three weeks to play non-stop. For the first two weeks, my timing is completely off but by the third week I am playing really well. Golf is the type of game that you can't expect to leave for a spell and hope to pick up again immediately.

Could I have been a professional? I don't know, but my handicap is down to one and I have never taken a golf lesson. I do sometimes wonder how good I could have been at the game if I had applied myself, but I have no regrets and when I am finished hurling I can devote much more time to the game. I play in Dromoland and Lahinch and both golf clubs treat me very well. My good friend John O'Halloran is just brilliant in Dromoland. He is a fanatical Clare supporter and before some of our games, he is even more nervous than I am. Dromoland's Managing Director, Mark Nolan, has been very supportive of the Clare team and very good to me too. Dromoland is my home club, the surroundings are beautiful and it is a great place to unwind. I go out on that golf course, hit the ball and my problems seem to drift away. Golf is a great release for me from hurling because out on the course, I am the same as any other Joe Soap.

Lahinch is a beautiful links course, which has been the home of the South of Ireland amateur championship since 1895. I will spend a lot of time in Lahinch when I retire from hurling but I will still try to fulfil a couple of remaining goals. With the golf, I had hoped to get my handicap down to single figures, to play in the South of Ireland championship, to go around a course level par, to shoot under par, to shoot a hole-in-one. I got that hole-in-one at Dromoland and I shot a three under par round there too. I went around the Woodstock course in Ennis one under par, and I have been level par in Shannon.

During the summer months, with the perfect golfing weather, I would like to be out on the course a lot more. I just have this thing in my head, that I won't play golf for two weeks before a big hurling match. Concentrate on one game, that's the way it should be.

I have to focus on one sport and nothing can be left to chance. Timing, catching, striking, reactions, footwork, puckouts, that's the hurling goalkeeper's lot.

***

The annual Poc Fada in the Cooley Mountains in Co Louth is a competition close to my heart and I am no stranger to the event, having competed for the last 14 years. I won the title in 1999, becoming the first ever Clare hurler to do so, and I won it again in 2002. The five kilometre course on Annaverna Mountain is a demanding one, a real test of skill, strength and stamina. The competition itself began back in 1961 when the late Fr Paul Johnston was the driving force. The Poc Fada wasn't contested between 1970 and 1980 but, since it was revived in 1981, it continues to go from strength to strength. I first competed in the competition back in 1992 and I can recall travelling up from Clare with Christy Ryan, a good friend of mine. Coming into Dundalk, Christy pointed up at the Cooley Mountains and smiled, 'That's where you'll be pucking a ball Davy.'

The late, great Tommy Quaid from Limerick won the competition in 1991 before Cork's Ger Cunningham captured the title for the next seven years on the trot. It was great just to puck a ball alongside men of that calibre who were as competitive on the mountain as they were at Semple Stadium, Páirc Uí Chaoimh or the Gaelic Grounds.

There are four stages to the Poc Fada. First, it's uphill to the top in rough terrain. Then we head across the top with a breathtaking view on each side, Carlingford Lough to the left and Dundalk to the right. The third stage takes competitors across a ravine, and in the final stage, we enter another ravine, 40 feet below sea level. It is an extraordinary test and it can take up to three and a half hours to complete the course.

When I first won the competition in 1999, I won on a shortened course because the weather conditions were so bad and I managed to cope best with the elements. In 2002, I won comfortably with 51 pocs, a record.

I am very loyal to the Poc Fada and there are some great characters involved. It's nice to meet up with old friends like Pat Hartnett from Limerick who is a great supporter of the competition, and Pat McGinn does a great job in organising the event. Martin Donnelly pumps in money for sponsorship and gear and it is a shame that the Poc Fada doesn't receive more recognition from the media because it is a serious competition.

I finished third in 2004 but I damaged ankle ligaments the night before as I trained for the event. I wouldn't have beaten Tipperary's

Brendan Cummins anyway because he was hitting the ball an absolute mile. Brendan is similar to me, he likes to prepare well, and because he had never won the competition before, I knew that he would be ultra competitive. I suspect that he worked on his upper body and practiced hard for the event because nobody could touch him. He set a new record of 48 pocs for the course, smashing my previous record by three pocs.

I would be delighted to win another Poc Fada because it is a prestigious tournament. The trophy and the All-Ireland medal do not matter to me on the Cooley Mountains, but pride does. It is about consistency because any guy can hit a long poc, but to do it over five kilometres is a serious achievement.

I always put serious time into preparing for the Poc Fada and the day before, I will go around the course. In 1994, I drove up in my Fiesta van with my friend Padraig McGrath from Clare and hit the mountain at 9.30 a.m. We went around the course twice but I still wasn't happy so we went up a third time. After that, I wanted to do it one more time. Padraig said, 'If you want to go around again, you're on your own!' We eventually reached a compromise and Padraig agreed to tackle part of the first stage. Looking back, that was complete madness on my part because we were on the mountain for nine hours. I slept for 12 hours when I got back to the nearby Carrickdale Hotel.

When my playing career finally comes to an end, I will cry. After wiping away the tears, I will then begin thinking of ways to fill the gaping void in my life. I will spend much more time with my son Colm, I can pursue my business interests further and I might give the golf a serious lash. But nothing will compare to running out in that Clare jersey, hitting the crossbar a lash and hearing the roar of the crowd at my back.

The more people at the game and the louder the roar of the crowd, the better. This is my arena and I love it. I am always second out of the tunnel, behind our team captain, and at the point of impact the feeling in my cheeks and in my stomach is indescribable.

When I listen to the national anthem before the game, I clutch the medals hanging from my neck and pull them close to my heart. My chain with two crucifixes and an ingot attached; I grab them and think about the people who gave them to me – my parents, my sister Helen, my son Colm, Ciara and Sheila Considine. On the back of my goalkeeper's shirt this year, the letters C, O, S, T, S and Ⓕ were printed, the initials of those closest to me.

I think of those people on my back, they are my inspiration and I need their help in a battle. People say I wear my heart on my sleeve, you could say that I wear it on my back. Those people are the reason why I am out there playing, I feel they are with me.

The GAA pisses me off, of course it does, and why wouldn't it with those suspensions? But I would go through it all again without hesitation.

Instead of being remembered as a nutcase, I would like people to remember a down to earth person who didn't get too carried away. A person who had good people around him, people who cared and helped him. A man who enjoyed the simple things. I have made plenty of mistakes in my life, but I have always tried to put things right if I have done wrong. People talk about me behind my back but I won't engage in that sort of behaviour. I have regrets, everybody does, but doing things from the heart is important too. I have my faults but you have to learn from experience and by Christ, I have had plenty of experience.

You can like me or dislike me but I am not going away. I am Davy Fitzgerald from 3 Thomond Terrace, Sixmilebridge and I am proud of it. I do not like being branded and that is why I spend more and more time by myself these days. Out of sight, out of mind. The main problem with being an inter-county player is that you don't have a private life anymore. People form their own opinions and when the rumour mill goes into overdrive, you are helpless. The people that dish out the abuse should take a long, hard look at themselves. Never judge a man until you meet him face to face.

I still firmly believe that Clare can win an All-Ireland hurling title over the next few seasons and I hope Anthony Daly is the man that leads us back to the promised land. I believe there is something big in this group of players. I wish that certain individuals would stop knocking our players and telling them to retire when they don't need to. Let the players themselves decide if they don't have the appetite for it anymore. Journalists and supporters should not make that decision under any circumstances.

Seánie McMahon, Brian Lohan, Colin Lynch and Frank Lohan will make up their own minds. And we will be straight about it because none of us want to be second best. After the 2002 All Ireland final I was asked if that was the end of Clare? What a load of crap, we are still here and we're not going anywhere!

The future is bright, a lot brighter than in other counties. We are safe in the knowledge that we will always be competitive. There is no doubt that we still have a team capable of doing the business.

Hurling is my life and it has kept me going through the bad times. My mind needs to be active and I have been used to hurling, hurling and more hurling since I was a young boy pucking a ball with John Lynch in the Old Mill at Sixmilebridge. I am getting better at sitting down and relaxing these days but I don't necessarily like it. I feel that I am wasting time just sitting around. My mind doesn't switch off from one end of the day to the other, it is always scheming.

What I will miss most when I retire is the inner sanctum of the Clare dressing room just minutes before the throw-in. Brian Lohan bandages up the knee and the last thing he'll do is pull down that red helmet over his head. Then, you know he's ready for war. Seánie Mac's on the table, getting his rub. I am sitting just inside the door at Cusack Park, first seat on the way in. I have my own spot in every dressing room: Semple Stadium, Páirc Uí Chaoimh, the Gaelic Grounds and Croke Park. I am a creature of habit.

Lohan and Seánie are stretching now but Colin Lynch takes stretching to new limits. Lynch is jogging on his toes, Seánie goes to a few lads, taps them on the back. Lohan lets off a bark occasionally and, just by looking at him, I know he is ready.

Ger Loughnane's presence in a dressing room is unbelievable. He walks around with an air of invincibility. Everything revolves around him, he is the man. 'Is everything done?' he asks. Everything is ready, you don't dare cross Loughnane. 'Now girls, warm-up in two or three minutes,' shouts Mike McNamara. On our toes, we're all looking at each other. Loughnane talks, Dalo talks. I go to every player and give them a hug before we get out on the field. I look each one straight in the eye and wish him the best.

'We'll leave everything out on that field,' we say to each other. We pray for the Clare jersey and clutch it tight. Passion and pride. That buzz of excitement before leaving the dressing room is incredible.

I will miss this more than anything. It's unique. We're standing in a huddle, Doc Quinn is nervously looking up and down, he is ready too. Colm Flynn, the heart and soul of it, my father Pat standing in the background. It is a fortress in here. Dalo in the middle of us and when he talks, it's from the heart. Passion, pride, the Clare jersey, your mother, your father, your sisters, your brothers, all of these are key words when you're going out playing for Clare. Die for each other, we are family – they are our words. We hold together in this huddle, so tight. Then, into the light, second out behind the captain. Showtime.

DAVID FITZGERALD
CHAMPIONSHIP HISTORY

1990 Limerick 2-16 Clare 1-5

1991 Limerick 0-21 Clare 1-15

1992 Clare 3-10 Waterford 2-13; Waterford 0-16 Clare 0-14 (replay)

1993 Clare 3-16 Limerick 3-12; Clare 2-7 Cork 0-10; Tipperary 3-27 Clare 2-12 (Munster final)

1994 Clare 2-11 Tipperary 0-13; Clare 2-16 Kerry 1-8; Limerick 0-25 Clare 2-10 (Munster final)

1995 Clare 2-13 Cork 3-9; Clare 1-17 Limerick 0-11 (Munster final); Clare 3-12 Galway 1-13 (All-Ireland semi-final); Clare 1-13 Offaly 2-8 (All-Ireland final)

1996 Limerick 1-13 Clare 0-15

1997 Clare 3-24 Kerry 1-6; Clare 1-19 Cork 0-18; Clare 1-18 Tipperary 0-18 (Munster final); Clare 1-17 Kilkenny 1-13 (All-Ireland semi-final); Clare 0-20 Tipperary 2-13 (All-Ireland final)

1998 Clare 0-21 Cork 0-13; Clare 1-16 Waterford 3-10 (Munster final); Clare 2-16 Waterford 0-10 (replay); Clare 1-13 Offaly 1-13 (All-Ireland semi-final); Clare 1-16 Offaly 2-10 (unfinished replay); Offaly 0-16 Clare 0-13 (2nd replay)

1999 Clare 2-12 Tipperary 0-18; Clare 1-21 Tipperary 1-11 (replay); Cork 1-15 Clare 0-14 (Munster final); Clare 3-15 Galway 2-18 (All-Ireland quarter-final); Clare 3-18 Galway 2-14 (replay); Kilkenny 2-14 Clare 1-13 (All-Ireland semi-final)

2000 Tipperary 2-19 Clare 1-14

2001 Tipperary 0-15 Clare 0-14

2002 Tipperary 1-18 Clare 2-13; Clare 3-22 Dublin 1-8; Clare 3-15 Wexford 3-7; Clare 1-15 Galway 1-14 (All-Ireland quarter-final); Clare 1-16 Waterford 1-13 (All-Ireland semi-final); Kilkenny 2-20 Clare 0-19 (All-Ireland Final)

2003 Clare 2-17 Tipperary 0-14; Cork 1-18 Clare 0-10; Galway 1-15 Clare 2-11.

2004 Waterford 3-21 Clare 1-8; Clare 7-19 Laois 2-15; Clare 3-16 Offaly 2-10; Kilkenny 1-13 Clare 1-13 (All-Ireland quarter-final); Kilkenny 1-11 Clare 0-9 (replay)

2005 Tipperary 2-14 Clare 0-14; Clare 1-23 Dublin 0-9; Clare 1-12 Offaly 1-11; Clare 4-14 Waterford 0-21; Clare 1-20 Wexford 0-12 (All-Ireland quarter-final), Clare 0-15 Cork 0-16 (All-Ireland semi-final)

Summary: played 54, won 29, drawn 5, lost 19, unfinished 1